THE ENCYCLOPEDIA OF

TRAINS & LOCOMOTIVES

C.J. RILEY

MetroBooks

MetroBooks

An Imprint of Friedman/Fairfax Publishers

© 1995 by Michael Friedman Publishing Group, Inc.

Library of Congress Cataloging-in-Publication Data

Riley, C. J., date
    The encyclopedia of trains & locomotives / C.J. Riley.
        p.   cm.
    "A Friedman Group book"--T.p. verso.
    Includes bibliographical references and index.
    ISBN 1-56799-087-8
    1. Railroads--Encyclopedias.   2. Locomotives--Encyclopedias.
I. Title.   II. Title: Encyclopedia of trains and locomotives.
TF9.R52   1995
625.1'003--dc20   94-1826
                                                                      CIP.

Editor: Nathaniel Marunas
Art Director: Jeff Batzli
Designer: Kevin Ullrich
Photography Editor: Emilya Naymark

Typeset by Classic Type, Inc.
Color separations by Bright Arts (Singapore) Pte. Ltd.
Printed and bound in China by Leefung-Asco Printers Ltd.

For bulk purchases and special sales, please contact:
Friedman/Fairfax Publishers
Attention: Sales Department
15 West 26th Street
New York, NY 10010
212/685-6610 FAX 212/685-1307

Photo Credits

© Dean Abramson: pp. 20 left, 22, 39, 86, 107
© Aerial Photography Services, Inc.: p. 28
Courtesy of Alaska State Library: pp. 67 bottom, 147
Courtesy of the American Association of Railroads: pp. 24-25, 40 top, 157 bottom, 192, 204
AP/Wide World Photos: Back endpaper, pp. 27 top, 29 top, 51 top, 55 bottom, 56-57, 58 all, 84, 98, 137, 141, 142 top, 152 bottom, 155 bottom, 162, 195
Archive Photos: pp. 19 top, 75 bottom, 78, 83 top, 167, 168; Archive Photos/London Daily Express: p. 71; Archive Photos/Welgos: p. 93; Archive Photos/Lionel Green: p. 174; Archive Photos/Herbert: p. 175 top
Courtesy of the Australian Information Service/Photography by Norman Plant: p. 35
© John C. Benson: pp. 20 right, 26 bottom, 30, 31, 33, 36, 37, 38 all, 51 bottom, 67 top, 100 bottom, 116, 119 top, 131 top, 183
© G. M. Best/Collection of W. Raia: pp. 12-13

Courtesy of Canadian Pacific Limited: #A-4402: p. 63; #485: p. 66 bottom; #8617: p. 69 background; #A-4420: p. 70
© Harold H. Carstens: pp. 103, 193 bottom
© Jack Casement/Envision: p. 105
© David Michael Davis/FPG International: p. 68
© Ron Dorman/FPG International: p. 180 top
© Robert K. Durham: pp. 90 top and middle, 121, 132 top
© Harold Edmonson: pp. 13 top, 138, 139 all
FPG International: pp. 46-47, 85 top, 99 bottom, 161, 175 bottom, 188
© Full Frame Photo Library: pp. 92 right, 150 all; Bruce Jenkins Photography: 149 top
© Colin Garratt/Railways of the World/Milepost 92 1/2: pp. 43
© Mark E. Gibson: p. 1
© Steve Glischinsky: pp. 6, 60, 73, 146 top, 152 top, 164
© James Golightly: pp. 65 top, 101, 165
© Steve Greenwood: pp. 25, 75 top
© Lara Hartley: pp. 99 top, 100 top, 176 top
© Don Heimburger/Heimburger House Publishing Co.: Front endpaper; pp. 55 top, 57 top, 85 bottom, 132 bottom, 142 bottom, 163 bottom, 178 bottom
© Jean Higgins/Envision: pp. 76 top, 97, 113 top
© M. Howell/Superstock: p. 135 bottom
© G. Hunter/Superstock: p. 61
© Mark Harland Johnson: pp. 41, 94-95, 129
© Wolfgang Kaehler: pp. 154 top, 197, 202 all
© S. Kanno/FPG International: p. 131 bottom
© Kugler/FPG International: p. 136
© Lee Kuhn/FPG International: pp. 2-3, 72
Courtesy of The Library of Congress: pp. 17 all, 18 all, 19 bottom, 153, 158 bottom
© Robert Lima/Envision: p. 80
Mirror Syndication International: pp. 48, 50 bottom, 102 bottom, 104 bottom, 179 top, 180 bottom, 181, 198, 199
Courtesy of the Musée Français, Mulhouse, Alsace: p. 77
Courtesy of the National Archives of Canada: #PA44742: p. 62 bottom; #PA44978: p. 64 top; #PA29691: p. 64 bottom; #PA48413: p. 65 bottom; #C46983: p. 111
Courtesy of the National Archives of New Zealand: pp. 148, 149 bottom
Courtesy of the National Railway Museum, York: pp. 104 top, 133, 134, 168 top, 171
New York Public Library: pp. 154 bottom, 193 top, 200
Courtesy of the Northumbria Tourist Board/Darlington Borough Council: p. 172
North Wind Picture Archives: pp. 69 inset, 79 top, 81, 135 top, 163 left, 166
© Maria Pape/FPG International: p. 54
© Ronald E. Partis/Envision: p. 50 top
© R. Pauli/Superstock: p. 82
© Chuck Place: pp. 163 right, 191
Courtesy of the Railroad Museum of Pennsylvania (PHMC): pp. 9, 27 bottom, 34, 40 bottom, 42, 76 bottom, 90 bottom, 113 bottom, 114 bottom, 120 all, 123 all, 143 all, 144, 145 top, 146 bottom, 176-177, 205
© D. Randy Riggs: p. 52
© C.J. Riley: p. 115
© Ernest H. Robl: pp. 102 top, 108 top, 112 top
© K. Scholz/Superstock: pp. 155 top, 196 bottom
© The Science Museum, London: pp. 125 bottom, 126
© Clyde H. Smith/FPG International: p. 106
© Chris Sorensen: p. 114 top
Courtesy of Steam Traction Limited, England: pp. 194 all, 196 top
Courtesy of Stockton-on-Tees Borough Council/Painting by John Wigton: p. 173 all
© M. Sutton/FPG International: p. 32
© John Terranova: pp. 29 bottom, 156, 210
© Alan Tillotson: pp. 4-5, 21, 23, 24 top, 26 top, 56 top, 59, 62 top, 66 top, 87, 88, 91, 92 left, 96, 99 middle, 108, 109, 117, 118, 124, 160
© Tokyo Photo Agency, Ltd./Superstock: p. 130
Courtesy of Union Pacific Railroad Museum Collection: pp. 44, 45; A.J. Russel Photo: 190
Dipl. -Ing. Michael Welke: pp. 10-11, 177, 178 top
© Ulrike Welsch: p. 184 all
Courtesy of the Western History Collections, University of Oklahoma Library: pp. 53, 110-111
© Michael Wootton: p. 182 top

Grateful acknowledgment is given to authors, publishers, and photographers for permission to reprint material. Every effort has been made to determine copyright owners of the reprinted material. In the case of any omissions, the Publishers will be pleased to make suitable acknowledgments in future editions.

Dedication

This book is dedicated to the fond memory of my father, Cliff, and to my mother, Alice, without whose early influence and encouragement I would not have embarked on a most rewarding lifetime of study, creativity, and personal growth.

Acknowledgments

I wish to offer my most heartfelt appreciation to the following, without whose knowledge and assistance this book could not have been completed:

Hal Carstens
Bud Charles
Bob & Cecile Kaminski
L. E. Kline
Bruce Metcalf
Kalmbach Memorial Library
Bill Metzger
John Roberts
Jim Ruffing
Bill Schaumburg
A.W. Thompson
The staff of the Michael Friedman Group, including:
Editor Nathaniel Marunas
Photo Editor Emilya Naymark
Designer Kevin Ullrich
Production Editor Loretta Mowat

And thanks to my wife, Denise, and sons Kegan and Morgan, whose benign tolerance was often as important as their active encouragement.

Contents

The Awakening of a Rail Fan

The warm half-light of dusk caressed the man and the boy as they stood, hand in hand, in a silence broken only by singing crickets, along the mainline of the Southern Pacific Railroad.

"Why are we here, Dad?"

"To see something special—a steam locomotive!"

The boy smiled wistfully as he remembered the little switchers chuffing happily around the Canadian National yard back in Toronto. His family stopped there often on pleasant Sunday afternoons to spend a few minutes watching the seemingly aimless activity. His uncle Roy, a CN employee, once wangled a ride for him in the cab of one of those "teakettles." Its unfathomable maze of pipes, valves, gauges, and levers fascinated and awed him. The heat that spewed from the firebox door as the fireman threw in a shovelful of coal inspired a long series of unsettling dreams. Those steam locomotives were wonderful, familiar, friendly little critters, and the boy marveled at them.

"But why is this one special, Dad?"

At that moment, a spiraling light pierced the gathering gloom far down the track. What sort of headlight was this? A low-pitched, mournful wail filled the air, a warning for the nearby grade crossing. It didn't sound like the shrill, tooting whistles the boy remembered. As the locomotive drew closer, he noticed the broad, flat front, much like a grinning face with glowing eyes, not like the round boiler fronts he knew.

Then the specter was upon them, flickering firelight reflecting off the ballast, the sound and the fury felt more than heard. Boiling water, roaring oil fire, throbbing pumps, whining generator, clanking rods and valve gear, escaping steam, and barking exhaust melded into a single, ear-straining, earthshaking cacophony, a sound one would expect from the passing of the Devil himself.

The boy's legs tensed. Fear forced his pounding heart into his throat and parched his tongue. He knew he had to run, to escape this screaming, roaring horror that bore steadily down on him. But his father's grip tightened and held firm. Wide eyes saw the face transformed, the grin becoming a snowplow pilot, the eyes lighted windows. A smiling man, wearing a familiar striped cap and red bandanna, leaned out and waved as the locomotive flashed by.

Wonder replaced fear as the boy realized that this was indeed a special locomotive. The cab lay in front of an immense boiler that stretched back an incredible distance over two sets of drivers and cylinders. The smoke box and stack were back by the tender, a huge, rectangular mass riding on six-wheel trucks. An endless string of yellow refrigerator cars trailed effortlessly, the staccato rhythm of wheels on rail joints a sharp contrast to the disciplined clamor of the quickly disappearing locomotive.

"What was it?"

"A cab-in-front, articulated locomotive. It's designed to keep the smoke away from the crew in the long tunnels and snowsheds of the Sierras. No other railroad has them, and these are about to be retired, cut up for scrap...replaced by diesels."

Oil smoke hung heavily in the night air as the caboose, markers glowing red, clattered into the darkness. The crickets broke again into a song as father and son walked silently, still hand in hand, back to the car. The boy's mind reeled with what he had seen and heard—and felt. An incredible machine was about to die, never again to tear joyfully through the night to the astonishment of young boys.

He knew—he already knew for certain—that he loved them.

Originally published in Railroad Model Craftsman. *Used with permission of Carstens Publications.*

Right and below: The cab-forward articulated locomotives of the Southern Pacific began with two conventional 197-ton (177 t) 2-8-8-2 class MC-1 (Mallet Consolidation) locomotives built by Baldwin in 1909. Slogging 1,200 tons (1,080 t) over the Sierra Nevada Range at 10 mph (16 kph), the noxious fumes and 750° F (400° C) heat emitted from the stack were devastating to the crews in the miles of tunnels and snow sheds, but reversing the construction of the oil-fired locomotives so that the cab was in front of the stack offered protection. The converted MC-1s were followed by fifty-nine new cab-forwards of the MC class. A successful experiment that converted the Mallets to single expansion preceded the construction of 195 additional AC class (Articulated Consolidation) locomotives, beginning in 1927. The cab-forwards were the backbone of the Southern Pacific fleet in the mountain regions, from the Siskiyous to Tehachapi, until AC-12 No. 4274 made the final run over the Sierras on December 1, 1956. The final cab-forward built, No. 4294, has been preserved at the California State Railroad Museum in Sacramento.

Foreword

Many of us have had our lives changed by a chance encounter with the technology that revolutionized the nature of land transportation in virtually every country in the world. Whether it's the French TGV flashing by at 200 kilometers per hour (125 mph) or a steam-powered Shay slogging up a mountain at a top speed of 12 miles per hour (19.2 kph)—but sounding like it should be going faster—a train excites deep passions in much of humankind.

The intense love of steam power often exhibited by its devotees represents more than a love of history or obsolete technology; rather, it is a passion for machinery that seems strangely human. A steam locomotive breathes, gurgles, and sighs at rest; grunts, pants, and labors when heavily loaded; and sings happily when running at speed. The warm chords of a well-designed steam whistle (with apologies to the devotees of European "peepers") come surprisingly close to song. Even the deep-throated roar of a six-unit diesel lash-up commands deep respect for the power and dependability such a noise implies.

The clickety-clack of steel wheels rolling on rail jointed every 39 feet (11.9 m) may be gone from the welded trackage of today's heavily traveled main lines, but there are plenty of secondary and tourist lines where that welcome sound can still be heard. Even today, a multichime air horn blowing for a crossing a mile (1.6 km) away on a warm summer night tugs at the heart of younger rail fans the way the mournful wail of a steam whistle, controlled by the skillful hand of an old-time, hickory-striped hogger, entranced generations before them.

But railroads are more than just machinery and twin ribbons of steel rail. They are brought to life by people, from yard clerks to brakemen to the top of the heap—the engineers. The daily toil of these people keeps the trains rolling yet goes almost unnoticed in our fascination with bigger and better machinery. James McCague said it best in *The Big Ivy*, his novel of life on the railroad in the early years, when he described a scene in a trackside cemetery:

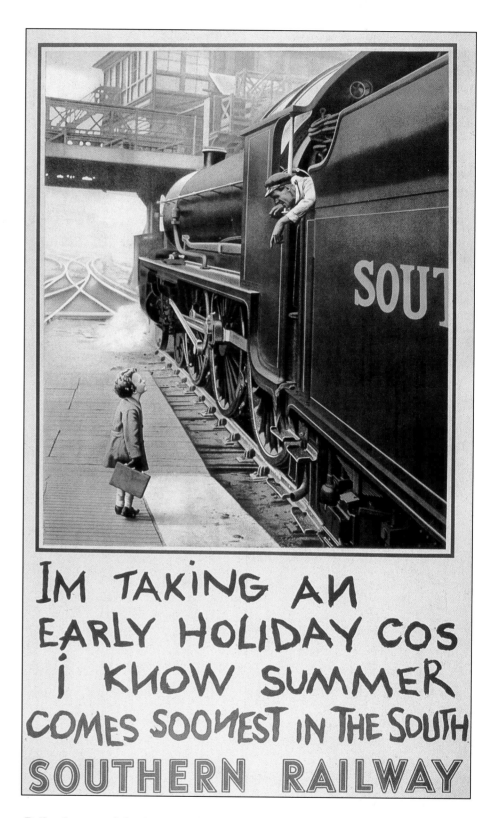

Railroads promoted the pleasures of rail travel, and the use of posters became a common method of spreading the word. The fascination children have for railroading is captured in this poster (above) for Britain's *Southern Railway, while London North Eastern Railway echoes the Southern's message in its own version (opposite page) promoting travel to the north.*

"It used to be that whenever an old mainline hogger was laid away, they'd time the ceremony so that [the train] would whistle a requiem in passing...and the smokestack would lay a rolling pall of smoke across the land, and the long mourning of the whistle and the rolling rumble of steel on steel would drown out the minister's last few words. And the mourners would be reminded then that their departing brother was one who had regularly, through most of the days of his life, lived on terms of easy intimacy with danger, surrounded by the thrashing pound of iron massively fashioned, breathing live steam, hurtling across the miles at his command faster than lesser men ever went their whole lives long.

"It set him somehow apart. The machine age brought few enough heroes, and he was one, and if he had too often partaken of the fiery waters in Fallon's Saloon, to the detriment of his family's happiness and the public peace....If his conversation had been studded with casual blasphemies, his will had been stubborn beyond belief, and his temper habitually carried a short fuse....Well, what does that amount to, against the fact that he had been a man among men."

Trains have brought us our milk and newspapers in time for breakfast, our refrigerators and our automobiles, and the coal to heat and light our homes. They carried our fathers and brothers off to war—and brought them home again. They were (and still are) an integral part of life in the industrialized world. But that does not explain the appeal that transcends just necessity or practicality. It wasn't trucks or airplanes about which Edna St. Vincent Millay was thinking when she included these significant lines in *Travel*:

> *My Heart is warm with the friends*
> *I make,*
> *And better friends I'll not be*
> *knowing;*
> *Yet there isn't a train I wouldn't*
> *take,*
> *No matter where it's going.*

It is not possible to capture the vast amount of information and romance that make up the history of railroading in a single volume, so I have selected for inclusion a limited number of entries presented in detail rather than a wider collection of surface treatments. The selection is varied enough that important equipment, locales, people, and legends are represented.

This encyclopedia, then, includes the illustrations, the history, the facts, and the anecdotes that, woven together, demonstrate the appeal—the romance—of the iron horse. From the *Locomotion* of 1825 to the General Electric Dash 8 diesels of the 1990s, this is the story of railroads and locomotives and how they, along with railroaders, changed the world.

C.J. Riley
Pittsburgh, Pennsylvania
November 1993

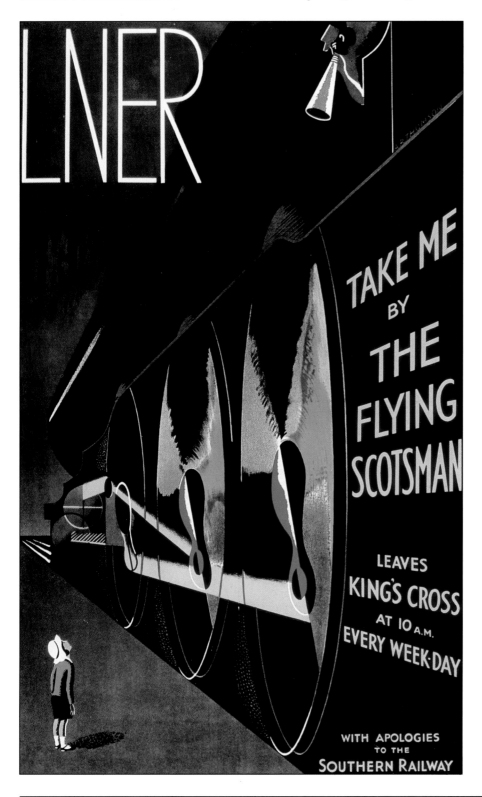

A

Aeolipile

The earliest known prototype steam machine, named for Aeolus, the Greek god of the winds, was first described in about 200 B.C. by Hero of Alexandria, a Greek mathematician and physicist. His *Spiritalia seu Pneumatica*, a book exploring the harnessing of air and water power, included a curious device that took advantage of the expansion of steam from water boiling in a tightly closed caldron, which traveled up two hollow columns and into a hollow copper sphere. By exhausting the steam from two right-angled pipes placed 180 degrees apart, the sphere was spun on its axis. Built solely for amusement, many of these devices became scientific curiosities in the aristocratic houses of Europe, and it was centuries before steam power was tamed for practical purposes.

See also: *Branca, Giovanni.*

Aeolus

In 1937, the owners of the Chicago, Burlington & Quincy—the Burlington Route—whose pioneering diesel-powered streamliner, Zephyr, was suffering mechanical difficulties, decided backup power was necessary. Seven-year-old Hudson 3002 went into the West Burlington shops and came out dressed in a stainless-steel streamlined shroud, similar in design to the Zephyr rolling stock. The mythological name Aeolus, Greek god of the winds, was chosen to complement the diesel units named after Zephyrus, god of the west wind, and Pegasus. The nickname "Big Alice the Goon" (after a somewhat ungainly popular comic-strip character of that era) was soon irreverently applied and, now renumbered 4000, it was assigned to regular service on the Aristocrat and Exposition Flyer, between Chicago and Denver. The shrouding was removed in 1941, but the nickname stuck. A second Aeolus, No. 4001, was converted in 1938.

See also: *Kuhler, Otto; Loewy, Raymond; Streamlined Steam Locomotives; Zephyr.*

American Civil War Railroads (1861–1865)

The American War Between the States was the first armed conflict in which the railroads played a significant role in the outcome. As the opening salvo fell on Fort Sumter, the North was already blessed with 22,000 miles (35,200 km) of operating railroad, with scores of locomotive builders, foundries, car builders, and the skilled mechanics and materials necessary to support them. The South, to its ultimate dismay, had only 9,000 miles (14,400 km) of mixed-gauge railroad and only the Tredegar ironworks in Richmond. This disparity caused grievous damage to the South as the Confederacy, outnumbered, surrounded and virtually cut off from the sea, was most dependent on quick and efficient railway transportation. The break in gauge meant that when a train reached a junction with an adjoining railroad of a different gauge, troops had to disembark and equipment and shipments had to be transferred to cars of the new railroad. This was not only a waste of time and manpower, it also prevented excess rolling stock in one area of the South to be transferred to another area where it might be desperately needed.

While most railroads, both North and South, prospered during the war, railroads in the border states, particularly the Baltimore & Ohio (B&O), suffered from constant theft and destruction at the hands of raiding parties from both sides. In 1861, the B&O yard at Martinsburg (now in West Virginia), virtually in no-man's-land and a vital link to the Union forces in the west,

Right: Maintenance and operation of vital rail arteries were assigned by President Lincoln to the U.S. Military Railroad. Troops guard a hastily erected temporary wooden trestle that has replaced the more substantial truss bridge that formerly spanned the stream. Inset: Locomotives and rolling stock were always in short supply during the Civil War due to theft and destruction by the opposing armies. Muscle power substitutes for a lack of heavy equipment as workers struggle to drag this intentionally derailed locomotive up an embankment to the tracks.

Soo Line Railroad (Soo). Originally the Minneapolis, St. Paul & Saulte Ste. Marie, the former nickname "Soo Line" came from the phonetic spelling of Saulte. Having dropped most of the original lines in Michigan and Wisconsin, the Soo reaches from Chicago to Duluth and points in Manitoba and Saskatchewan as well as south to Louisville and Kansas City. Having bought and scaled back the bankrupt Milwaukee Road in 1985, spinning off a number of regionals and adding service to southern Ontario via trackage rights on CSX to Detroit, Soo now operates 5,807 miles (9,300 km) of track in ten states from headquarters in Minneapolis. Canadian Pacific, having owned 56 percent of the Soo for a long time, assumed full ownership in 1990.

Southern Pacific Lines* (SP). Successor to the Central Pacific, the western section of the first transcontinental railway, SP forms an arc from Portland through San Francisco and Los Angeles to New Orleans, and maintains the original 1869 leg from Sacramento to Ogden, Utah. Subsidiary St. Louis Southwestern (SSW), known as "The Cotton Belt," extended service from northeastern Texas to St. Louis and Memphis. Recent affiliation with the Denver & Rio Grande Western (D&RGW) connected Salt Lake City and Ogden with Denver and provided a connection east to Kansas City via trackage rights. Additional purchases provided lines to Chicago from both Kansas City and St. Louis. System-wide trackage now stands at 14,600 miles (23,400 km). The three components operate as subsidiaries with headquarters in San Francisco.

Union Pacific Railroad* (UP). Begun as the eastern link of the transcontinental, running from headquarters in Omaha to Ogden, Utah, UP added lines to Kansas City, Denver, Los Angeles, Portland, and Seattle. Acquisition of the Western Pacific and the Missouri Pacific in 1982 provided access to San Francisco, Kansas City, Pueblo, Memphis, New Orleans, and all major Texas cities. Addition of the Missouri-Kansas-Texas (the Katy) provided a St. Louis to Houston line parallel to their Mopac. The system totals 21,882 miles (35,000 km).

Above: The rugged climb over Tehachapi Pass, in Southern California, forced the Southern Pacific to loop over itself, yet this train still requires five locomotives to make the trek. EMD SD40T-2 No. 8279 is equipped with a "tunnel motor," with lowered air intakes to avoid the heat under the ceilings of the miles of tunnels and snow sheds on the SP.

Below: A New York Central streamlined 4-6-4 Hudson poses for a formal portrait along the shore of its namesake river with the Twentieth Century Limited in tow. The classic lines of the locomotive shrouding, as well as the rest of the train, were styled by the noted industrial designer Henry Dreyfuss.

American Locomotive Works (Alco)

This major American locomotive builder was formed in 1901, when eight smaller builders (which dated to the 1850s) merged to counter the competition of the ever-expanding Baldwin works. Alco comprised the Brooks Locomotive Works of Dunkirk, New York; Cooke Locomotive and Machine Works of Paterson, New Jersey; Dickson Manufacturing Company of Scranton, Pennsylvania; Manchester Locomotive Works of Manchester, New Hampshire; Pittsburg Locomotive & Car Works of Pittsburgh, Pennsylvania (the company eventually added a final *b* to match the spelling of the city); Rhode Island Locomotive Works of Providence, Rhode Island; Richmond Locomotive Works of Richmond, Virginia; and the Schenectady Locomotive Works of Schenectady, New York. They were joined a short time later by the Locomotive & Machine Company of Montreal, Quebec (Canada), in 1902, and the Rogers Locomotive Works of Paterson, New Jersey, in 1905. Alco continued to manufacture locomotives at most of these plants until the 1920s, but production was eventually consolidated at Schenectady in 1929.

The Great Depression almost halted locomotive construction, but production increased with the last great steam locomotive boom beginning in the late 1930s. Alco was known for its superb 4-6-4 Hudsons and 4-8-4 Niagaras for the New York Central and the massive 4-6-6-4 Challengers and 4-8-8-4 Big Boys of the Union Pacific. The final domestic steam locomotives built at Schenectady were seven 2-8-4s for the New York Central affiliate Pittsburgh & Lake Erie.

Cooperative ventures in electric locomotive design with neighbor General Electric were inevitable, the earliest designs dating to 1906. The partners joined with Ingersoll-Rand to produce the first standardized diesel-electric locomotives from 1924 to 1928.

Inset: Union Pacific No. 3985, a 4-6-6-4 Challenger, was built by Alco in July 1943. After retirement for display at the Cheyenne, Wyoming, depot, it was restored by the railroad's employees and returned to service in 1981. The 633,000-pound (287,000 kg) locomotive operates regularly in excursion service.

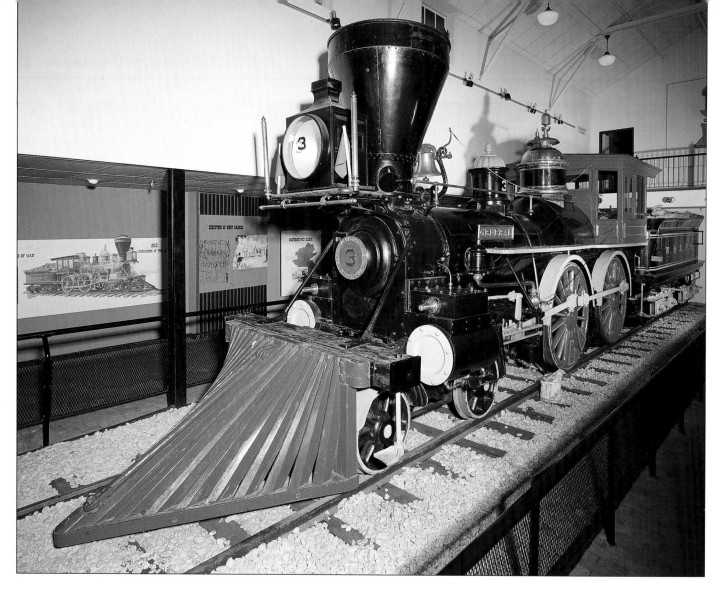

Andrews' Raid (The Great Locomotive Chase)

Raids against the railroads serving the other side were common during the American Civil War, but the mission of Union captain J. J. Andrews against the Western & Atlantic (W&A) is probably the best-known example. Two films, an early Buster Keaton effort, *The General*, and a much later Walt Disney production, *The Great Locomotive Chase*, which chronicled the story, contributed considerably to the legend.

In April 1862, Andrews led nineteen Federal soldiers, dressed in civilian clothing and claiming to be refugees, into the heart of the South, determined to sever the rails that were the lifeline of the Confederate troops at Chattanooga. Climbing aboard a northbound W&A mixed train some 20 miles (32 km) out of Atlanta, the raiders gathered in small, apparently unrelated, groups and waited for the Chattanooga-bound train's normal breakfast stop at Big Shanty, Georgia. As the passengers and crew left the train, Andrews' men moved

The General *survived its brush with Andrews' raiders but was severely damaged later in the Civil War. After a rebuilding that altered its appearance, it served for many more years before retirement and preservation.*

quietly toward the locomotive, named *General*, uncoupled the passenger cars, and hightailed the locomotive and freight cars north. Their intention was to continue to the Union lines at Chattanooga, burning bridges and disrupting the railroad as they went.

The plan was a good one, but they hadn't taken into consideration some extremely wet weather and an uncommonly tenacious conductor. At first, suspecting deserters from the nearby Confederate camp had commandeered his train and would abandon it shortly, William Fuller ran down the tracks in pursuit, much to the amusement of onlookers. Upon reaching the next station, he learned that telegraph wires had been cut and track

tools taken. Fuller immediately suspected saboteurs, and the chase began in earnest. Joined by his engine crew, who had followed him up the line, he continued the pursuit on a hand-propelled track car. When they reached a section of track where Andrews had removed the rail, the hand car was carried across the gap and the chase continued to Etowah, where an old yard switcher, the Yonah, sat under steam. A posse of outraged citizens and six Confederate soldiers joined the party, and they all piled onto the locomotive, increasing their speed under steam power, but running tender first.

Andrews, meanwhile, had persuaded a railroad agent that his train was carrying ammunition urgently needed by the Confederate forces, and all southbound trains were ordered to clear the tracks for his passage. The *General* moved swiftly northward, at speeds up to 60 mph (96 kph) on the light unballasted track, stopping only to tear out some rail. The pursuers, their numbers depleted after running several miles past the damaged section, reached

With the Texas *in close pursuit and the stolen* General *out of fuel and water, James Andrews and his band of saboteurs abandon their prize and run for the woods. Andrews and six others were captured and hanged as spies.*

the *Texas*, a locomotive on one of the southbound freights. The chase continued with the *Texas* in reverse, pushing the freight cars to the nearest siding, and then continuing tender first, dodging cross ties that had been dumped on the tracks and carefully crossing partially burned bridges. The weeks of rain had so saturated the wooden structures that complete destruction was not possible. Once Fuller and his men came within sight of the *General*, Andrews cut loose two boxcars to roll on a downgrade toward the *Texas*. A third boxcar was set

afire and cut loose. Fuller handled these impediments by carefully stopping them and then pushing the cars to a siding.

The pursuit had lasted for a hundred miles (160 km), and the *General* was running out of fuel and water. Fuller's pursuit prevented Andrews from stopping to reload, as well as from doing a proper job of destroying the line. As the stolen locomotive slowed to a stop, the raiders took to the woods. Most were captured, and Andrews and six men were hanged two months later. At that point, the *General* was once again busy hauling ammunition and hospital trains, having been saved only by William Fuller's bulldog determination and the inclement weather. In this case, at least, the Confederacy had been saved.

Both locomotives survived the war—although the *General* was badly damaged—

and were ultimately restored. The *General* can be seen at the Kenesaw Museum in Georgia, and the *Texas* is displayed at Grant Park, Atlanta.

Atlantic-type Locomotive

Vulcan Iron Works of Wilkes-Barre, Pennsylvania, built the first 4-4-2 locomotive, in 1888, designed by George S. Strong for the Lehigh Valley. The wheel arrangement became known as "Atlantic" at the suggestion of J. K. Kenly, general manager of the Atlantic Coast Line, which received an 1894 order of 4-4-2s from Baldwin.

The type became very popular in fast passenger service and was built as conventional tender locomotives, tank engines, and Camelbacks. The final Atlantics were also the largest and fastest constructed. American Locomotive Works (Alco) turned out four oil-fired streamlined locomotives for the Milwaukee Road's Hiawatha. These magnificent orange, maroon, and gray locomotives, styled by the renowned Otto Kuhler, were designed to run at 100 mph (160 kph) and frequently exceeded 120 mph (192 kph).

The high-wheeled 4-4-2 Atlantic was the standard passenger power in flat territory for many years. Chicago & Northwestern No. 125 was built at Alco's Schenectady Works in December 1908.

Australian Railways

Australia is roughly oval in shape—1,500 miles (2,400 km) north to south and 2,000 miles (3,200 km) east to west—and its population is concentrated along the coasts, particularly the southeast and eastern shore, where rainfall is plentiful and temperatures are moderate. Much of the interior, as well as the northwest corner, is quite dry and barren; in fact, 75 percent of the country could be called desert. Fifteen and a half million of the seventeen and a half million inhabitants live in the eastern half of the country, most of them in the major cities: Sydney, Melbourne, Adelaide, and Brisbane.

Australia has been a unified federation only since 1901, and when railway construction began in 1850, each state developed its own independent railroad to serve individual needs, with a cavalier and parochial attitude to the possibility of future connection. Gauge became a problem when both Victoria and South Australia hired Irish engineers, who chose 5 feet 3 inches, the Irish standard gauge; New South Wales insisted on the British standard gauge of 4 feet 8 1/2 inches. Queensland and Western Australia decided to save money with 3-foot-6-inch gauge, and backsliding South Australia built a third of its final mileage in that narrow gauge as well. Added to this was some mountain trackage in Victoria that was set at 2 feet 6 inches (0.8 m). That meant that except for a line between Melbourne and Adelaide, state boundaries ended where gauge changed.

The inconvenience caused by break of gauge is well known and has doomed many promising rail systems to isolation and even failure, but in a country where no gauge was an obvious minority, and where rail systems served primarily their immediate areas, all four gauges survived, and three now function as part of a national rail system. Unification of the gauges was first proposed in the 1880s and continued to be discussed for years. Lord Kitchener pointed out the defense difficulties in 1911, and a Royal Commission proposed a solution in 1921. Unfortunately, the country, though unified, struggled for consensus on many issues; considering the tremendous cost of railway standardization, agreement between the much separated state governments could not be easily reached.

The New South Wales standard-gauge line was extended 70 miles (112 km) from the border to Brisbane in 1930. Thirty years later, the Victoria broad gauge was paralleled with a new standard gauge for 190 miles (304 km) to Melbourne. A transcontinental link was built to standard gauge across southern Australia in 1917, but it connected to the narrow gauge at Port Augusta in the east and at Kalgoorlie in the west. The true standard-gauge transcontinental link did not come until 1969, and Adelaide was not part of it until the mid-1980s.

The states are generally responsible for rail management, with the Commonwealth government controlling the central desert sections of the east-west transcontinental line and the north-south transcontinental line, which runs to Alice Springs, in

Above: An apparition out of the heyday of the North American passenger train, this stainless steel train set of the Australian National Railways is being hauled by a pair of Australian copies of GM's legendary F Unit. Left: The Mount Newman iron ore railway is a classic example of a modern "conveyor belt" operation. No. 5513 leads a 150-car train loaded with 15,000 tons (13,500 t) of ore down to Port Hedland.

the center of Australia. In 1973, the Commonwealth offered to assume responsibility for all the states' railways under the Australian National Railway (ANR) Commission, but only Tasmania and South Australia (non-suburban lines) had done so by 1978. ANR was left with scattered rail lines in three gauges, but envisages ANR freight trains running into all mainland capital cities now served by rail.

The Australian railways, some of which were heavily influenced by British practices, have styles unique to each state, as the following descriptions illustrate. Many locomotives were constructed in Australia under license from U.S. manufacturers and look quite American. Alco-MLW units were built by Clyde Engineering; EMD designs, notably the F Unit, were built by the A.E. Goodwin Shops.

Australian National Railways (ANR).

Formerly Commonwealth Railways, ANR includes the Trans-Australian, 1,100 miles (1,760 km) of standard gauge between Port Augusta and Kalgoorlie, which includes the famous 300-mile (480 km) straight track across the Nullarbor Plain that serves no major settlement in between. This is the route of the remarkable Indian-Pacific, a Perth-to-Sydney streamliner in the style of the finest American luxury trains of the 1950s. A relatively new standard-gauge line has been com-

pleted north from the transcontinental route to the center of the continent at Alice Springs; a closed section goes south 300 miles (480 km) from Darwin to "a tin shed" that comprises the town of Birdum. The Alice Springs section replaces a 3-foot 6-inch gauge line on another route, via Maree, and carries an even more luxurious train, the Ghan. ANR also operates a 3-foot 6-inch-gauge freight-only network in Tasmania.

The Indian-Pacific: Australia's Transcontinental Passenger Train.

It wasn't until 1944 that the gauge problem began to be seriously addressed by the national government, but it was 1970 before the first east-west transcontinental passenger train, the Indian-Pacific, was inaugurated between Sydney and Perth. Prior to that, one could not cross the country on a single train. The journey involved five separate trains, because of multiple gauges, and passengers often had to leave one train at an ungodly hour to cross a platform and board another.

Modern diesels on the New South Wales rail lines are very reminiscent of American designs. Here, a passenger train leaves Henty, NSW, pulled by No. 4405.

Much reconstruction and even relocation of existing lines was needed to accommodate high-speed passenger trains. The Parkes–Broken Hill section of the New South Wales Railway was rebuilt to replace the pioneer standard light rail and earth ballast. Beyond Broken Hill, a new line was built to bypass the route of the Silverton Tramway to Cockburn, on the South Australian border.

The South Australian Railways line was originally built to 3-foot 6-inch gauge, so the 218 miles (350 km) of trackage to Port Pirie was converted to standard gauge for the coming of the Indian-Pacific. Port Pirie to Port Augusta involves 50 miles (80 km) of the Commonwealth Railways. From there, the original 1917 section of the standard-gauge Trans-Australia Railway runs 1,050 miles (1,680 km) across the Nullarbor Plain to Kalgoorlie.

This barren section includes many settlements along the route named for political figures: Curtin, Chifley, Hughs, Cook, Fisher, Watson, Barton, and Lyons (all Australian prime ministers); Kitchener and Haig (prominent figures in World War I). Those settlements carrying Aboriginal names are more intriguing: Wirrappa ("two little girls and a rock hole"), Wirramina ("see the gum tree"), Coondambo ("small kangaroo rat"), Kingoonya ("Nardoo seeds"), and Malboomba ("wind").

Kalgoorlie was formerly the final train change, to the 3-foot 6-inch track of the Western Australian Government Railways for the run to Perth. Although conversion of this line had long been a dream of the West Australians, the discovery of substantial iron ore deposits at Koolyanobbing provided the impetus. A new standard-gauge line was constructed from Kwinana to Koolyanobbing, swinging northward to reach Koolyanobbing and bypassing the former stations east of Southern Cross before turning back south to Kalgoorlie.

The transcontinental route was completed with this final 427-mile (688 km) stretch, constructed at a cost of £431 million. Six new trains were built to service the line. Each train has one car of first-class "roomettes," two cars of first-class "twinnette" suites, and three cars of second-class "twinnettes." There are also a dining car, cafeteria car, club car, and a lounge car for

first-class passengers. Three additional cars house power equipment, mail, and dormitory space for the crew of twenty. The train includes a honeymoon suite and a fully equipped sick bay.

On March 1, 1970, the first Indian-Pacific departed Sydney on its 2,362-mile (3,780 km), four-day, three-night journey across the southern portion of the Australian continent. Only twenty years later, the destiny of the train is in doubt, as discussions are under way to determine the future of the Indian-Pacific.

See also: *Australian Railways: Iron Ore Railways of Australia, Puffing Billy; Heavy Harry.*

Iron Ore Railways of Australia.

Perhaps the most impressive railroading in Australia is found on the ponderous iron ore lines in northwest Western Australia. The standard-gauge track on the 263-mile

(425 km) Mount Newman to Port Hedland line sees 150-car ore trains weighing almost 20,000 gross tons (18,000 t) pulled by three locomotives at almost 40 mph (64 kph). This mine-to-port railway carries more annual tonnage than the entire Western Australia Government Railways does.

The line was built in the late 1960s to extraordinarily high standards, with 263-foot (80 m) lengths of the heaviest rail ever used in Australia. Substantial jarrah-wood ties (sleepers) were set in high-grade granite ballast, and the curves were kept to three degrees—about a 340-foot (103 m) radius —with the grade limited to 0.55 percent in the loaded direction. After a record-breaking construction effort, the line was officially opened by the premier of Western Australia, Sir Davis Brand, on January 22, 1969.

Loaded trains have the right-of-way during the twenty-hour trip from mine to port and back. Two hours are allowed for

turnaround at the mine, loading, and crew change; the actual time taken for dumping 14,750 tons (13,275 t) of ore into 150 cars is seventy minutes. The journey to Port Hedland takes nine hours, running through the Opthalmia Range at Ethel Gorge, turning west for 90 miles (145 km) down the Fortescue Valley, then swinging northward for the 15-mile (25 km) climb over the Chichester Range. Down the other side, the line drops 700 feet (215 m) in 15 miles (25 km) before leveling out for the remaining run across the coastal plains to the port.

Once at Port Hedland, the first two cars are placed in the dumper before the locomotives are removed for servicing. The

A Hammersley iron ore train with six diesel locomotives rolls across the massive 540-foot (165 m) steel arch on the Mount Tom Price line, headed for Dampier.

crew is changed, the ore is dumped in four hours, and the empties are sent back on the nine-hour return to Mount Newman. The return train will wait at a passing siding for any portbound trains.

Hammersley Iron runs another line from Mount Tom Price 180 miles (295 km) to the port of Dampier. This line opened in 1966 and features a 540-foot (165 m) trussed arch bridge over a 150-foot (45 m)-deep gorge.

At the turn of the century, a Mount Newman partner, the Broken Hill Proprietary Company, built a 3-foot 6-inch gauge tram railway between Iron Knob and Whyhalla to carry "iron stone" to the company's smelter at Port Pirie. When the Newcastle steel works opened in 1915, the line carried greatly increased quantities of iron ore, and it is still used to transport ore from Iron Knob to Whyhalla for shipment to other Broken Hill works and for export.

Like the railroads serving the Messabe Range in the United States, the Australian iron-ore railways perfected hauling unusually dense commodities in conveyor-belt fashion, supplying the vital raw materials flowing to the heavy industries of Western Australia.

See also: *Australian Railways: Indian-Pacific, Puffing Billy of Australia; Heavy Harry.*

Puffing Billy of Australia.

The depression of the 1890s brought Victoria's railway-building spree to an end, but the fever remained, fed by the narrow-gauge bug. Some politicians believed the economy of 2 feet between the rails, as opposed to the colony's established broad-gauge

standard of 5 feet 3 inches, would allow for additional services, particularly on branch lines in hilly country.

The Parliamentary Standing Committee on Railways, despite the strong opposition of the Victorian Railways Department, recommended that "providing transport from sparsely settled districts to the main lines might be attained by the use of narrow gauge railways or tramways, properly constructed, adequately equipped for the traffic to be accommodated, and properly managed." The gauge recommended: 2 feet.

Four routes were selected: through the King River Valley, in northeastern Victoria; to Beech Forest, in southwestern Victoria's Otway Range; to Gembrook, in the Dandenong Range; and to Warburton, in the valley of the Yarra River. John Mathieson, the railway commissioner, was so enraged by the political interference that when construction began in November 1899, he succeeded in getting the Warburton line built as broad gauge. The committee held fast for narrow gauge on the other three lines, but the railroaders managed

When Victoria began the narrow-gauge system, two Baldwin 2-6-2 tank engines were imported, along with a supply of spare parts. Two additional locos were assembled from the parts at the Victorian Railways' Newport Workshops, followed by thirteen more brand-new copies. The round builder's plate on the smokebox indicates this is a Baldwin product.

to force one concession—the gauge was increased to 2 feet 6 inches. The engineer-in-chief complained he was given the choice of making the narrow-gauge lines "a laughing stock, a failure, or a fiasco."

The narrow-gauge spree began with the line along the King River, from Wangaratta to Whitfield, which opened for business March 14, 1899. The going was easy, and a broad-gauge line could have been built for little additional cost, but narrow gauge was chosen in anticipation of an extension through the rugged country to Tolmie. The extension was surveyed but not built.

Second in line was the route through Upper Ferntree Gully to Gembrook, which provided rail access to the popular holiday destinations of the Dandenong

The oval plate on the cab and the locking handle on the smoke-box front identify No. 4A as a Newport-built copy. Steam plumes from the stack as this Puffing Billy swings a train of excursionists across the wooden trestle near Belgrave on the preserved line.

Ranges. Although cost estimates for a broad-gauge line were less than 20 percent more than those for narrow gauge, the line was built at 2 feet 6 inches and opened for traffic on December 18, 1900.

Mathieson continued his vociferous opposition, but the Victorian government proceeded nonetheless. Settlers in the Otway Ranges were anxious for a way to market the valuable timber they had been simply

burning off, and a line was built from Colac to Beech Forest. The opening of the line, in February 1902, was celebrated with a special train of dignitaries, including the governor. On arrival at Beech Forest, the official party was forced to sprint through the rain to a tent, where a ceremonial felling of a tree spattered them with mud. In 1911, the line was extended to Crowes.

The fourth narrow-gauge line to be constructed was the Walhalla line, which connected that gold-mining town with the main line at Moe. Although construction began in 1904, financing was appropriated in small amounts, and completion was delayed for a number of years. Construction was relatively simple at the beginning, as the line was pushed to Upper Moondarra, but the final 7¹/₂ miles (12 km) clung to steep fern-tangled slopes and crossed the Thompson River on a three-span girder bridge with wooden trestle approaches. The final leg to Walhalla was along the bed of Stringer's Creek on another series of high wooden trestles, and the depot was built on a platform spanning the creek. It was not until May 3, 1910, that loco 9A pulled the first official train into Walhalla.

Victoria's only other narrow-gauge line was a 3-mile (4.8 km) horse-drawn line between Welshpool and Port Welshpool, which ran from 1905 to 1940.

The first locomotives used on the Victorian narrow gauge were a pair of Baldwin 2-6-2 tank engines, imported from Philadelphia in 1898. Two duplicates of the Baldwins were built in Victorian Railways' Newport Shops, using the original locomotives' spare parts. Thirteen additional copies were ultimately built there.

Looking for more powerful locomotives —longer and heavier trains would reduce train mileage—two 2-6-0 + 0-6-2 Garratts were purchased from Beyer, Peacock & Company of Manchester, England. They were assembled at the Newport Shops and put in service on the Beech Forest and Walhalla lines in 1926.

Over the years, Victorian Railways rostered a full complement of goods wagons (freight cars) and passenger coaches, peaking at 298 cars in 1920—all built at Newport.

None of the Victorian narrow-gauge lines ever turned a profit and were shut down one by one. The Walhalla line was cut back to Plantina in 1944, to Erica in 1952, and was finally abandoned in 1954. The line to Whitfield was shut down in 1953. Dismantling of the Beech Forest line began in 1961, and the last train operated in 1962.

The scenic line through Upper Ferntree Gully to Gembrook was closed in 1953, when the track was buried by a landslide between Selby and Menzies. However, passengers still ride the line from Belgrade through Menzies Creek to Lakeside. In Melbourne, children, as well as more than a few adults with cameras and tape recorders, flock to ride the restored trains now operated by the Puffing Billy Preser-

vation Society, which also maintains a museum at Menzies.

The society was formed when Victorian Railways decided clearing the Selby slide was not cost-effective and closed the line, but they were persuaded to operate for tourists from Upper Ferntree Gully to Belgrave. Then-expanding Melbourne appropriated the right-of-way for a broad-gauge electrified transit line, and Puffing Billy went into retirement.

Australia's Citizen Military Forces joined in the rescue. Needing an engineering exercise, they took on the job of building a bypass around the slide, and soon Puffing Billy's red trains were running the opposite way, from Belgrave to Menzies Creek. Later, additional volunteers reopened the line to Lakeside.

Today, Puffing Billy continues to operate 365 days per year, thanks to the many volunteer navvies and other unpaid enthusiasts who provide most of the necessary personnel. The train crews, however, are paid professional railroaders—rostered employees of Victorian Railways.

See also: *Australian Railways: Indian-Pacific, Iron Ore Railways of Australia; Beyer-Garratt Locomotive; Gauge.*

Queensland Railways. There are some 6,000 route miles (9,600 km) of 3-foot 6-inch gauge based on the 1,040-mile (1,664 km) main line along the east coast between Brisbane and Cairns. Five major

branch lines totaling 500 miles (800 km) climb the mountains to the interior and service much of the state. Electrification of the Brisbane suburban lines required new coaches, as the original equipment, which, although purchased in anticipation of electrification (without electric motors), was worn out from being hauled by 4-6-4T steam locomotives and diesels for thirty years before the electrification project was completed. Electrification now extends north to Rockhampton, on the Tropic of Capricorn, some 400 miles (640 km) from Brisbane.

South Australian State Transport Authority—Rail Division. The broad-gauge South Australia Railways never developed much beyond the southeast corner of the state around Adelaide. There was a detached 3-foot 6-inch-gauge line on the Eyre Peninsula at Port Lincoln and a now-closed network of the same gauge serving the east and northeast of the state. The only other rail is the standard gauge put down by the Commonwealth Railway for the transcontinental route.

The smallest of the mainland systems, the SAR peaked at about 1,600 miles

Queensland Railways No. 2401, a class GL 22C-2, rests between assignments at Brisbane.

(2,560 km) of 5-foot 3-inch gauge and 1,000 miles (1,600 km) of narrow gauge; all but the Adelaide suburban service was transferred to the Australian National Railways in 1978. In the steam days, SAR had a modern fleet of American-designed (but British-built) locomotives that operated alongside nineteenth-century brass-trimmed steam pots. The fleet included smooth shark-nosed 4-8-4s reminiscent of the Pennsylvania Railroad's T-1s, as well as Beyer-Garratts and handsome English Electric diesels that were visually similar to Alco PAs. Signaling was based on American practice.

State Rail Authority of New South Wales.

This 6,000-mile (9,600 km) standard-gauge system is Australia's most important. Sydney is the center of the essential main lines that radiate north 600 miles (960 km) to Brisbane via Newcastle and the coal country, west 700 miles (1,120 km) to Broken Hill, and southwest 400 miles (640 km) to Albury, where it connects with the Victorian standard-gauge line to Melbourne and the Victorian system. A branch line connects with Canberra, the federal capital, which is 200 miles (320 km) from Sydney. Numerous branches and secondary lines that once guaranteed coverage for all but the western third of the state are no longer in service.

It was the New South Wales system that followed British practices most closely, with signaling stations, and rolling stock that could pass for English, particularly in the early steam era. The heavy 4-8-2s and Beyer-Garratts are long gone, replaced in part by locally built American-design diesels. Sydney suburban service is electrified using double-deck multiple units. Some of these operate as far as Newcastle, 100 miles (160 km) to the north; Lithgow, 100 miles (160 km) to the west; and Wollongong, 50 miles (80 km) to the south. Electric locomotives pull mainline freight trains on the climb to the Blue Mountains and on other intercity trunk routes. American-built Budd RDC self-propelled railcars were assigned to passenger service from Sydney to Nowra, but now most long-distance passenger trains are pulled by push-pull XPT trains.

Tasman Peninsula Railway.

Captain O'Hara Booth was the commandant of the Van Diemen's Land convict settlement at Port Arthur, on the Tasman Island state of Australia (off the southeast coast), in the early nineteenth century. To travel from Hobart to Port Arthur, ships had to sail out and around Cape Raoul—"Rounding Raoul," in the parlance of the day, was likened to rounding the Horn. Captain Booth resolved to build a railway across the peninsula to lessen the ordeal.

Steam power was unknown, and horses were rare, but convicts were more than plentiful, and manpower would do perfectly well for the 4.3-mile (7 km) distance. In 1836, construction began. The wooden rails, cut locally from gum trees, were laid following the rolling contour of the natural terrain, and earthworks were minimal. The gauge was set at 4 feet 8 1/2 inches, and the wooden sleepers were spaced at 8 feet (2.4 m). Small wooden carts, with two benches, rode on four cast-iron wheels. Long handles projected from the corners of the cart for the four convicts to push against while climbing grades. When the summit was reached, the puffing prisoners hopped aboard for the careering ride down the other side. On one 1 3/4-mile (3 km) downhill stretch, speeds reached 40 mph

Modern Australian passenger service is illustrated by this Australian National Railway Commission train, led by diesel locomotive EL-62, in Dry Creek, South Australia, on August 24, 1992.

(65 kph), with only a rudimentary log drag brake for control.

Rest huts were provided at both ends of the route and at the middle for the twenty prisoners who operated the line. A typical workday was three trips out and back, with a crew change halfway, or 31 miles (50 km) per day of toil and struggle. It might be noted that free laborers in the nineteenth century fared no better.

Completion of Australia's first railway allowed coastal passengers to avoid rounding Raoul by being boated ashore at Norfolk Bay and taking a seat in the "carriage" at what is now Taranna. After being propelled across the peninsula to Long Bay (present-day Oakwood), they were only 3 miles (4.8 km) from Port Arthur, by beach or sea.

A Captain Stoner, in his book *A Year in Tasmania*, described the crew of the French frigate *Artimise* when they rode the Tasman Peninsula Railroad. They were "in ecstasies with their descent, which on a larger scale, reminded them of the Montagnes Russes of Paris: down they went, hallooing, shouting, screaming like madmen."

Victorian Government Railways.

The smallest state, only 500 miles (800 km) east to west and half as much north to south, Victoria boasted 4,400 miles (7,000 km) of broad-gauge railway that served all but the mountainous area northeast of Melbourne. Most lines no longer carry passengers, and many have ceased to operate, but one long-distance electrified line serves the eastern coalfields. Wooden passenger coaches were still used in the 1980s. The railroad also once maintained a modern fleet of Indian-influenced steam locomotives, and dieselization brought a fleet of cab units almost identical to American F Units.

The steam era of the narrow gauge is represented by Puffing Billy, a restored passenger train running between Lakeside and Belgrave in the Dandenong Ranges, near Melbourne. The railway was restored and is managed by the Puffing Billy Preservation Society.

Right, top: The Victorian Railways switched to diesel with a fleet of locomotives of American design built locally under license. The Clyde Works turned out the double-ended A66 based on General Motors' revolutionary F Unit. It was painted to commemorate the Australian Bicentenary in 1988. Right, middle: Commuter lines were serviced by push-pull units like N459, shown with a passenger train at Dry Creek, South Australia. A push-pull arrangement allows for operation in reverse by an engineer using an extra set of controls located in the rear passenger car, eliminating the necessity to turn entire trains at the end of the line. Right, bottom: Another F Unit clone, Victoria Line A73, is pulling into Melbourne with a passenger train. These diesels were once painted in a scheme highly reminiscent of the Erie Railroad locomotives of the 1950s, but as in America, the classic paint has succumbed to less pleasing, contemporary graphics.

Westrail (Western Australian Government Railways). Fifty years ago, the railway was entirely 3-foot 6-inch gauge with much mileage in little-used branch lines that looped around, connecting many points by multiple routes, all revolving around Perth. In 1957, a total of 800 miles (1,280 km) of lightly used branches were simultaneously abandoned—and even that drastic measure closed only those lines carrying fewer than one train per week.

Today, the system includes 3,800 route miles (6,100 km), of which 80 percent remains narrow gauge and the rest a gauge of 4 feet 8¹/₂ inches. The use of standard gauge began when the Perth-Kalgoorlie section was dual gauged to accommodate connection with the Commonwealth Railway's transcontinental line, and then some branches in the eastern part of the state were converted.

The mineral boom of the 1960s greatly increased traffic and inspired the construction of brand-new isolated private railways, all built to handle large quantities of iron ore from mines in the northern part of the state to port. Heavy trains of up to 18,000 tons (16,200 t) operate under CTC control, on primarily single track, through arid semi-desert with no towns within a thousand miles. The operations are straightforward, a matter of putting two or three diesels onto 175 to 200 loaded ore cars and hauling the loads to the coast, with the empties returning inland in a continuous flow. Hammersley Iron Company did import an English Castle class 4-6-0 in 1978 to operate excursion trains and amuse the mechanical staff.

On Westrail, locomotives have always been unremarkable—small steam locos on the narrow gauge and basic diesels. The last steams, however, were the V-class 2-8-2s of 1955, bought to replace the original order of poorly performing diesels. In 1938, the old transcontinental express did offer hot showers on the narrow-gauge Perth-Kalgoorlie leg. Today, the same run provides one of the fastest average speeds— 50 mph (80 kph) in Australia, on standard-gauge track.

See also: *Australian Railways: Indian-Pacific, Iron Ore Railroads of Australia, Puffing Billy of Australia; Gauge; RDC; Trans-Australia Railway.*

Autotrain

In the face of declining passenger traffic in the United States, a new service common in Europe was imported. The Autotrain Corporation was formed in 1969 to offer long-distance rail service for passengers and their automobiles. It was one service planes and buses could not compete with. Families could arrive at a vacation destination without the fatigue of long-distance driving, but still have their car available for use while there.

There were several difficulties to overcome in setting up the U.S. version of the service. While Amtrak's exclusive rights to passenger service meant Autotrain could be barred from their routes, Amtrak could not implement an auto-carrying service of its own because the railroads that owned the trackage on which Amtrak operated would not permit the passenger trains to haul "freight." Autotrain was able to negotiate its own agreements on routes roughly parallel to Amtrak's.

The service proved to be as popular in the United States as it was in Europe, where similar trains operated on 143 routes. Autotrain ran from Lorton, Virginia, outside of Washington, to Sanford, Florida, near the popular destination of Disneyworld. With twelve purple-and-white diesel locomotives and a fleet of 182 passenger and 315 auto-carrying cars, the service carried a quarter of a million passengers annually.

A second route was opened up to meet the needs of the Midwest-to-Florida traffic, and the future looked as bright for the American Autotrain as it had been for its European counterparts. Unfortunately, a series of disastrous derailments and economic woes conspired against the company, and it folded in 1981. Two years later, Amtrak took over the Washington to Florida route, which continues to be popular today.

The takeover by Amtrak meant the white, purple, and red design of Autotrain was to disappear under red, white, and blue paint, but the service hardly changed—passengers and their cars are still being whisked through Ashland, Virginia on their way south.

B

Baldwin, Matthias William (1795–1866)

Born in Elizabeth, New Jersey, Baldwin began his career as a jeweler, and created an improved gold-plating process. Unhappy with the prospects of his trade, however, he entered a partnership that manufactured bookbinders' tools and calico-printing cylinders. Needing to mechanize the successful business, Baldwin discarded a purchased steam engine that proved unsatisfactory and built his own, combining an ingenious vertical boiler and cylinders to conserve floor space. The unique design and quality of workmanship earned a number of orders for similar equipment, causing a shift in the business and an end to the partnership.

By 1830, the use of steam power on railroads was being explored as a few locomotives were imported from England and one unsuccessful example was constructed by the West Point Foundry in New York. The proprietor of the Philadelphia Museum asked Baldwin to construct a miniature locomotive and two carriages to demonstrate steam power. Having only a description of the locomotives used in the Rainhill Trials in England, Baldwin completed the model in 1831, and it operated successfully, carrying four passengers at a time through the rooms of the museum.

The Philadelphia, Germantown & Norristown was sufficiently impressed to order a locomotive to replace horses on a 6-mile

Matthias Baldwin's early experiments with steam power led to the founding of one of the world's great industrial giants—the Baldwin Locomotive Works, of Philadelphia. Unfortunately, the company that thrived with steam power could not compete in the diesel era with newcomers General Motors and General Electric.

(9.6 km) railway. Baldwin paid a visit to the Camden & Amboy Railroad to inspect a yet-to-be-assembled locomotive imported from England. After careful examination of the parts—and armed with little more than a few notes and the experience of the completed model—Baldwin began work on *Old Ironsides*, based on the design of the Stephenson Planet-type.

Despite the need to create new tools and processes and to train assistants, Baldwin was able to complete *Old Ironsides*, and it was tested on November 23, 1832. Despite a few problems and imperfections, the 5-ton (4.5 t) locomotive was considered a success and was placed into service, operat-

ing for twenty years. Due to the "defects," Baldwin had some difficulty collecting the agreed-upon $4,000, but when corrections were made, a compromise amount of $3,500 was paid.

The second Baldwin locomotive was the 7-ton (6.3 t) *E. L. Miller* of 1834. After examining other locomotives, Baldwin included a number of improvements over *Old Ironsides*, including solid metal wheels (although they were cast in brass, which proved too soft) rather than compound wood and iron. A "half-crank" axle that placed a crank offset on the back of each wheel, integral with the spokes and outside the frame (the bearings remained on the axle end outside the wheel), enabled the connecting rods and cylinders to be outside the frame as well, which allowed a larger boiler to be mounted lower in the frame.

The Commonwealth of Pennsylvania was building a railway and asked Baldwin to provide steam power to replace horses, which led to the 9-ton (8.1 t) *Lancaster*, completed in June 1834. It was so successful that the state ordered two more and the Philadelphia & Trenton ordered another, making a total of five locomotives delivered in 1834. The company moved into a new shop, and fourteen locomotives were completed in 1835, forty in both 1836 and 1837, twenty-six in 1839, and nine in 1840, with one exported to Austria. Most of these

The most handsome of the Baldwin diesels, appropriately labeled Sharks, were purchased by the Pennsylvania, New York Central, and Baltimore & Ohio. These diesels were built in both passenger and freight versions. The demonstrator paint scheme on No. 6001 was especially striking. This unit eventually went to the B&O.

were of the same early design. With three hundred employees, the Baldwin Locomotive Works was becoming a force in the North American locomotive market.

An early association with the legendary Ross Winans of the Baltimore & Ohio (B&O) produced the ungainly "Crab" design of 1842. In 1852, Baldwin secured a contract with the Pennsylvania Railroad for a dozen 28-ton (25.2 t) locomotives, signaling an arrangement that lasted until Baldwin left the diesel locomotive market.

The company continued to grow and prosper, surviving several partnership and name changes and contributing numerous revolutionary advances in locomotive design. Matthias Baldwin died in September 1866, and the company continued to operate as the Baldwin Locomotive Works.

A detailed history of the evolution of steam locomotive design and Baldwin's contributions is well beyond this entry, but it can safely be said that the Baldwin Works, as one of the "Big Three" (with Alco and Lima), was at the center of steam locomotive development for more than one hundred years. The company was also involved with Westinghouse Electric in the development of heavy traction locomotives; it experimented with steam turbines and entered the diesel locomotive business in 1939.

Baldwin's prowess in steam locomotives was well demonstrated by the thirty EM-1 2-8-8-4s turned out for the Baltimore & Ohio in 1944 and 1945. The 314-ton (282.6 t) articulated locomotive thunders across the Potomac River at historic Harper's Ferry with a westbound fast freight.

Baldwin, like other steam builders, could not adequately compete with General Motors' Electro-Motive Division (EMD), but produced several noteworthy locomotives. The "Sharknose" diesel was a classic inspired by the Raymond Loewy designs for streamlining the Pennsy's steam locos, but the Baldwin Works, in addition to their large steam locomotives, is also noted for their oversized diesels. The "Centipede" DR-12-8s were 3,000-hp behemoths that rode on twelve axles (twenty-four wheels). The Pennsylvania bought twenty-four units and coupled them in pairs, making a 6,000-hp unit crawling on twenty-four visible wheels—thus the nickname. Many of the other diesel designs also had unusual appearances.

After a 1950 merger with arch-rival Lima, the company became the Baldwin-Lima-Hamilton Corporation. However, its fortunes did not improve, and the company left the locomotive business. But in

1956, a comeback attempt was made. In conjunction with car builder Pullman-Standard, the lightweight streamlined Train-X was built. The 1,000-hp locomotives used a German twelve-cylinder Maybach engine along with a Mek-hydro (hydraulic) transmission. Three train sets were built, two for the New Haven and one for the New York Central. These experiments marked the end of 125 years of locomotive production.

Baltimore & Ohio Railroad (B&O)

Generally conceded to be the first American railroad to operate and build a line for general traffic, the B&O also holds the rare distinction of retaining its original name throughout its 150-year history. A number of Baltimore merchants met on February 2, 1827, to develop the project, and incorporation soon followed. The states of Virginia and Pennsylvania soon confirmed the charter.

Charles Carroll of Carrollton, the last surviving signer of the Declaration of Independence, was present at the laying of a cornerstone on July 4, 1828. Despite opposition, including the United States Congress, financing was secured and 13 miles (21 km) of construction was completed to Ellicott Mills, Maryland. Operation began, using horses as power, in May 1830.

Steam power arrived three months later, with a successful run by *Tom Thumb*, an experimental locomotive. April 1, 1832, saw the line complete to Point of Rocks, on the Potomac River some 72 miles (115 km) from Baltimore. On December 1, 1834, the B&O reached Harpers Ferry. A branch from Baltimore to Washington was completed in 1835, and the main line was extended to Cumberland, "Queen City of the Alleghenies," 178 miles (285 km) from Baltimore, in 1842.

Expansion to the Ohio River at Wheeling, (West) Virginia, took eleven difficult years. Eleven tunnels, thirteen major bridges, and a tortuous temporary switchback were needed to conquer the Allegheny Mountains, but Wheeling was reached on January 1, 1853. The Parkersburg extension was completed in 1857, and by connections with other lines, St. Louis, on the Mississippi River, was reached later that year.

The B&O became embroiled in the Civil War, as the Union and Confederate armies swept back and forth across its route. Track and bridges were destroyed, locomotives stolen, and rolling stock burned. Following the war, expansion and consolidation with other railroads created a great network of trackage spreading from Baltimore to St. Louis and Chicago on the west, Buffalo on the north, and New York City on the east.

Unfortunately, the competition from mergers and deregulation ultimately doomed the B&O, and the proud railroad was finally absorbed into the Chessie System, which became a part of CSX Transportation.

Berkshire-type Locomotive

The 2-8-4 type was first built by Lima Locomotive Works of Lima, Ohio. It was the beginning of Lima's evolutionary Super Power series, which combined power and speed. The first order went to the Boston & Albany for use in the Berkshire Mountains, thus providing the name. The Nickel Plate Road operated fast freights through the American Midwest and ordered 65 S Class Berkshires between 1942 and 1948, many of which were in use until 1958. Several were preserved, including the Fort Wayne Historical Society's No. 765, which operates regularly in excursion service. Another large fleet of Berkshires was owned by the Chesapeake & Ohio; their No. 2716 was restored by the Norfolk Southern for excursions.

Often called the epitome of "Super Power" steam, Lima Locomotive Works supplied these 2-8-4 Berkshire locomotives to numerous American railroads. The New York, Chicago & St. Louis, more commonly known as "The Nickel Plate Road," was noted for the fast freights hauled across the Midwest by No. 756 and other Berkshire-type locomotives. Several Lima "Berks" still operate in fan trip service.

Beyer-Garratt Locomotive

In 1908, a consulting engineer named Herbert W. Garratt took out a patent for a novel articulated locomotive. This new design featured two completely independent engine units, practically identical in arrangement and weight, that supported a single large cradle-mounted boiler slung between them. The boiler and firebox sizes were not restricted by the space between the wheels, as in a conventional design; therefore, an ideal, short-barreled boiler of maximum diameter heated with a wide firebox was possible. This boiler design, coupled with the flexibility of the articulated chassis, made for superb tracking on sharp curves and free-steaming characteristics for efficient power generation. The weight, being distributed over a large number of drivers, allowed for good traction as well as light loading on the rail.

Beyer, Peacock & Company, a British locomotive builder, was quick to recognize the design's potential and licensed the design from Garratt at a fee of £2 per ton to him and his heirs. The first Garratts were small 2-foot-gauge 0-4-0 + 0-4-0s, built for the Tasmanian Government Railways in 1909, later followed by a similar design for the Darjeeling-Himalayan Railway in 1911. The second order was placed by the West Australian Government Railway, also in 1911, for six 2-6-0 + 0-6-2s at a gauge of 3 feet 6 inches. Foreign railway builders were reluctant to accept the new design, but Beyer, Peacock persuaded the South African Railways to test a large 2-6-0 + 0-6-2 type against a huge four-cylinder

compound Mallet. The Mallet weighed 179 1/2 tons (161 t) and produced a nominal tractive effort of 65,000 pounds (29,445 kg), while the smaller Garratt produced 47,385 pounds (21,465 kg) and weighed 133 1/2 tons (120 t). It seemed that the Garratt was outmatched on the 27-mile (43 km) climb up the 1 in 58 grade from South Coast Junction (near Durban) to Botha's Hill.

The more powerful Mallet could not utilize this advantage because of steaming problems inherent to the design, but the free-steaming Garratt exceeded expectations. The incredulous railroaders arranged for an extended test: a three-month trial between Ladysmith and Glencoe Junction in the spring of 1922. Both locomotives made fifty-eight round trips of 88 miles (140 km) each, pulling approximately 825 tons (742.5 t) per trip. In addition to recording the round-trip times, detailed measurements were taken on the three

The powerful British-built Beyer-Garratt-type articulated locomotive was exported throughout the world, and in numerous sizes successfully served railroads of virtually all gauges. The search for increased tractive effort took many paths, from increasing the number of drive wheels to increasing the weight on them.

worst grades. The aggregate time for all fifty-eight trips was 5,358 minutes for the Mallet, but only 4,130 minutes for the Garratt, which also used three quarters of a ton less coal for each round trip.

It was a stunning triumph, and the Beyer-Garratt type, as it became known, was exported throughout the world, in sizes from light narrow-gauge locos to the South African GL Class monsters. The design was never developed for high speed, but the Garratt earned a well-deserved reputation as a dependable slogger in the

tough conditions and light trackage often found in developing countries.

Australia chose the Garratt design during World War II, as the northward rush of troops and supplies created a need for new, powerful, but lightly treading locomotives. First came the War Department's Class CLTB of 1941. Commonly known as the Australian Standard Garratt, or ASG, it was a 4-8-2 + 2-8-4 of 3-foot 6-inch gauge and had a 9.4 ton (8.5 t) axle loading for the lightweight rail that was hastily thrown down to support the war effort. Sixty-five of these locos were constructed between 1943 and 1945. After the war, three were sold to Tasmania and three more to South Australia, where they operated until dieselization. Another unit went to the Australian Portland Cement Company, but the remainder were scrapped.

In 1950, the Queensland Government Railways purchased the 1000 Class Garrett, a larger, more powerful version of the ASG, with increased coal and water capacity for the long haul across the dry Queensland plains. The Railways of the State of New South Wales needed heavy power for hauling minerals from inland mines on the central plains to the coast, at Sydney. These standard-gauge 4-8-4 + 4-8-4 giants, designated the AD60 class, were the first Garratts to have a cast-steel engine-bed frame, which included integral cylinders. They weighed 264 tons (238 t) and remained in operation until March 1973.

The largest Garratt built was the Class Ya-01 4-8-2 + 2-8-4 of the USSR railways. They stood 17 feet (5.2 m) high, with a boiler diameter of 7 feet 6 inches (2.3 m), and weighed 262.5 tons (236 t). In contrast, the smallest were two 0-6-0 + 0-6-0s built in 1913 for the Arakan Flotilla Company of Burma. They weighed 23.5 tons (21 t) and operated on 2-foot 6-inch gauge track. That there are Garratts still in operation today is a tribute to the British heavy-engineering industry.

Even standing still Big Boy is impressive, the clean lines and sheer size reflecting one of steam power's finest.

Big Boy

The world's largest conventional steam locomotives, twenty-five Big Boys were built by the American Locomotive Works (Alco) between 1941 and 1944 for the Union Pacific Railroad. Appropriately named after the chalk marking applied to an uncompleted locomotive by an unknown employee, they had a 4-8-8-4 wheel arrangement and the four cylinders operated simply. Designed for hauling fast, heavy freights on the railroad's Sherman Hill grade, they could run at 80 mph (129 kph). With a length of 130 feet 9 inches (39.9 m), a height of 16 feet 2½ in (4.9 m), and a weight (including tender) of 1,120,000 pounds (508,020 kg), they generated 7,000 hp at 300 pounds of steam pressure. To accommodate the massive locomotives, the world's largest turntables, 135 feet (41 m), were installed at Green River, Wyoming, and Ogden, Utah, in 1945.

Bloomers

J. E. McConnell, locomotive superintendent of the London & North Western's Southern Division, was one of the few designers willing to take on Brunel and Gooch in the search for speed. He created a new design for an inside-frame 2-2-2 express locomotive that, for the first time, completely exposed the wheels without the skirting that had come to be expected on a "decent" locomotive.

Immediately nicknamed "Bloomers," after the popular ladies' undergarment of the day, they were eventually produced in three sizes—small, large, and extra large. Bloomers were a clear success, riding smoothly (unlike the yawing of the Stephenson "long Boilers"), and they didn't pound the rails like the low-center-of-gravity Cramptons. With their large boilers and their wheels spread about the long rigid wheelbase, the Bloomers "rode like a swing, easily and comfortably, and their drivers took full advantage of this to make them fly." It must be remembered that the Bloomers rode on the world's straightest

and best-maintained tracks, however, and locomotive design in the rest of the world took quite a different direction.

See also: *Brunel, Isambard Kingdom; Crampton, Thomas Russell; Gooch, Daniel; Stephenson, George.*

Branca, Giovanni (1571–1645)

This early-seventeenth-century inventor adapted Hero's aeolipile, a parlor amusement for centuries, and created what we know today as the impulse turbine. Water was boiled in a hollow casting in the shape of a cigar-smoking Indian. The steam collected in the head, escaped as a jet from a hole in the end of the cigar, and turned a

small windmill. A series of reduction gears converted the energy of the windmill into power, which drove a pair of cams that raised and lowered two pestles in two mortar bowls.

Branca's machine, like its predecessor aeolipile, remained in the category of scientific curiosity, but he envisioned larger models operating water pumps. The increasing needs of the burgeoning industrial age created a greater demand for coal and ore, and the mining industry depended on manually operated piston pumps to remove water. This machine was neither efficient nor powerful enough to operate a a large mining pump, and the first practical steam engine waited for another day.

See also: *Aeolipile; Newcomen, Thomas.*

The name Big Boy says it all. The Union Pacific was (and still is) fond of oversize locomotives for use in the wide open spaces of Wyoming. Big Boys were the largest conventional steam locomotives ever built —twenty-five of the 4-8-8-4 articulated monsters were produced by American Locomotive Works between 1941 and 1945. Although articulated, the engines were not Mallets because new steam was used in all four cylinders. These powerful locomotives were at home hauling hundred-car fast freights up the grade of Union Pacific's (or "Uncle Pete's") Sherman Hill. No. 4017, brother to No. 4019 (above), is preserved at the National Railroad Museum in Green Bay, Wisconsin.

Brotherhood of Railroad Trainmen

Immediately following the American War Between the States, railroading was so hazardous that employment as a trainman was sufficient reason to be denied insurance, and seven out of ten train crew members were seriously injured or killed on the job. There was no workmen's compensation, Social Security, unemployment insurance, Medicare, or minimum wage, nor was there an eight-hour day or a forty-hour week.

Organized labor had made no inroads. Strikes were quickly, sometimes brutally, suppressed, and strikers were blackballed. There was no redress for a worker from an employer's negligence. In this grim atmosphere, eight determined men met on September 13, 1883, in Delaware & Hudson (D&H) caboose No. 10, which was parked in the freight yard at Oneonta, New York. The car was assigned to conductor Charles J. Woodworth. Meeting with him that day were William Gurney, Daniel Hopkins, Daniel J. and Eugene McCarty, Union C. Osterhout, and Elmer Wessel and H.S. Wilbur. The group's modest objectives were summed up by Wessel: "We want better working conditions and some kind of insurance for those who might be stricken by illness, injury, or death." Woodworth was chosen as the first grand master of the organization, then called the Brotherhood of Railroad Brakemen, and the movement spread rapidly as local lodges sprang up across the country.

In 1889, the name was changed to Brotherhood of Railroad Trainmen, and

The men who toiled for the railroads worked under conditions that would be incomprehensible today. This 1868 photograph of a Union Pacific camp clearly shows both the isolation and the primitive facilities at the site that was to become the railroad town of Green River, Wyoming. The comfort and safety of employees were not high priorities in the efforts to knit the web of rails that would one day service the entire country.

the BRT, headquartered in Cleveland, Ohio, became the largest of the rail operating unions.

Caboose No. 10 was later restored by the D&H and placed on display, under cover, in a park in Oneonta.

Brunel, Isambard Kingdom (1806–1859)

Brunel was the first chief engineer of Britain's Great Western Railway (GWR), but he knew little of railroads, his construction experience having been confined to bridges and docks. Nonetheless, it was Brunel who was selected to build the Great Western from London to Bristol. Perhaps because of his lack of experience, but also, possibly, because of his unique vision, Brunel insisted in varying from common practice at any opportunity.

Despite the clearly established standard gauge of 4 feet 8 1/2 inches, Brunel disregarded all warnings and advice and insisted on a broad gauge of 7 feet for the Great Western. Even in 1835, it was becoming obvious that the various rail lines spreading throughout Great Britain would eventually need to be knitted together into a connecting system, and the proposed broad gauge of the GWR would put it at a disadvantage. Initial construction costs would be higher for both right-of-way and rolling stock as well.

Brunel prevailed on the matter of gauge, however, and also pursued a fetish for easy grades, further compounding construction difficulties. He limited the grade to 1 in 660 west of London as the Great Western avoided the established population centers of Newbury, Hungerford, and Devizes, making a wide sweep to the north through the Vale of the White Horse and climbing the watershed between the Thames and Avon rivers. As the GWR ran along the limestone flanks of the Cotswold Hills, Brunel ignored his preference for easy grades when he tunneled through Box Hill, 96 miles (153 km) west of London. Rather than climb the ridge and descend the far side at a low grade for 7 or 8 miles (11 or 13 km), the GWR circled to the south and tunneled deep under Box Hill at a slope of 1 in 100, reaching the floor of the next valley in just 2 miles (3.2 km).

Isambard Kingdom Brunel, one of the world's greatest engineers and well known for his work on British railways, poses in front of the **Great Eastern,** *his acclaimed steam ship.*

This extreme bit of engineering was inconsistent with Brunel's often expressed theories and was far more costly than the alternatives, but can be explained by the vanity and showmanship of the brilliant engineer himself. Each year, on the anniversary of Brunel's birth, the sun shines through the tunnel from end to end. Accomplishment of this feat required the slope of 1 in 100 to match the angle of the sun's rays.

The Great Western's Bristol line was completed in 1841, and subsequent new construction and amalgamations of existing lines of several gauges led to a Great Western system that ultimately included 600 miles (960 km) of broad-gauge track, 230 miles (368 km) of mixed-gauge, and 420 miles (672 km) of narrow-gauge. Brunel's vision was in question as this mixture of gauges proved to be a serious handicap. Shippers signed petitions requesting standardization because wide-gauge goods wagons were rarely filled and were therefore uneconomical to use. The GWR began to convert to standard gauge in 1868, and finished in 1892, ending the battle of the gauges in Great Britain.

Brunel continued his eccentric ways, experimenting with longitudinal rather than the standard transverse sleepers (ties), but the rigidity of the rails, with none of the resilience allowed by the spacing of ordinary sleepers, caused broken locomotive springs and tracking problems.

Adapting the system of Clegg and Samuda, he built an "atmospheric traction" propulsion system for the South Devon Railway in 1848. A piston, carried in an iron pipe between the rails, was attached through a slot sealed with a greased leather flap to a railroad carriage. Large stationary steam engines, located at intervals along the track, operated large pumps that exhausted the air from the pipe in front of the piston. Atmospheric pressure entered the pipe behind the piston and pushed the carriage along the rails. George Stephenson derogatorily referred to the invention as "the great humbug." While observers marveled at the high speeds attained, junctions proved difficult, rats feasted on the greased leather seals, and the expensive experiment was abandoned after operating for several months.

Brunel was at his best when he applied his immense talent to engineering bridges and structures, so primary responsibility for locomotive design on the Great Western was left with John Gooch. But Brunel built two locomotives, *Ajax* and *Hurricane*, which had 10-foot (3 m) driving wheels. They were retired after two years, while Brunel's magnificent bridges, viaducts, and stations endure today.

There was an unprecedented architectural splendor about the larger stations of his GWR. The elegant hammer-beam timber roof at Bristol spanned five broad-gauge tracks, and the second terminal at Paddington, completed in 1854, provided for lateral transfer of carriages between rail-

Above, top: Brunel's Box Hill Tunnel, nearly 2 miles (3.2 km) long, terrified early passengers who rode through it in the dark for twenty minutes. He cleverly oriented the tunnel so that the sun shone through the entire length on his birthday. Above: Due to navigational considerations, Maidenhead Bridge, which crosses the Thames, was limited to one central pier in its 300 feet (91 m). The low elevation of the approaches meant that Brunel was forced to build the flattest and longest brick arches ever attempted, and the bridge was expected to collapse. It wasn't until the "temporary" wood centering was blown down in a storm more than a year after completion that doubters were convinced.

roads by the use of turntables and transverse tracks. The handsome skylit arched roof overlooks broad roadways that anticipated motor transport.

Perhaps the apex of Brunel's skill was his Royal Albert Bridge, Saltash, connecting Devon with Cornwall. It is a clever composite of a tubular structure with a stiffened suspension bridge. Two enormous oblong tubes arch high over the water, with the deck gracefully suspended from these arches. Tall stone piers support a series of deck girders on the long viaduct approach to the main spans. Each span was constructed off site, and floated into place on the hulks of retired ships. Hydraulic jacks then lifted the spans to the tops of the piers. One of the tubes neatly deflected a German bomb during World War II. The Royal Albert Bridge was completed in 1859, shortly before the engineer's demise. As did many of the Victorian engineers, Brunel worked himself to death. After hearing of an accident involving his great ship, the *Great Eastern*, he suffered a stroke. His workers lifted him into an armchair and

placed it in a wagon. Brunel made his final journey, slowly crossing his bridge from Devon into Cornwall—and then he died, a great artist and an engineering giant.

The Budd Company

The youngest of the three major American passenger-car builders was also the most innovative. The Edward G. Budd Company, of Philadelphia, was a builder of steel automotive bodies when railroad car building experiments began, in 1931. The first product—lightweight, self-propelled cars riding on pneumatic tires—was not successful, but it pioneered the concept that led to Budd's ultimate success: spot-welded stainless steel car bodies.

Budd's entry into the rail business was a three-car, articulated, diesel-powered streamliner: the Chicago, Burlington & Quincy's Zephyr of 1934. Three more orders quickly followed—one for the Maine Central and two more for the Burlington route. In 1936, Budd turned out the first full-size stainless steel coach, Santa Fe 3070, which still operated in 1984 in New Jersey Transit commuter service.

They closed out the 1930s by producing sleek, shiny streamliners for the Burlington, Santa Fe, Seaboard, and Atlantic Coast lines. Budd broke with the company's tradition with the Tuscan red–painted South

The "drumhead" bearing the mark of the New York, Susquehanna & Western is positioned on the classic round end of a fluted stainless steel dome-observation car manufactured by the Budd Company.

Wind of the Pennsylvania, and turned to war work after completing the 1941 Empire State Express for the New York Central.

Although not the precursors of the dome car, the Budd-built Vista-Domes were the standard set for other builders. During the late 1940s, Budd produced twice as many dome cars as the competition, and reached its zenith with multiple-dome cars built for the famous California Zephyr.

During the following two decades, Budd built RDCs, high-level cars for the Santa Fe, multiple-unit (MU) commuter cars, gallery-style bi-level commuter coaches, the high-speed electric Metroliners for Amtrak, and rapid-transit cars for New York, Chicago, and Philadelphia. Production continued through the 1970s with 620 MU cars for the Long Island, 168 gallery coaches for Chicago commuter service, and Amtrak's Amfleet cars. Budd closed their legendary Red Lion plant after completing 150 Amfleet II cars for Amtrak in the early 1980s. Unlike the other major American car builders, Budd never built freight cars.

See also: *RDC.*

The Royal Albert (or Saltash) Bridge was the final accomplishment of the renowned British engineer I. K. Brunel. It is neither a true tubular bridge nor a true stiffened suspension bridge, but a clever combination of the two concepts. Built in 1859, it is still in use.

Above: The comfortable interior of a Budd dome-lounge shows why trains in the days of the streamliners are acknowledged as the pinnacle of elegant travel in the United States. Right: The Budd RDC, a self-propelled railcar, was a last attempt to reduce costs on lightly traveled lines. The cars could be coupled for multiple unit (MU) operation if traffic warranted.

Caboose

The little red caboose bringing up the rear of a train is inevitably the first piece of railroad rolling stock that is recognized by a child, and still remains the traditional symbol of "the end." The origins of the caboose are in dispute. The word is likened to words in several other languages each meaning, more or less, "a little room or hut." Spelled *caboose*, it has multiple meanings, including "an open-air cooking oven," "a kitchen on the deck of a ship," and "a galley." In addition to its railroad functions as the conductor's cabin and kitchen, the caboose also served in its nautical function as "the fo'csle and the crow's nest," or "lookout."

The first recorded use of a caboose in concept was in the 1840s on the Auburn & Syracuse, a short line absorbed by the New York Central. Conductor Nat Williams carried out his business while sitting on a wooden box at an upended barrel in an old boxcar, which also contained his tools, chains, lanterns, and flares, that was tacked on to the end of a mixed freight-passenger train.

The earliest known use of *caboose* as a word, in 1855, was in reference to the conductors' cars on the Buffalo, Corning & New York (later absorbed by the Erie-Lackawanna and then Conrail). In 1889, *The New York Times* reported that a New York Central predecessor, the New York & Harlem Railway of Commodore Vanderbilt, had been sued by an employee named Edgerton for injuries received in a "caboose car" in 1859.

The earliest cabooses were often flatcars with a shanty or cabin built on the deck (a number of railroads still call them "cabin cars"), but more common was a boxcar fitted with windows, side doors, bunks, stove, desk, and equipment storage. They sometimes doubled as baggage or passenger cars. These early cars still lacked the distinctive, charming identifier of the caboose—the cupola—which is credited to conductor T. B. Watson of the Chicago & Northwestern.

In a widely accepted version of the cupola's origin, Mr. Watson's regular, flat-topped caboose had been temporarily assigned to a work train, so an old boxcar was tacked onto the rear of his Cedar Rapids to Clinton freight train one sunny Iowa summer day in 1863. The car had a large hole in the roof, and Mr. Watson, in his whimsical way, piled up some boxes so he could sit on top with his head and shoulders projecting above the roof. From this precarious perch he was able to watch the passing parade of grazing cattle and farmers at work in their fields, wave at

The caboose functioned as an office for the conductor of a freight train; it performed similar duties, along with tool and material storage, on work trains.

pretty girls, and, incidentally, keep a watchful eye on the train rattling along ahead. Realizing the benefit of this "crow's nest," he reportedly sought out the C&NW master mechanic in Clinton, where two new cabooses were under construction, and suggested that the "lookout" be included. The official agreed, the cabooses were built, and the C&NW became the first railroad to operate cupolaed cabooses.

The use of cupolas was originally a strictly local custom. There were no cupolas on either the Central Pacific or the Union Pacific in 1869, when the tracks of the American transcontinental railroad were joined at Promontory, Utah. The first edition of *Master Carbuilder's Dictionary* in 1873 listed the word *caboose*, but

On lightly traveled lines, a mixed train might carry passengers, baggage, and LCL (less than carload) freight in the caboose. The side door in this Santa Fe caboose was beneficial in loading and unloading bulky items.

did not mention cupola. The 1884 second edition stated, "Cabooses are often made with lookouts for displaying train signals to locomotives and following trains, and to give trainmen a view of their train."

It is not known when the cupola became universal, but the well-known caboose of song and story from the glory days of railroading was always wood and always had a cupola. As trains grew longer and cars became taller, air brakes replaced hand

CABOOSE

"What is a caboose? Formally, it's the punctuation mark that concludes every freight train...a mobile office...a lookout post. It's also the most vulnerable victim of the ugly, often terrifying backlash of slack action. Or the only shelter when the flanger gets on the ground and snow closes in the line ahead and behind. Or a coffin if the second section overruns your flagman in the fog."

—David P. Morgan

SERVICE STARS

During World War II, it was common practice to display "service stars"—banners with a star for each member of a household that was serving in the military—in a window. Caboose 0673 of the Milwaukee Road displayed a star, thanks to conductor G.A. Volkman, who was proud of the service record of his furloughed flagman, Gene Koebel.

brakes, and railroad workers began to communicate via shortwave radio. By 1937, the need for a high perch in the "sun parlor" to signal the engineer and provide access to the car roofs to set hand brakes diminished, as the difficulty of looking over tall boxcars and trying to see cars almost a mile (1.6 km) ahead became impossible. The railroads were building steel cabooses then, and as they recognized the danger of snapping slack action and the "crack the whip" effect, which caused frequent falls from the cupola, the bay window evolved as a safer and more effective location for a trainman to ride. Australian cabooses often had a periscope, safely giving the crew a rooftop view of the train, and some British passenger cars also had a periscope.

The International Car Company produced a hybrid caboose, wherein the cupola itself had a bay window. In these newer cars, electric lights, kerosene or propane heat, double-pane windows, chemical toilets, and foam insulation all contributed to an increase in comfort and safety.

Caboose was originally a nautical term for "little house on a ship's deck" and eventually one caboose served both on land and at sea. No. 4259, an Erie four-wheeled "bobber" built in 1892, was damaged in a wreck, losing its wheels. It was shipped on a flat car to Susquehanna, Pennsylvania, for scrapping, where it was spotted by Captain Robert E. Peary, U.S.

For most of the history of railroads, the "little red caboose" signified both the end of the train and the warmth and romance of railroading. More practically, it was an office and home for the crew.

Navy, then visiting the president of the railroad. Noting that except for the shearing off of its wheels, it was undamaged and quite snug, Peary "borrowed" the bobber "for winter headquarters in Greenland." Once again loaded on a flat car, 4259 was shipped to New York, where, on July 4, 1898, it was hoisted onto the deck of the steamship windward and bolted down as protection from heavy seas. On the trip north, little 4259 served as a deck house until August 1898, when it was hauled to the top of a cliff at Etah, Greenland, to serve the explorer until the summer of 1901. Peary eventually returned 4259 to the Erie, who restored the caboose and displayed it as a commemorative exhibit until it was destroyed by fire in 1940. Marie Peary, the explorer's daughter, described the adventure in her book *North Pole Caboose*.

Above: This classic wooden caboose has been fitted as a dynamometer car to collect data on the power of locomotives. It exhibits all of the characteristics of the classic wooden caboose—end platforms, cupola, vertical wood siding, and stove pipe. Missing is the "possum belly," or tool box, under the frame.

Above: The Baltimore & Ohio's experiments with lightweight equipment that produced the round roof boxcar led them to a radically new caboose design as well. By adding a bay window instead of a cupola, the B&O shops' classic 1936 design would survive until the end of the caboose era, although it was not adopted by any other railroad.

The caboose, although merely picturesque to observers, has been critical to crews on long-distance trains, where eating and sleeping facilities may be few and far between. Thus, cabooses on the Trans-Siberian Railway, which travels through sparsely populated areas, provide eating and sleeping facilities for the crews during the grueling journey. Western Europe, however, does not have wide-open spaces comparable to North America or Australia. The comforts of home are not essential on a run between, say, London and Leeds, so European cabooses are different in history and design.

In Britain, the trainman in charge is a *guard*, rides in a *brake van*, and has authority over the engine driver. A highballing British train is under the control of the locomotive driver, subject, of course, to trackside signals and operating rules. The guard's job, much like that of an early-day American brakeman, is to apply hand brakes in case of a "drawbar snatching" (broken coupling) or to stretch the coupler slack in rolling country, and to carry marker lamps so the head-end crew can tell if the train has separated at night. Brake vans typically had four wheels, although the Great Western Railway used six-wheelers, and eight-wheeled brake vans were used on the Southern and a few others. Early British brake vans carried a form of cupola, but in England it was called a "birdcage."

In Germany, cabooses are known as *Güterzugpackwagen* (literally, "freight-train passenger car") and went into service in the 1840s with the beginning of non–mixed-freight trains. As in Britain and the rest of Europe, where trains travel short distances, the caboose is small and simple, with an open area like a baggage room (for which it once functioned). The *Güterzugpackwagen* has always been coupled directly behind the locomotive and provides office space for the conductor on longer runs, but a switching crew is not required since German freights generally run between terminals without switching.

With conductor space provided in locomotives, the caboose has disappeared from most freight trains around the world. In North America, the function of rear-end vigilance has been assigned to an "end of train" (EOT) flasher, or "flashing rear end

It seems unlikely that future generations will have the same sense of nostalgia regarding the end-of-train (EOT) device as we have for the caboose, but the little computerized device and the last car on the train had many of the same functions.

device" (FRED), a battery-powered electronic wizard in a metal box mounted on the rear coupler. FRED measures air-brake pressure (thus continuity of the train), radios the information to the cab, and provides a flashing warning light for following trains.

This, along with other measures of economy, has allowed for reduced crew size and the attendant dollar savings but has caused delays. With all crew in the locomotive, a mechanical problem in the rear portion of a mile (1.6 km)-long train that causes the train to stop leads to considerable loss of time before the defect can be reached and repaired. Thus, the caboose has come full circle, with several American railroads pulling them from the scrap line for refurbishment. The day of the little red caboose providing the "exclamation point" at the end of the train is not yet gone forever, and these charming anachronisms continue to serve a purpose in contemporary railroading.

See also: *Glossary of Railroad Terminology (for alternate caboose names)*.

Camelback Locomotives (Mother Hubbards)

Ross Winans' Camel concepts went through several phases of development as anthracite coal became more important. Several other builders made significant improvements in locomotive combustion capabilities, but one of the most significant was the Wootten firebox.

John Wootten began as an apprentice at Baldwin and rose to general manager of the Philadelphia & Reading (P&R). He became aware of the potential value in the vast heaps of waste anthracite coal surrounding the mines and breakers of eastern Pennsylvania. This culm, or buckwheat anthracite, was largely the breakage from handling, too fine for general use, and was thought to represent 18 to 20 percent of the total production at the time. Wootten began to use the material in stationary boilers, reporting the use of nearly 7,000 tons (6,300 t) of the material in heating the shops and depots of the railroad. Experiments with a locomotive proved the need for a larger grate area if the culm was to burn satisfactorily.

The first locomotive equipped with the extraordinarily wide Wootten firebox was P&R 4-6-0 No. 408, completed in January 1877. Although the culm still would not burn well until a rough cleaning lowered the 15 to 20 percent shale content, the yearly fuel bill for a ten-wheeler was

reduced by nearly $2,000 from normal anthracite. By 1883, with 171 working Wootten-boilered locomotives, the P&R saved $378,000 on its total yearly anthracite bill.

The disadvantage of the Wootten design was the lack of room for a cab at the rear of the boiler, although the earliest Woottens managed to squeeze one on. But the boiler and wheel diameters were increasing to meet the need for speed, leaving no room at the rear, and mounting the cab on top of the boiler, Camel style, would make the locomotive top heavy. Thus the cab draped over and around the boiler, in front of the wide firebox, producing the Camelback

Right: Reading No. 676 rains cinders down on the trailing coaches as the train accelerates to speed. Below: The wide fireboxes required to properly burn anthracite coal inspired the Camelback design, in which the cab straddles the boiler. Central of New Jersey No. 592, built in 1901, set passenger-train speed records between Philadelphia and New York before retirement in 1949. It can still be seen at the Baltimore & Ohio Museum.

design, also called "Mother Hubbard." As in the Camel, the fireman was separated from the engineer and had to work from a covered platform at the rear of the firebox.

The Camelback design permeated the rosters of the eastern roads and even went west when stone coal and lignite were encountered. They were produced in most wheel arrangements: 0-4-0 to 0-8-0 switchers; 4-4-0 and 4-6-0 fast passenger locomotives; 2-8-0 freight haulers; and even a massive pair of Alco-built 0-8-8-0s for helper service on the Erie. Virtually all common wheel arrangements were seen, and the locomotives were used in everyday service of all types.

Despite their widespread use, there were other drawbacks besides the remoteness of the fireman. The engineer had little room for movement, and a steam leak from a broken gauge or leaking joint was deadly. The position above the rapidly rotating wheels meant that a flailing broken siderod was virtually fatal, and there was little opportunity to jump free from an imminent collision. In 1818, the Interstate Commerce Commission banned the further construction of Mother Hubbards, although there were a few exceptions. More than 3,000 were built, and the locomotives remained in operation until the end of steam. There were still forty-seven operating on Class 1 roads in 1953 (almost all on the Central of New Jersey), but the last seven were retired in 1954, although CRRNJ No. 774 ran on excursions for a while longer.

There are still three Camelbacks in existence: Lackawanna 4-4-0 No. 952 at the National Transportation Museum in St. Louis; CRRNJ No. 592 at the B&O Museum in Baltimore; and an 0-4-0 from the Colorado Fuel & Iron Co., formerly Philadelphia & Reading No. 1187, at the Strasburg Railroad near Lancaster, Pennsylvania.

Camel Locomotives

The difference between a Camel locomotive, as typified by the Ross Winans designs for the Baltimore & Ohio Railroad (B&O), and a Camelback (Mother Hubbard) is basic. The Camel was a slow-speed locomotive with a narrow firebox and the cab perched on top of the boiler, while the Camelback had a wide Wootten firebox with the cab straddling the boiler and was built in a variety of types, including high-speed express configurations.

Development of the Camel coincided with the change from wood to coal as locomotive fuel. Some of the first attempts

Below: The John Hancock, *built in 1836, was one of the first locomotives with a cab for protection of the crew and the first of six Baltimore & Ohio Grasshopper types manufactured at the Mount Clare Shops. It now resides at the B&O Museum and is occasionally run during special events. Below, bottom: The Baltimore & Ohio No. 217 is an 1873 design of J.C. Davis, master of machinery at the railroad's Mount Clare shops. A 4-6-0, or "ten wheeler," it follows the pattern set by Ross Winans, with the cab perched on top of the wide boiler. It is no wonder that this style of locomotive was called Camel.*

at burning anthracite in the American Northeast resulted in locomotives that did not cope well with their new diet. Scant bituminous coal was available in the mid-nineteenth century, but anthracite, or stone coal, which burned slowly with little flame and smoke, had been mined and shipped in Pennsylvania since the Revolution. Unfortunately, in the small simple locomotives of the 1830s, if an anthracite fire burned low while a locomotive was standing or coasting, it was very difficult to get it up again—wood was more dependable. As a result of growing industrialization and cheap water transportation, anthracite coal became both readily available and cheap by the 1840s, just as the cost of wood cut in the depleted forests was rising.

The early coal burners were vertical-boilered Crabs and Grasshoppers, but their design provided only limited opportunity for combustion improvement, although a primitive steam turbine blower was employed for improved draft. Ross Winans developed the "mud-digger" design, which used a horizontal boiler but a normal-size firebox, thereby limiting service to slow coal drags; a dozen were built.

Winans' Camel eliminated the gears and dummy crankshafts inherent in the earlier designs and replaced them with the now-familiar arrangement of horizontal cylinders and connecting rods. To provide more grate area for a better fire, Winans increased the length of the firebox, the width being restricted by the wheels. This forced the engineer into a "pulpit" on top of the horizontal multitube boiler, with the fireman operating from a perch between the firebox and the tender. The first of these ungainly locomotives was an 0-8-0 built in 1848. Because of its odd appearance it was named Camel, giving the name for the class of locomotives that followed. They were at their best on slow-speed trains or in helper service. Although not having a major impact on the development of the steam locomotive, the Camels were the first to successfully burn anthracite, and 300 were built in the following twenty years, including 119 for the B&O and nearly 50 for the Philadelphia & Reading. B&O No. 217, although not an original Winans, is preserved at the B&O Museum in Baltimore.

Canadian Railways

Because of proximity to the United States and the amount of interchange traffic, Canada adopted the standards and practices of American railroads, rather than those of Britain. In many ways, the major Canadian roads are just two more American Class 1 lines, with track both above and below the border.

The main differences are the predominantly east-west nature of the traffic, since so much of the population is located close to the border, and the competition between the government-owned Canadian National (CN) and the privately held Canadian Pacific (CP). The ratio of 190 miles (351

CP Rail SD40-2 leads three other units past Mount Stephens on August 5, 1989. The Canadian Pacific rostered 479 of these locomotives in 1992.

km) of line per thousand people is the highest in the world, but because of the vast areas of sparse population, the ratio of rail miles per square mile is quite low.

Passenger service is provided through a government-sponsored entity called Via Rail Canada, which absorbed both the former CN and CP trains and has been rationalizing routes, removing the premier coast-to-coast train, the daily Montreal to

Vancouver Canadian. Much protest accompanied the last run of this fabled train, on January 14, 1990. Once called the Trans-Canada Limited and then the Dominion, the train represented all that was good with Canadian railways—good food and great scenery on a ride that was packed in the summer and empty in the winter. But the Canadian was more than a train; it symbolized the national dream of unity in the vast country. But, as in other large industrialized countries, a growing highway system and the advent of jets began to lure away railway passengers. The spectacle of the Canadian Rocky Mountain scenery continued to draw tourists, but the government could no longer support two transcontinental passenger trains.

While the great age of Canadian passenger trains is gone, Via Rail continues to provide critical service, and freight traffic remains strong. The vast mineral deposits, forests, and wheat fields of the prairies supplement the heavy manufacturing of the urbanized areas to provide a solid base for traffic. Each of the major railroads will be dealt with separately to best illustrate their unique qualities.

Algoma Central (ACR). Another northward-running railroad, Algoma Central starts at Saulte St. Marie, Ontario, on the connection between Lakes Huron and Superior. The northern terminus is 325 miles (520 km) away, at Hearst, on the Canadian National, once again serving an area with few roads. While holding an important place in the region, freight operations are also somewhat connected with the needs of Algoma Steel Corporation, the major industry on the line. Passenger service is provided, and tourists looking forward to the scenery of Agawa Canyon mingle with the fishermen, canoers, and locals.

The ACR roster includes 34 diesels, 40 passenger cars, and 2,000 freight cars. The railroad hauls 190,000 passengers and 4 million tons (3.6 million t) of freight per year.

British Columbia Railway (BCR). The former Pacific Great Eastern was rescued by the provincial government as a necessary service along the Canadian Pacific coast. Running 600 miles (960 km) north from Vancouver, it serves the undeveloped mineral- and resource-rich area along the route to Fort Nelson and has a long branch line from Prince George (a Canadian National connection) to Dease Lake.

BCR operates 107 diesels, 10 passenger cars, and 9,000 freight cars on a total of 870 miles (1,400 km) of track, hauling 45,000 passengers and more than 6 million tons (5.4 million t) of freight. Stainless steel Budd RDCs operate to Prince George, and the restored Canadian Pacific Royal Hudson operates excursion trains out of Vancouver.

Canadian National Railways (CN). The government-owned railway was formed in January 1923, when all of the previous government lines were merged under the name that had been in actual use since 1918. The oldest of these

The Algoma Central provides critical service to the generally roadless area of northwestern Ontario. A General Motors–built 2,000-hp GP38-2 leads a quartet of diesels at Heyden, Ontario.

lines was the Grand Trunk Railway of Canada, which dated to 1853. The original component of GT, a 14-mile (25 km) line from Laprairie, Quebec, to St. John, New Brunswick, opened on July 24, 1836. Its connection to the Richelieu River provides access to the Hudson and allowed for a rail-steamboat route between the St. Lawrence River and New York. From that base, the Grand Trunk developed a web of rails across eastern Canada with additional lines into the United States in Michigan, Indiana, and New England. The Grand Trunk Western, an associated line, began operation inland from Prince Rupert on the Pacific coast, and the two companies were taken over by the government between 1919 and 1920.

Other components of the Canadian National included the Canadian Northern,

A Canadian National Railways grain train, loaded with wheat for export, follows the Thompson River through the mountains of British Columbia.

which came under government control in 1916 (following severe financial problems), and several government-built lines: the Intercolonial Railway in Nova Scotia and New Brunswick; the Prince Edward Island Railway; and the National Transcontinental Railway, from Quebec to Winnipeg on a northern route.

The grouping of these railroads into the Canadian National system created a 24,000-mile (38,400 km) coast-to-coast system that was bigger than any other in North America until the 1960s mergers in the United States. One of its lines went

north from Winnipeg to Hudson Bay and another north from Edmonton to the mines near Great Slave Lake. The easternmost point is on the 3-foot 6-inch gauge ex–Newfoundland Railway, where trucks were exchanged on freight cars so they could run on the narrow-gauge track. The narrow gauge was also famous for its "crack" passenger train the Caribou, commonly known as the "Newfie Bullet," which trundled over the 547-mile (875 km) line from Port-au-Basques to St. John's.

Because the government funding was intended to open up new land to settlers, the CN main line runs farther north than the CP and serves many small towns and villages accessible only by train or float plane. Despite the isolated country at the northern part of the railroads' route, there is little notable construction. An exception

Above, top: Via Rail's No. 6453, one of twenty-six F40PH-2 diesels built by General Motors' Electro-Motive Division, provides a visual treat for the passengers along Lake Louise in the Canadian Rockies. Above: Quebec Bridge, the world's longest cantilever span, carries the trains of Canadian National across the St. Lawrence River. Opened December 3, 1917, the bridge includes a main span of 1,800 feet

(548 m) in the total length of 3,238 feet (987 m). Two accidents marred construction at the site. A 1907 attempt to complete the bridge was abandoned after the south cantilever collapsed, killing seventy-five men. When the central span was being hoisted into place on the current bridge, its collapse killed ten men; that structure still lies on the bottom of the river.

is the steel cantilever bridge over the St. Lawrence River at Quebec, the longest rail bridge in the world, with a span of 1,810 feet (547.2 m).

Likewise, with a crossing of the Rockies that was easier than CP's, the motive power is also straightforward. CN did, however, roster more 4-8-4s, the ultimate passenger locomotive, than any other Canadian railroad. These were massive steamers, with Vanderbilt tenders and the horizontal cylinder of the feed-water heaters laid across the top of the boiler in front of the stack. No. 6060, a semistreamlined 4-8-2 called *Bullet Nosed Betty*, earned fame as the last Canadian National steam locomotive when it ran in excursion service from Toronto to Niagara Falls in the 1970s.

Dieselization was complete by 1960, but in 1928, the first 1,000-hp road units in North America went into service on the CN, with Beardmore engines, generators, electric motors, and multiple-unit capability. A small amount of electrification is in place for Montreal suburban service. CN also devoted considerable effort to make practical use of the somewhat difficult operation of the turbo-trains—despite the

advanced technology, the turbo-train is a return to the idea of a fixed train-set and power-car arrangement.

Along with the turbos, CN still operates considerable passenger service under the Via Rail Canada despite the cutbacks of 1990. Its premier cross-country train—between Montreal and Vancouver—had first been the Continental and then the Super Continental. Rationalization of passenger service under Via Rail will likely affect even this train.

Canadian Pacific Limited (CP Rail).
The first of the Canadian transcontinentals, CP began with the St. Andrews and Quebec, but it came to prominence in compliance with treaty demands made by the stubborn residents of British Columbia in 1871. As the price

for joining the new Dominion of Canada, they wanted a transportation connection with the east, and the government, which was dominated by easterners, agreed to start the railroad within two years and complete it within ten. The project began on June 1, 1875, on the banks of the Kaministiqua River at what would become Fort William, Ontario.

On the momentous day of the ground-breaking, no one really knew what hardship lay ahead. Scandal investigations caused the fall of the government, weather conditions and the terrain presented far more difficulty than expected, political intrigue affected the route selection, and the $25 million originally appropriated by the government proved inadequate.

The members of the syndicate were approaching personal bankruptcy in the spring of 1885, when the half-French, half-

Indian rebel Louis Riel, a specter from the Canadian past, organized his second uprising and led his followers against the authorities in the western part of the country. Seizing the moment, the CP offered its services to the government, and troops were dispatched from Ottawa. Using boats and sleds over incomplete sections of the railway, the massive force moved across northern Ontario and arrived in Winnipeg in only four days, putting down the rebellion before any momentum developed. Recognizing the security value of the rail-

The rugged granite of the North Superior Shore proved a formidable barrier to the transcontinental builders. The numerous tunnels and cuts consumed as much as three tons (2.7 t) of dynamite per day; Jackfish Tunnel was no exception.

way, Ottawa relented and additional funds were reluctantly approved.

On November 7, 1885, the final spike was driven in the wilderness of British Columbia, at Craigellachie. The last spike was plain iron, and in the words of Van Horne "as good as any other on the line." A simple stone cairn marks the spot, 28 miles (45 km) west of Revelstoke and 2,529 miles (4,046 km) from Montreal. The following day, the special train that had carried the dignitaries to the ceremony arrived at Port Moody, British Columbia, the first to travel across Canada from the Atlantic to the Pacific. It was not until the following summer that the first regularly scheduled train, the Pacific Express, began service from Montreal to Port Moody, and another year before completion of an extension allowed trains into Vancouver.

A century later, the Canadian Pacific, now known as CP Rail in deference to the parent company's other ventures, operates a system totaling 21,000 miles (33,600 km) that extends east to Halifax, Nova Scotia, and into the United States. Route improvements were many: an alternate

Above: Gilded, garlanded, and bunted Canadian Pacific 4-4-0 celebrates both Queen Victoria's Jubilee and its successful inaugural trip across the trans-Canadian railway on July 4, 1886. Below: The 1909 Lethbridge Viaduct, the tallest railroad bridge in Canada, carries the trains of the Canadian Pacific over the Oldman (formerly Belly) River in Alberta. The 5,327-foot (1,624 m)-long, dead-straight bridge includes thirty-four spans supported on steel towers, 314 feet (96 m) above the valley.*

route was built through the Rockies, using Crow's Nest Pass; the often temporary construction was rebuilt, including replacement of huge timber trestles with steel bridges—Stoney Creek Viaduct is 307 feet (93 m) high with a span of 336 feet (102 m), the 5-mile (8 km) Connaught Tunnel and two spiral tunnels under Kicking Horse Pass helped to reduce some horrendous grades; and a mile (1.6 km)-long

steel viaduct at Lethbridge, Alberta, soars across the valley of the Oldman River at a height of 314 feet (95 m). The luxurious Empress steamship service was begun to continue passenger service across the Pacific. Today, CP Air has taken over that service, but CP Ships continues to carry intermodal cargo.

The steam locomotives of the CP, while similar to American designs, were more

British in appearance. Basic black paint was replaced by "crimson lake" on their passenger locomotives, including the magnificent semistreamlined 2-10-4s they called Selkirks. Along with the Royal Hudson 4-6-4s, they were the pride of the fleet, snaking matching passenger consists across the prairies and over the Rockies. The CP also rostered a batch of 4-4-4s, built in 1938 for high-speed service between Montreal and

Above: The restored Royal Hudson, so called because the class was used to pull the train of the visiting royal family in 1939. No. 2860 still works in excursion service out of Vancouver, British Columbia.

Below: A handsome 4-6-2 Pacific leads a train of Canadian Pacific heavyweight passenger cars out of Montreal on its way to the west.

Toronto. A Royal Hudson operating out of Vancouver continues in excursion service.

Dieselization began in the Rockies in 1948 and was complete by 1954. Today, it is possible to see 10,000-ton (9,000 t) coal trains hauled by eleven diesel units—eight on the head and three more radio-controlled slave units cut into the middle. On the prairies, wheat is moved from elevator to port 21,000 tons (18,900 t) at a time—that's 250 freight cars with seven locomotives on a train that is 2 1/2 miles (4 km) long! CP currently rosters 1,260 diesels and 76,000 freight cars, which haul 87 million tons (78.3 million t) of freight.

Canadian Transcontinental. The financial strain of building the Canadian Pacific Railway overwhelmed the backers on more than one occasion. At the close of construction season, with the snows of winter already isolating the construction crews, the railroad announced that robberies of the payroll train had forced the company to switch from cash to payroll checks. The management knew full well that the workers would be unable to leave the camps without cash, so they would still be available

Above, top: The ubiquitous EMD SD40-2 (almost 4,000 were built) adds 3,000 hp to the drawbars of a Canadian Pacific Railway (now CP Rail) train as it climbs above scenic Lake Louise, in the Canadian Rockies.

Above: It took the incredible efforts of rugged men to push the railroads west. A typical construction camp on the Canadian Transcontinental illustrates the primitive living conditions in the remote wilderness.

in the spring; furthermore, they would be unable to cash the checks until then, giving the syndicate time to raise enough money to cover the payroll.

Ontario Northland Railway (ONR).

An absence of roads in northern Ontario has helped to keep the Ontario Northland viable. Built from North Bay, on Lake Nipissing near Lake Huron, to Moosonee, the site of a proposed ocean port on Hudson Bay, the line was completed in 1932. Through-passenger service from Toronto, including an overnight sleeping-car train called the Northland, is provided via Canadian National Railways to North Bay and over ONR to Cochrane, 480 miles (768 km) north. From there, the Polar Bear continues north for the last 186 miles (300 km) to Hudson Bay. Ontario Northland also has created interest by using a TEE train set retired from the Dutch railways and can bring out a steam engine for excursions. Its current roster includes 34 diesels, 34 passenger cars, and 1,000 freight cars, which transport a quarter of a million passengers and more than 5 million tons (4.5 million t) of freight.

Quebec, North Shore & Labrador Railway/Cartier Railway (QNS&L).

These separate railways deliver iron ore to adjacent ports on the St. Lawrence River in Quebec. QNS&L is the older of the two friendly rivals, having been completed for the Iron Ore Company of Canada in 1954. Loads are delivered to the port of Sept-Iles in 260-car trains of 23,400 tons (21,060 t) over 360 miles (576 km) from a mine at Schefferville and in 165-car trains on the 265-mile (424 km) Carol Lake line. Radio-controlled mid-train helpers are added to the Schefferville trains to reduce coupler stresses. Branches to Wabush Lake and Pointe Noire served the mines of another ore company.

The Quebec Cartier Mining Company opened their 190-mile (304 km) railway in 1961 between Port Cartier and Lac Jeannine with a 1976 extension of 85 miles (136 km) to Mount Wright, where continuous loading equipment was installed. A moving train of 156 cars can be loaded

with 14,000 tons (12,600 t) of ore in less than an hour. A close-fitting chute and car-actuated switches control the flow of the ore. At the port, automatic equipment and rotary couplers allow cars to be turned over and dumped two at a time.

The two railways are vital to the developing mineral industry of an otherwise barren territory and can handle more than 50 million tons (45 million t) of ore per year.

White Pass & Yukon Railway (WP&Y).

This 3-foot-gauge railroad was hurriedly built to serve the great Klondike gold rush and opened July 21,

Above, top: The cloudy sky promises rain as Ontario Northland SD40-2 uses its full 3,000 hp to haul freight in June 1986. Note the "ditch lights" above the pilot that help warn the crew of right-of-way obstructions that could cause a derailment. Above: The parallels between the White Pass & Yukon 3-foot gauge and the Colorado narrow-gauge lines are obvious. Both were built through rugged and remote country to aid in the extraction of precious metals.

1898. It began at the port of Skagway, in Alaska, and had reached Whitehorse, Yukon Territory, 111 miles (178 km) inland, by 1899. From there, sternwheeled steamboats took the prospectors 460 miles (736 km) farther up the Yukon River to Dawson City.

An early innovator, the WP&Y relied heavily on containerization, having purchased the world's first container ship in 1953 and an airline in 1937. Having no direct interchange with another railroad helped, but it was the quick loading and unloading of containers that would keep the railroad viable, and within ten years, more than half of the WP&Y traffic was in containers.

Passenger equipment included wooden coaches, and passengers' automobiles could be carried on the train. The railroad dieselized, and at the peak rostered 21 locomotives, 30 passenger cars, and 420 freight cars. Unfortunately, financial problems shut the railroad down, although throughout the 1980s several attempts were made to restart it.

Canadian Transcontinental Railway

The basis for government sponsorship of a transcontinental railroad was the same in both the United States and Canada. The U.S. Congress wanted to protect and unify California, while the Canadian Parliament was forced into taking action by a treaty. The hardheaded residents of British Columbia, isolated from the rest of Canada by the rugged Rocky Mountains and the vast prairie, were more aligned economically with the American Northwest, and there was fear in Ottawa of a political alliance as well. To bring the two colonies (Vancouver Island was separate from BC)

White Pass & Yukon steam power was influenced by the British interests that built the railroad, but Mikado No. 73, shown in Skagway, is a 1947 Baldwin product.

into the new confederation authorized by the 1867 British North America Act, the premier, John Macdonald, agreed to a treaty that provided a new railroad.

Typical of politically sensitive and horrendously expensive projects, after a formal ground-breaking at the site of the future Fort William, the start was delayed until the Canadian Pacific Railway was incorporated by an act of the British Parliament in 1882. The fledgling company was to receive $25 million in cash, 25 million acres (10,000,000 ha) of land, and title to 700 miles (1,120 km) of completed railway. The founders included George Stephen, president of the Bank of Montreal; R. B.

While some labor-saving equipment was available to help with the heaviest work, such as moving large boulders (inset), the Canadian Pacific was built by the strong arms of the construction crews. Trees, rock, dirt, ballast, ties, and rail were ultimately moved and placed almost entirely by muscle power (above).

Angus, his general manager; Donald Smith, of the Hudson Bay Company; and American railroad builder James J. Hill, who later became known as "The Empire Builder."

Sandford Fleming, builder of the Intercolonial Railway, had been given the task of finding a route through the Rockies and selected a low-grade route through Yellowhead pass and down the canyons of the Thompson and Frazer rivers. After a number of years of indecision, it was determined that the route was too far north and that the colonizing effect of the line could be diluted by American settlers moving north. The only other known possibility was through Crow's Nest Pass, which was too close to the border for strategic safety.

A new surveyor, A. B. Rogers, set off to find a route as close as possible to the straight line that an agitated J. J. Hill had drawn with a ruler between Winnipeg and Kamloops, and William Cornelius Van Horne was hired to manage the construction.

Van Horne's future was as a giant of North American railroading, but in 1882 his job was simple—get the railroad built! The 2,000-mile (3,200 km) venture divided itself neatly into three compo-

The need for minimal grades meant bridges had to be built over every large valley and stream. This is the Little Pic River bridge, under construction on the Superior shore.

nents: the Rockies over Rogers' new route; the relatively easy going across the prairies; and the connection of the prairies with the St. Lawrence basin. The prairie section was completed to Calgary by 1883, but the route east from Fort William was the subject of much controversy: Hill insisted on a route south of the Great Lakes, which would nicely complement lines in which he held an interest, and Stephen demanded an all-Canadian route. Hill resigned and Van Horne was forced to deal with the rugged granite of the North Superior shore, a route that proved almost as difficult as the Rockies.

Even after Rogers had discovered the pass that bears his name, the problems had just begun. An investigation into the for-

mation of the partnership that was to build the line and the resulting "Pacific Scandal" caused the fall of Sir John Macdonald's conservative government. Ottawa's cash subsidy of $25 million was an immense sum, but was not sufficient to keep the partners from the brink of personal bankruptcy.

Donald Smith and his cousin George Stephen sold or mortgaged everything they owned after the railway had swallowed their considerable personal fortunes. Expecting the creditors to close in, Stephen told his cousin, "Donald, when they come they must not find us with a dollar." While waiting for the politicians to authorize further subsidy, a resolute Smith sent a one-word telegram, "Craigellachie," in reference to the war cry of Clan Grant in his native Scotland—"Stand fast Craigellachie."

Weather provided its own impediments: mosquitoes and black flies harassed the workers in summer; winter temperatures of minus 40 degrees (F and C are identical) meant spikes had to be heated to keep the heads from shattering. The frozen ties often split from end to end when a spike twisted. Muskeg that was frozen solid in winter would swallow up track and roadbed in the spring thaw.

The project might have been abandoned had it not been for a French-Indian renegade named Louis Riel. When Riel marched with his band of followers against the local authorities (for the second time in fifteen years), the military was granted unrestricted access to the uncompleted railway. By improvising sled routes between unfinished sections and rushing to lay track ahead of the advancing army, the Canadian Pacific was able to complete the deployment of the militia from Ottawa to Winnipeg in four days; the rebellion was crushed. The value of the railway to internal security had been firmly established, and the grateful government provided enough funds to finish the line. Cynics within the company proposed the erection of a statue in honor of Riel, the "savior" of the Canadian Pacific.

After much struggle, the final spike of the transcontinental railway was driven in; although the spike was made of iron and came to rest in the wilds of British Colum-

Cecil Rhodes earned his early fortune in the gold and diamond fields of South Africa. His vision of a Cape to Cairo railway has yet to be realized, but the completed portions are vital to the region's economy.

bia (at a place called Craigellachie), the event was one of immense significance for an entire continent. The spot is marked (albeit modestly) by a stone cairn. (These historic events are detailed in a well-known book by Pierre Burton called *The Last Spike*.)

Cape to Cairo Railway

The ability of railroads to bring civilization and therefore to tame a rough country was recognized early. An English clergyman's son named Cecil Rhodes decided he was the man to bring civilization to Africa. With a large fortune earned in the diamond mines and additional funds bullied from the government, Rhodes made considerable progress toward the goal of linking Cape Town and Cairo with steel rails before his death.

Original impetus for a rail line came from Rhodes' need to connect his diamond mines at Kimberley to established seaports, but his imperial vision of rails running the length of Africa was always at the back of his mind, as reflected in his famous remark: "The railway is my right hand, and the telegraph my voice." Cape Town to Kimberley was completed first, and when gold was discovered in the Trans-

vaal, an extension to the now booming town of Johannesburg was completed in 1892, despite the best efforts of the Boer settlers to thwart the Rhodes-backed line in favor of one being built by their government.

The 3-foot 6-inch gauge railroad reached Bulawayo (in what is now called Rhodesia) in 1897 and pressed northeastward to the Congo (Zaïre) town of Bukama, 2,600 miles (4,160 km) from Cape Town but still 3,500 miles (5,600 km) from Rhodes' destination when the visionary imperialist died in 1902.

The loss of Rhodes' influence and money thwarted progress, and much of the momentum was lost. After World War I, British control over the region reduced the political problems with expansion, but money was in short supply. Since World War II, the economy has improved and new construction in Tanzania, Uganda, and Zambia has filled in some gaps, but the current political difficulties have interfered with completion and have created barriers at some borders along existing track.

While the railroad's builders managed to avoid heavy earthworks on the long climb to the interior, they ultimately reached the mighty Zambezi River, which had cut a deep gorge through the African plateau and formed the breathtaking Victoria Falls, on the border between Zambia and Rhodesia. The falls had remained undiscovered by the outside world until 1855, when David Livingstone reported: "Creeping with awe to the verge, I peered down into a large rent which had been made from bank to bank of the broad Zambezi." Rhodes never saw the falls, but he was so moved by the vivid descriptions that he decreed his railway would cross the Zambezi within sight of Victoria Falls—higher and wider than Niagara Falls—and close enough to feel the constant mist.

The "boiling pot" was where the falls dropped 350 feet (106 m) into the mile (1.6 km) -wide gorge. The two-hinged spandrel-braced trussed arch that was to stretch across the gorge below the falls had a span of 500 feet (152 m) and a length of 650 feet (200 m). To build the cantilevered arch from each side, a cableway with a 10-ton (9 t) capacity was constructed adjacent to the bridge site so building materials could

be transported across the gorge. Rhodes insisted that the railway proceed north without waiting for the bridge; a mile (1.6 km) of track was laid per day. The bridge was finished in 1905, three years after the death of Cecil Rhodes.

Although the Cape to Cairo Railway was never completed, Rhodes' route could be followed through Kimberley and Mafeking to Bulawayo and across the Zambezi, truly in the spray of Victoria Falls. At Kapiri-Mposhi one must divert from the original route to the Tan-Zam line to Dar-es-Salaam on the Tanzanian coast, where a switch to meter gauge is made. Continuing northward on the East African Railways (which will eventually convert to 3-foot 6-inch gauge), Kenya is entered near Mount Kilimanjaro, and, following the original Uganda Railway, one arrives at Gulu, near the Sudanese border. A short 100 miles (160 km) by road to Juba and a Sudan Railways steamboat is the beginning of a nine-day and 900-mile (1,440 km) journey to Kosti near Khartoum. Then the Sudan Railway—its 3-foot 6-inch gauge had

A National Railways of Zimbabwe Beyer-Garratt, No. 414, pauses at Victoria Falls, one of the scenic wonders along Cecil Rhodes' ambitious but uncompleted Cape to Cairo railroad.

anticipated rail connection at each end—carries passengers on one more boat ride on the Nile before the final leg of the 4-foot 8½-inch line into Cairo.

The Cape to Cairo Railway has yet to reach the point envisioned by Rhodes a century ago, but the continuing growth of the African economy may yet force the completion of this ambitious undertaking.

Cascade Tunnel

When it was opened in 1929, about 55 miles (88 km) northeast of Seattle, Washington, the 7.79-mile (12.5 km) Cascade Tunnel was the longest outside of Europe. It was built by the Great Northern Railroad and cuts through the Cascade Range, under Stevens Pass, between the tiny settle-

ments of Scenic and Berne, and reduced some 43 miles (69 km) of steep track to 34 miles (55 km) of high-speed railroad. Construction began in 1925 and was completed in late 1928. President Calvin Coolidge set off the final explosive charge by remote control, from Washington, D.C. The first train ran through on January 12, 1929.

The tunnel replaced an earlier bore at a higher elevation. The first Cascade Tunnel was 2.63 miles (4.2 km) long and opened in 1900. In 1909, the installation of a 134-mile (215 km) electrified district on the approaches to the tunnel eliminated the severe steam locomotive exhaust problem. The 25-cycle AC electrification remained in operation until 1956, after the advent of the diesel rendered it superfluous.

Chapelon, André (1892–1978)

The Paris-Orléans Railway employed André Chapelon after World War I, and he was to have considerable impact on the postwar French locomotive fleet. It was on

the Orléans that the first European Pacific was introduced in 1907, and it was a class of larger-wheeled Pacifics built in 1912 that provided Chapelon with his opportunity. The entire French railway system was in need of massive rebuilding from wartime damage, but there was little capital available, so Chapelon looked to rebuilding these locomotives.

The compound locomotive used steam twice: the exhaust steam from smaller, high-pressure cylinders being directed to the larger, low-pressure cylinders before being sent up the stack. Ideally, the steam pressure and cylinder size are balanced so that the same horsepower is developed in each cylinder of a set, but Chapelon applied scientific measuring devices to a working locomotive and found that, under a moderate output of 1,000 hp, the low-pressure cylinders were doing very little work. On a 375-ton (337.5 t) train moving at 66 mph (105 kph) the high-pressure cylinders produced 918 hp, while the low-pressure cylinders produced only 59. At a harder output it was 1,460 hp versus 390,

One of the 232 SD40-2s of the Burlington Northern leads a fast intermodal train out of the Cascade Tunnel in Washington State. Note the length of continuous welded rail along the ballast, ready for a replacement project on the heavily used line.

still a great discrepancy and not efficient. The locomotive had to be modified to better use the exhaust steam.

Using the money available for the rebuilding of one locomotive, Chapelon applied new cylinder castings that contained streamlined ports and passages and modified the valves so that steam could flow more smoothly. He also put a larger superheater (which increases the temperature and volume of the steam) in the boiler and a twin orifice and blast pipe in the smoke box. While the completed locomotive, with its exposed piping and appliances, still looked very French by British standards, its performance was magically transformed. With an ability to just stretch

for 1,800 hp originally, the rebuilt locomotive easily topped the 3,000 hp mark, with an almost perfect distribution of power between the high-pressure and low-pressure cylinders. Once finished with the Pacific, Chapelon turned to the earlier Pacific of 1907 and applied the same techniques, but also converted the 4-6-2 wheel arrangement to 4-8-0. The result was an astonishing 4,000 hp.

The results of the tests were widely published in the English technical press and attracted the interest of the legendary Sir Nigel Gresley, of the London & Northwestern, as well as steam designers in America. The British took much more advantage of Chapelon's work with compound cylinder design, as the direction in the United States turned toward Mallet-articulated compounds and simple articulated locomotives.

Chapelon, however, became the champion of steam power in France, and French locomotives became noted for wringing every ounce of power out of a ton (0.9 t) of coal. When nationalization of the railroads came to France in 1938, Chapelon was placed in charge of all future development. His final accomplishment, flying in the face of widespread electrification, came in 1947 with the conversion of a twenty-year-old 4-8-2 into a dazzling 4-8-4 that clearly outperformed the new electrics. He had prepared a remarkable series of designs for postwar production that would have advanced steam locomotive design several stages forward, but the distinguished engineer was doomed to disappointment. The commitment had been made, and the rapid conversion to electric power rendered Chapelon's magnificent steam locomotives obsolete.

Commodore Vanderbilt

New York Central's founder was memorialized in December 1934 when three-year-old J-1e Hudson 5344, originally a product of Alco, emerged from New York Central's West Albany Shops as America's first streamlined steam locomotive. Cleveland's Case School of Science, under the guidance of Norman F. Zapf, designed the jet black with silver trim shroud inspired by the Burlington's diesel-powered streamliner, Zephyr. Refitted with Scullin double-disc drivers and Timken roller bearing rods, the Commodore Vanderbilt was stripped of shroud and name in a 1939 restyling that brought 5344 more into compliance with the Henry Dreyfus semi-streamlined styling applied to the roads J-3a and Hudson's 5445–5454 for the Twentieth Century Limited. Finished in a single gray shade, 5344 spent her final years assigned to the Chicago Mercury running between Chicago and Detroit on New York's subsidiary Michigan Central.

See also: *Alco; Hudson-type Locomotive; Streamlined Steam Locomotives.*

Consolidation-type Locomotive

The first 2-8-0 locomotive was named "Consolidation," in honor of the merger between the Lehigh Valley and the Lehigh & Mahanoy railroads. Designed by Alexander Mitchell and built at the Baldwin Works in 1866, its name was applied to the wheel arrangement, and the Consolidation

became the most ubiquitous steam locomotive in the United States. The Western Maryland Railway was typical of the lines that were enamored of this type and continued to build and operate them until the end of steam.

Couplers

The power of the locomotives—whether it's the few hundred hp put out by an industrial switcher, or the 16,000 hp put out by a quartet of G. E. Dash 8-40Cs on a hundred-car coal train—is transferred through the train by the couplers. Early American couplers were a simple single link of chain connected to sockets on the cars by steel pins. The European coupler was originally a chain and buffer system, with the chain eventually replaced by a screw coupling device. The coupler must be capable of not only pulling the next car (and all the following cars) but also of pushing on a backing train, being coupled and uncoupled, and withstanding the

stresses of the impacts of buffing and slack action (the tendencies of cars to bang together or jerk apart).

The link and pin was strong enough to pull the short trains of the nineteenth century, but was dangerous to life and limb for the trainman. Coupling required the brakeman to step between the cars to insert the link into the empty socket and drop the pin at the right moment. Any error in communication or braking could crush the fingers, arms, or entire bodies of the hapless worker. The buffers that were developed by the British were some protection, but even there a worker had to expose himself

The infamous link-and-pin coupler maimed many early railroaders. The brakeman's hazardous job was to guide the chain link into the slot in the adjacent car as the locomotive moved slowly. The invention of the automatic knuckle coupler made this occupational hazard a thing of the past.

to the dangers between the cars, whether he was manipulating chains or screw-type connections.

The United States Congress passed the Federal Safety Appliance Act of 1893, which required the railroads to adopt a coupler that would connect on impact, thus eliminating the necessity for putting a man between the cars. Of the many inventions that were patented in the following years, the railroads selected a swinging "knuckle" coupler designed by Major Eli

H. Janney as the standard for interchange. The Janney-design Type D coupler featured interchangeable cast-iron parts that could be manufactured by many industry suppliers.

Ongoing design improvements included devices to prevent differential vertical movement of the couplers, which could cause uncoupling in a derailment, resulting in couplers puncturing cars or the jackknifing and rolling over of passenger cars. Various cast-iron shelves were added to the Type E

and Type F couplers, greatly reducing uncouplings and the resulting hazardous material leaks during derailments.

The couplers do not fit tightly, and there is a small amount of space, called slack, in each coupling. This slack must be carefully handled by train crews, as the locomotives on a long train will have traveled a considerable distance before the rear cars begin to move. Likewise, once the slack is stretched out, the engineer must be careful to keep it so, sometimes requiring such incongruities as applying the brakes on the train (but keeping the throttle open) while approaching the crest of a hill, so that gravity won't force out the slack as the cars roll onto the downhill track. Special complex machined interlockings on the Type H "tight-lock" couplers have greatly reduced the incidents of passenger car jackknifings and overturnings during derailments, with a resultant reduction in injuries.

Several deficiencies still exist in the design, and research has never stopped. Metallurgical improvements, further

Left: The classic "hand-clasped" design of the knuckle coupler is little changed since first proposed by Eli Janney. The bar-and-chain link raises a pin that allows the knuckle to open for uncoupling. Below: The 1934 Commodore Vanderbilt, *the first American streamlined steam locomotive, contrasts with ancestor* Dewitt Clinton *of 1831, one of the first American locomotives.*

Walter Scott became a railroad legend as "Death Valley Scotty" when his 1905 record-breaking run from Los Angeles to Chicago was completed in under forty-five hours.

a special train faster than any cowpuncher rode before."

Running at speeds up to 90 mph (150 kph), the special averaged 72 mph (115 kph) for the 300 miles (480 km) to Fort Madison, Iowa, and had already set records, but the best was yet to come. Charlie Losee steamed the 510, a Baldwin-balanced compound Atlantic, up to 106 mph (170 kph) on the flat Illinois prairies, between Cameron and Surrey, running the 105 miles (168 km) from Fort Madison to Chillicothe in 101 minutes.

After losing 9 minutes in the stops at Chillicothe and South Joliet, the leg from Shopton to Chicago was back to speed— 239 miles (382 km) in 239 minutes. Arrival of the Coyote Special in Dearborn Station was at 11:54 A.M., July 11—2,267 miles (3,627 km) in 44 hours and 54 minutes —a new record.

Nineteen crews and locomotives were used in the run that covered two-thirds of the North American continent: nine Atlantics, four Prairies, three Pacifics, one ten-wheeler (all Baldwins), and two more ten-wheelers built by the Rhode Island Works. The Santa Fe was primarily single track, and traversed four mountain ranges. The train observed slow speed requirements

in yards and the speed limits of line-side towns. Full stops were made for fuel and water, loco and crew changes, and the addition of helpers and several hotboxes. Death Valley Scotty got his record, and his average speed of 50.4 miles per hour (81 kph) was a tribute to the teamwork of all the railroad workers along the route.

Denver & Rio Grande

The Rocky Mountains of Colorado posed a formidable barrier to development. A Russian immigrant named Otto Mears knew the old Indian trails well, and developed an early freight wagon business using them. Because of the inadequacy of these trails, Mears began building toll roads for the wagon freighters, but he recognized the limitations of roads and looked to the new railroads that were building to the eastern face of the Rockies. The approach to this barrier was relatively easy, but penetration of the steep and narrow canyons was another matter.

Enter former Confederate general William Jackson Palmer, a visionary with dreams of a railroad empire. He began to build south from Denver in 1871, planning to reach Santa Fe and then Mexico, and named his railroad the Denver & Rio Grande. Disdaining the accepted standard gauge of 4 feet 8½ inches, Palmer's road was the first important common carrier to adopt a gauge of 3 feet. The construction costs of this narrow gauge were considerably less than those of standard gauge, allowing more railroad to be built with the funds available.

By 1872, Palmer had pushed his railhead as far as Pueblo, where he organized the Central Colorado Improvement Company to create an industrial district south of town. Ten years later, the company was reorganized as the Colorado Fuel & Iron Company, an industrial giant that would become the Rio Grande's principal source of traffic for the next seventy-five years.

General Palmer's grand plan came to a halt with the panic of 1873. After a delay of several years, additional construction funds became available, but local citizens had helped the Atcheson, Topeka & Santa Fe occupy Raton Pass, the only practical route to the south.

Since the silver booms were in full swing at Silverton and Leadville, Palmer realized that future expansion must be to the west. The 3-foot rails pushed up the Sangre de Cristo Range and over Veta Pass, reaching Alamosa in 1878. From Alamosa, a route to Mexico might have been possible, but the silver ore of Leadville and Silverton was still to the west. The route to Leadville was up the Arkansas River, and once again the Santa Fe occupied the only possible road-bed in the narrow rock canyon. The Rio Grande had already surveyed and claimed the right-of-way and, after several armed confrontations, took the matter to court. Having lost a lower court decision, resulting in severe limits to the railroad's borrowing capabilities, and needing to protect his investors, Palmer leased the Rio Grande to the Santa Fe and sat back to await further developments.

On April 21, 1879, the U.S. Supreme Court ruled in favor of the Rio Grande, and the Colorado courts immediately ordered the lease terminated. Control was returned to Palmer, but the railroad's finances were in such disarray that a receiver was appointed in July. Stepping into the situation was the master financial manipulator Jay Gould.

Gould controlled the Union Pacific and was close to gaining control of the Denver, South Park & Pacific, which was building southwest from Denver—heading directly for Leadville and competition for the Rio Grande. The "Pacific" in the corporate name also indicated intentions of building farther southwest through the San Juan Mountains, which would lead to additional future conflict with Palmer's road. Buying Rio Grande securities at depressed prices gave Gould a strong position in the company and, with the general's agreement, a seat on the board.

Through his position on the Rio Grande board, Gould was able to interject himself into, and resolve, the potential conflicts with the South Park line. His position with the Union Pacific gave him the power to force a peace between the Rio Grande and the Santa Fe by threatening economic reprisal. Under the agreement, the Santa Fe agreed to stay away from Denver and Leadville if the Rio Grande stayed out of New Mexico. The narrow-gauge line also agreed to pay for the grading that the Santa Fe had finished in the Leadville area, and all lawsuits were withdrawn.

Gould also set the roles and futures for the Rio Grande and the South Park. Palmer was to extend into the coal, timber, and silver areas to help the region's development, but remain in a local role. The South Park was to cross the Continental Divide and push west, contributing to Gould's dream of a transcontinental empire. Unfortunately, the South Park's engineers deemed the Marshall Pass route to be unsuitable and, instead, set out to tunnel under Altman Pass, a decision that would destroy Gould's dream.

The South Park began construction of the Alpine Tunnel, a bold project that, although completed, took so much time and money that Palmer had to complete

Left: The desolate wilderness served by the Denver & Rio Grande is illustrated by the remote station in Clear Creek Canyon. The Colorado narrow-gauge lines were built to handle the vast quantities of valuable minerals hauled out of the rugged region. Below: The Santa Fe's Uncle Dick, *a 2-8-0 "saddle tank" engine, was designed for helper service up the switchbacks in Raton Pass in 1878. The 4,500th locomotive built by the Baldwin Works, it was named for "Uncle Dick" Wootton, an ornery character who controlled a toll road near the pass and cooperated in the building of the tunnel that eliminated the need for his namesake loco. After reassignment to less strenuous duties, No. 204 was retired in 1921.*

The Cumbres & Toltec Scenic Railroad operates excursion service on a section of the former Denver & Rio Grande out of Chama, New Mexico. No. 487 is a Baldwin 2-8-2 built in 1925.

over 800 miles (1,280 km) of railroad using considerable outside financing. Gould, whose money was tied up in the South Park construction, did not participate in this new capital, lost his financial leverage, and therefore his control of Palmer.

With a chance to be once again in charge of his own destiny, Palmer quickly forgot about gratitude, persuaded Otto Mears to sell his toll road over Marshall Pass, and put the new grade to good use as the new right-of-way for the Rio Grande. Gunnison was reached in 1881, a year ahead of the South Park, and Palmer pushed ahead into the Black Canyon, heading for the Great Salt Lake. Although Alpine Tunnel was eventually completed and operated, it was all but worthless, and Gould had been dealt a tremendous blow.

Narrow-Gauge Decline. At this time, Palmer decided to convert the principal Rio Grande routes to standard gauge and the remaining narrow gauge, isolated geographically and technologically, began a long, slow decline over the following half century. Although the railroad remained an important link to market for the ranchers and oil men after the silver boom died, the narrow-gauge Denver & Rio Grande was decaying as the standard-gauge Denver & Rio Grande blossomed.

After World War II, a number of movies were filmed using the railroad, including *Texas & Rio Grande*, *Colorado Territory*, *Around the World in Eighty Days*, and best of all, *Denver & Rio Grande*. Tourist traffic also helped to keep the narrow gauge steaming, but the less-used branch lines were torn up, one by one. As the freight business atrophied, the future seemed to be in tourism.

When the Denver & Rio Grande Western (D&RGW) finally began to give up on the antique railroad plant, unable to sustain mainline operations with almost nonexistent freight business, some preservationists, the National Park Service, and the legislatures of Colorado and New Mexico stepped in and began the dialogue that created the Cumbres & Toltec Scenic Railroad (CATS). Beginning operation of the Antonito to Chama portion of the route in 1970, CATS provided a ride that began in the valley at Antonito, clung precariously to the side of Toltec Gorge, climbed to the summit of Cumbres Pass, where 400 inches (10 m) of snow fell each year, and finished in the town of Chama.

Several years earlier, when the railroad petitioned for abandonment of the Silverton Branch, local opposition forced the parent line, now the Denver & Rio Grande Western, to keep it operating, and the D&RGW undertook extensive repairs. Even that arrangement was unraveling in the late 1970s, when the continuing maintenance costs forced a renewed attempt to abandon the line. A Florida citrus grower named Charles Bradshaw purchased the Silverton Branch in 1981, operating it for tourists as the Durango & Silverton Narrow Gauge Railway, saving another portion of the legendary line.

The most scenic branch of the Denver & Rio Grande ran from Durango to Silverton among remote 13,000-foot (3,960 m) peaks of the rugged Rockies. The train clings to narrow-gauge trackage on a ledge high on the wall of the canyon of the Rio de las Animas Perdidas (River of Lost Souls).

For tourists wishing to re-create a bit of the myth and romance of the San Juan Express, watch a rotary snowplow fling an arc of snow high into the sky, or simply listen to the clank and rattle of a string of wooden narrow-gauge freight cars, these two pieces of the past preserve the hardware, the people, and the setting of the early twentieth century.

Standard-Gauge Prosperity.

Despite the decline of the narrow gauge, the standard-gauge portion of the railroad continued to prosper. In 1890, a standard-gauge line was built over Tennessee Pass, the highest point reached by a standard-gauge main line in North America, and Palmer's dream of pushing west continued.

The Denver & Rio Grande Western operated a large fleet of narrow-gauge 2-8-2 Mikados. Built by the American Locomotive Works in 1923, No. 476 has been preserved for excursion service on the Durango & Silverton Railroad, a former D&RGW route in Durango, Colorado.

Bankruptcy came in 1910, when the Western Pacific, in which the Rio Grande had invested heavily, sought protection from its own creditors. When the railroad was sold in 1920, it took the name—Denver & Rio Grande Western—it carries today.

Merger with David Moffat's Denver & Salt Lake came in 1947, and with it came the long-sought route to Salt Lake City via the Moffat Tunnel. Shortly thereafter, the D&RGW began operation of another legend, the California Zephyr, operating between Chicago and San Francisco, in cooperation with the Western Pacific and the Chicago, Burlington & Quincy. With the creation of Amtrak, in 1971, the D&RGW declined to join and continued to operate the CZ until 1983, when Amtrak took over.

The Denver & Rio Grande Western prospers by hauling western coal and other minerals, as well as farm products and general merchandise on 1,840 miles (2,950 km) of track between Denver/Pueblo and Salt Lake City/Ogden. The affiliation of the D&RGW with the Southern Pacific provided direct access to both the Pacific coast and St. Louis, seemingly guaranteeing the railroad's future.

Diesel Locomotives

On other than electrified lines and the few rare roads still operating steam, the diesel (or more correctly, diesel-electric) locomotive is the worldwide freight hauler. An oil-burning internal-combustion engine (called the prime mover) actually turns a generator (or alternator), which produces electricity that operates the motors mounted on the trucks and powers the axles. There have been various attempts at direct mechanical connections from the engine to the trucks, and even diesel hydraulic drives, but at this time the diesel-electric is the standard, and references to a diesel locomotive refer to this arrangement.

Efficiency, flexibility, maintenance, and changing fuel costs ultimately doomed steam power in the industrialized world, and the high costs of capitalization for generating and distribution facilities made a significant increase in electrification unlikely outside of relatively short and heavily traveled corridors, or for special industrial and regulatory conditions. But these simple facts were not so obvious in the 1920s, when early experiments in internal combustion railroad equipment met with mixed results.

The diesel engine was invented by Rudolf Diesel (1858–1913), a German mechanical engineer who was born in Paris and educated in England. His 1893 book, *The Theory and Construction of a Rational Heat Motor*, describes his ideas on internal combustion power. Diesel survived the explosion of his first engine, which nevertheless proved the practicality of the principle. Many more failures preceded the first successful model, built in 1897.

Shortly thereafter, Adolphus Busch, the noted St. Louis brewer, purchased the manufacturing rights for the United States. Unfortunately, wealth eluded the inventor, as patent lawsuits and unscrupulous associates siphoned profits, and Rudolf Diesel died when he mysteriously fell overboard on a crossing of the English Channel.

The engine Diesel invented operates on oil, which is cheaper than gasoline, and has no spark plugs or carburetor. It depends on heat generated by compression of the intake air in the cylinder (to 500–600 psi), which raises its temperature to 1,000 degrees F (540° C). When oil is injected into the hot air, it ignites and the expanding gas forces the piston down (the power stroke), thereby turning the crankshaft and flywheel. As the momentum of the flywheel carries the piston back up, the burned gases are expelled, readying the cylinder for a new intake stroke.

Each piston movement, either up or down, is called a stroke, and each stroke has a job to do. The minimum number of strokes necessary to produce one power stroke is called a cycle—diesel engines are either two strokes per cycle or four strokes per cycle. The four-stroke engine takes in air on the first downstroke' compressing it as it returns to the top. The ignition happens at that time, driving the piston down on the power stroke. As it returns to the top, it forces out the exhaust and is ready for the next cycle. The two-cycle engine requires only a compression stroke and a power stroke; the intake happens at the end of the power stroke and helps to force out the exhaust before the compression stroke begins.

Some diesels have two opposed pistons in each cylinder, which move toward each other on the compression stroke. When the fuel is injected and ignites, the pistons are forced apart and turn a common shaft to which they are linked.

Above: The early experiments of Rudolf Diesel, inventor of the internal combustion engine named for him, were the beginning of the end of steam locomotives in most of the world. Below: After a number of experimental diesels and a successful tour by a General Electric/Ingersoll-Rand demonstrator, American Locomotive Works was added to the consortium that produced the first standardized line of diesel-electric locomotives. Five 60-ton (54 t) units were built for stock in 1924, and the first was sold to the Central Railroad of New Jersey (becoming CNJ 1000) the following year.

On a diesel locomotive, the energy of the turning crankshaft is connected to an alternator (for alternating current—AC) or to a generator (for direct current—DC). The two-stroke engines deliver a power stroke for each revolution of the crankshaft, but the four-strokes deliver power on alternate strokes and are therefore less efficient. The European invention of turbosupercharging saved the four-stroke diesel from obsolescence.

While fuel costs for diesels were low, the engines were very large and heavy, required skilled crews for operation and repair, and were suitable for stationary industrial engines and ships. A diesel engine with sufficient horsepower to pull a train, yet small enough to fit in the confined space of a locomotive, was beyond reach until Charles Kettering directed a project in the research facilities of General Motors (GM) that was experimenting with two-cycle diesels, and by 1930 had achieved the same horsepower in an engine 25 percent smaller and with a 20 percent weight reduction. In 1935, the 900-hp twelve-cylinder, two-cycle engine, designated 201-A, was produced with the help of new lightweight alloys. The diesel locomotive engine had left the experimental stage and become an industry reality.

Not to be outdone, the American Loco-motive Works (Alco), already well estab-lished as a builder of superb steam locomotives, also introduced a 900-hp engine but with only six cylinders and using a four-cycle unit with turbocharging. From that point, turbocharged four-cycle engines competed fully with two-cycle engines, mainly in the arena of mainte-nance costs since both designs performed very well.

GM, through its Electro-Motive Division (EMD), built a new plant at La Grange, Illinois, exclusively to manufac-ture diesel-electric locomotives. Early busi-ness at La Grange consisted primarily of switch engines powered by eight- and twelve-cylinder diesels still manufactured by the Winton Engine plant, the company

having been purchased by GM. A passen-ger locomotive, designated "TA" and built for the Rock Island in 1937, was the first locomotive with the car body built by GM, and it was followed by the stylish E Unit, both still Winton-powered.

By 1938, La Grange was ready for pro-duction of GM's own two-cycle engine, following years of exhaustive testing. GM was well aware that road failures of their new diesel, particularly in highly publi-cized premium service, would destroy the image and acceptability of the product. Corporate concern was strong enough that sleeping beds were installed in the engine rooms of the early units, so that EMD technicians could ride around the clock to ensure proper maintenance and handle emergency repairs.

Southern Railway No. 6100, the original EMD FT demonstrator set, swings across the Cumberland River near Burnside, Kentucky, in 1961. After a barnstorming tour on twenty railroads in thirty-five states, the units were purchased by Southern and operated for twenty years until retirement to the National Museum of Transportation in St. Louis.

Once General Motors sent their FT freight demonstrators on a wildly success-ful barnstorming tour of American rail-roads, steam power was doomed, despite the best efforts of the steam locomotive manufacturers to delay the inevitable. The fuel economy, lack of water stops, and the operational simplicity of a diesel locomotive—a single module that could be assembled into a block of horsepower matched to the weight of any train and controlled by one crew—were very appealing. When the components that make up an assembled locomotive are very much interchangeable between different models built by a manufacturer, then parts inventory and training for maintenance are also simplified.

Diesels performed at their best at low speeds, such as during switching, where steam was least efficient, so it was not surprising that low-horsepower switchers were the first market penetration. In round-the-clock yard service, a diesel switcher might operate almost continuously for several days before stopping for fuel and water. The lack of smoke made diesels the choice in urban areas with anti-smoke legislation. Further, large coaling, water, turning, and ash removal facilities could be eliminated, along with round-the-clock hostlers for tending fires and water levels.

In passenger service, streamlined diesels implied speed, modernity, comfort, and progress. Long-distance passenger trains began to be quickly dieselized in the late 1930s, but the early locomotives did not accelerate well above speeds of 15 or 20 mph (20 or 32 kph), the speed where steam engines were getting into stride. Once a train was started, a steam locomotive of 3,000 hp could easily outperform a diesel locomotive set of twice the horsepower, so the railroads were reluctant to replace steam on freights.

World War II came at a very opportune time for the diesel builders. Steam development was frozen while diesel engines, critical technology for ships, tanks, trucks, and a myriad of other wartime machinery, were given priority for development and improvement. Once the diesel builders were able to extract higher horsepower and smaller size from their units, they attained a technological lead against which developers of advanced steam concepts such as turbines could not compete. Steam power was relegated to high-efficiency stationary plants, while diesels became mobile.

North American passenger trains were quickly converted after the war, and diesel-

Above: The power plant of the Zephyr included this eight-cylinder diesel engine, which drove the cylindrical generator (on the far right), thereby providing electrical power to axle-mounted motors. This is the same combination that powers today's massive diesel-electric locomotives. Below: Gulf, Mobile & Ohio No. 733 was one of the first American Locomotive Works FA-1 diesels, built in 1945. The GM&O FAs differed from later production in having a smaller, lower grille around the headlight and a curved trim piece on the vent grille behind the door, which was typical of the PA-1 and PA-2 passenger versions of the locomotive.

Green and gold Central Vermont 4442, an Alco locomotive of the RS series, contrasts with the snow of New England as it leads a freight train.

ization was virtually complete by the mid-1950s. Coal haulers such as the Chesapeake & Ohio and the Norfolk & Western held on longer than most. Fast freight lines of the flatlands, like the Nickel Plate with its modern fleet of Lima's "Superpower" steam locomotives, were the last holdouts. The cost of keeping facilities for both steam and diesel power, and the large forces of semiskilled personnel necessary for steam maintenance overcame the higher initial cost of the diesels and the theoretical advantages of steam, and the conversion was all but complete in the United States by 1960.

The ultimate cost saving is open to argument. The postwar years saw major efforts at reductions of expenses and increases of efficiency, but, it is fair to say, the claim that diesel power saved the railroads from bankruptcy is probably exaggerated. The diesel locomotive has performed well, however, and has been equal to the task assigned to it.

Electrification, although common in Europe, has not been attempted on a large scale in North America since the Pennsylvania Railroad's New York to Washington and Philadelphia to Harrisburg projects of the 1930s. Light rail commuter operations and a few captive coal mine-to-power plant lines have been built or converted, but the overwhelming capital costs required have prevented any significant new installa-

tions. Continuing experiments with coal-fired steam such as the ACE 3000 project of the 1980s and other experiments with coal-burning diesel locomotives have not yet come into production, so it appears that the diesel-electric locomotive will continue to churn out the miles around the world for years to come.

See also: *Alco; Baldwin; General Electric Company; Ingalls Shipbuilding Company.*

Double-stack Trains

The 1980s saw great change in the American railroads. As truckers took more and more of the general merchandise hauling away from the rails, the railroads' early response was the "piggyback" train, where truck trailers were loaded onto special flatcars and then picked up at the terminal to continue the road haul.

As merchant shipping became containerized, and intermodal freight was deregulated by the Staggers Act, the railroads continued to adapt with new marketing strategies. At the beginning of the decade, watching a Union Pacific hotshot "piggyback" climbing Cajon Pass meant an end-

less parade of Trailer Train flatcars with mostly 40-foot (12 m) highway trailers mixed in with a few 45-foot (14 m) trailers and some containers. Ten years later, even the name "piggyback" is anachronistic; a solid train of "double-stack" container cars is the norm.

In addition to the equipment change, the international container shipping lines have entered the picture as "hands-on" customers of the railroads. These companies sell their services directly to the shippers, and then contract with the railroads for hauling the load, as opposed to the traditional contract being between the railroad and the shipper. The primary traffic is from Southeast Asia into West Coast American ports, and thence is distributed eastward via rail. Train capacity can be topped off with domestic traffic, and westbound loads can be used to minimize empty back hauls.

American President Lines was the first shipping line to contract with the railroads to operate a containerized unit train with its own equipment. The cars were all-purpose 89-foot (27 m) hitch/container flats leased from Itel Corp. Sea-Land also operated unit trains, but with equipment from the Trailer Train Company. As the traffic volume increased, so did the need for specialized equipment. Price sensitivity of this highly competitive business meant that all possible efficiencies had to be explored: thus the evolution of the double-stack container car.

The double-stack car was developed by the team of Sea-Land, Southern Pacific, and ACF Industries; the first was SP 513300, built in July 1977. Basically a well-hole flat, it allowed the container to fit into the car, between the side frames, so that a second container could fit on top without overhead-clearance problems. A triple-platform car, the first articulated double-stack, followed in 1979. Satisfied with the prototypes, SP ordered 42 five-unit articulated double-stack cars from ACF. Each group of cars weighed 199,100 pounds (90,390 kg) and carried the bottom container 14 inches (35 cm) above the rail.

In 1983, the Thrall Car Corporation built a three-platform prototype double-stack car with interbox connectors to secure the upper container to the lower,

Union Pacific 9352, a 4,000-hp GE-built Dash 8-40C (one of 256 on the UP), heads a double-stack train at Tobin, California, on the former Western Pacific.

thus eliminating the heavy bulkhead formerly used. Delivery of 86 five-unit articulated versions of these cars to American President Lines signaled the beginning of the double-stack revolution.

SP, Sea-Land, and ACF Industries pioneered the double-stack concept, while American President Line, Union Pacific Chicago & North Western, and Thrall added to the momentum. Gunderson stepped in by building a five-unit prototype in 1984; although lighter than the ACF cars, they still had bulkheads. Even lighter cars were built for Sea-Land in 1985 and ran from Tacoma, Washington, to Little Ferry, New Jersey, as the "Susquehanna Double Stack" unit trains while carrying Greenbrier Leasing or NYS&W markings.

In 1985, there were 2,655 double-stack platforms delivered, the orders split between Thrall and Gunderson, and the fleet totaled 3,672 platforms. Thrall supplied the first Trailer Train double-stack units for APL use on the Union Pacific. Trinity Industries, having purchased Pullman Standard, entered the market with a five-car unit, which was assigned to the UP

for Maersk Lines service between Tacoma and New Jersey. Trailer Train received 803 Thrall units and 870 more from Gunderson, giving TT control of 46 percent of the national fleet. By the end of 1986, there was a total of 6,640 units nationally.

The complexity of container traffic has forced the car builders to maintain flexibility in their designs. Containers come in 20-, 35-, 40-, 45-, 48-, and 53-foot (6, 10.5, 12, 13.5, 14.5, and 16 m) lengths, and it is difficult for a car to accommodate all of them. Typically, a car might handle a single 40-foot (12 m) or two 20-foot (6 m) containers in the well, with longer containers on top overhanging the end platforms and using adjustable flippers for support.

Double-stack cars are usually run in solid train consists—unit trains—under a single waybill, and may cross the country as a single train operating over several railroads and with pooled power. Santa Fe,

Five locomotives led by SD40T-2 8338 (a tunnel motor) head east with a Southern Pacific double-stack train.

Burlington Northern, and Southern Pacific also operate double-stacks in regularly scheduled freights.

It is very clear that the future of railroading in the United States is closely tied to intermodal traffic. The containerization of both import and export traffic means the car designs will keep evolving and the double-stacks, which can carry the equivalent cargo in a train only 60 percent as long as with standard equipment, will play an important role well into the future.

Dynamometer Car

Not every railroad owns a dynamometer car, but coupling one of these cars between a locomotive and a train (either steam or diesel—passenger or freight) can provide information about locomotive performance. Along with a continuous measurement of drawbar pull, the equipment can record steam loco water consumption, fuel consumption, steam pressure, air brake pressure, cylinder performance, temperature, and many other specialized measurements. All of this data is recorded during

a run and keyed with respect to mile posts, stations, and other landmarks that can later be related to grades and curves.

A dynamometer car allows a railroad to make decisions concerning locomotive capabilities based on scientifically collected data, rather than theoretical calculations or "seat of the pants" opinions. Locomotive tonnage ratings, helper districts, passing siding, and block-signal locations can all be determined with great accuracy. Testing of new devices under actual operating conditions can help determine their real value to the railroad.

The cars look much like a passenger car, although they may have a cupola or a bay window for better visibility. Recording equipment, computers, and a device for measuring drawbar pull are accommodated, as well as office, cooking, and sleeping facilities. These rare pieces of equipment are rarely seen today, but there are a number still operating, primarily for the locomotive builders.

See also: *Caboose.*

Eiffel, Alexandre Gustave (1832–1923)

While best known for his landmark tower (1887–1889) in Paris, Eiffel was responsible for many of the significant European iron railway bridges, including France's Sioule and Neuvial viaducts on the Orléans Railway (1887–1889), the Tagus Bridge on the Caceres Railway in Spain (1880), and the Tardes Viaduct (1883) in central France. In Portugal, the Douro Bridge (1875) first demonstrated his use of a great iron arch, and the finest example of that form is the Garabit Viaduct (1882) on the Southern Railway of France. Eiffel's bridges had absorbed 38,000 tons (34,200 t) of iron and steel by 1887.

Electrification

Although heavy main-line electrification was investigated in the United States long before it was considered in Europe, the amount of American electrification is but a fraction of what has become a major propulsion method for overseas railways. Thomas Davenport of Vermont built an electric traction engine in 1837, which he operated on a short stretch of track. By 1850, experiments had begun in Europe without any measurable results. These experiments did inspire the U.S. Congress, which authorized Professor Charles Page to build an electric locomotive. Unfortunately, government enthusiasm was premature as the design of electric motors was not sufficiently advanced, and no more funds were forthcoming.

The Berlin Exhibition of 1879 included a small electrically powered locomotive built by Ernst Werner von Siemens and Johann G. Halske, which pulled carriages around a circular track while drawing current from a middle third rail. Amazingly, the locomotive survived even the bombing during World War II and is on display in the Deutsches Museum, Munich. Siemens and Halske opened the first public service street railway in Lichterfelde, a suburb of Berlin. The early 1880s also saw electric traction installations in Brighton, England, and Portrush, Giant Causeway, Ireland.

In 1880, Thomas Edison demonstrated a small locomotive that reached a speed of 40 mph (64 kph). The 1885 electrification of the Richmond (Virginia) Union Passenger Railway inspired rapid growth in electric street railways. That was also the year that Frank Sprague patented a system in which several electrically powered streetcars could be controlled from a single motorman in the lead car. This is the basis of the control system used in virtually every commuter railroad and transit system today.

In 1895, the Baltimore & Ohio (B&O) became the first American railroad to take advantage of electrification. Responding to an ordinance banning steam locomotives and their smoke within the limits of Baltimore, the B&O at first used horses to haul trains through the city. Seeking a more efficient system, the B&O electrified 3 3/4 miles (6 km) of track, including a tunnel running the length of Howard Street. The 600-volt system used a small General Electric locomotive to haul trains, with their steam locomotives, into and out of Baltimore's Mount Royal station.

In New York City, the polluting steam locomotive was likewise banned south of

Many early electrification projects were undertaken to eliminate smoke pollution. The B&O built a 3 3/4-mile (6 km) mostly underground connection, including the 1 1/2-mile (2.5 km) Howard Street Tunnel, to accommodate rail traffic across downtown Baltimore. General Electric built tunnel motor No. 1 in 1894 to pull steam trains up the tunnel grade, thereby avoiding exhaust problems.

the Harlem River after 1908, causing the New York Central to electrify its track with a third-rail DC system between Grand Central Terminal and Croton, New York, allowing for an open cut to be converted to a tunnel along Park Avenue.

Westinghouse Electric favored AC power, as opposed to competitor General Electric, which continued founder Thomas Edison's preference for DC. Their first AC project in North America was for the New York, New Haven & Hartford in 1907. This 11,000-volt, 250-cycle system is still used by Amtrak.

The argument over AC versus DC was fierce. AC is easier and more economical to transmit over long distances, but DC traction motors are simpler and less expensive than AC motors. The New Haven's electric locomotives were among the first to be operable with either AC or DC. A device

Left, top: The L5 electrics of the Pennsylvania Railroad were intended as a multipurpose locomotive, capable of easily being converted from passenger to freight service, AC to DC, and overhead wire to third rail pick-up shoe. The third rail shoe–equipped 3930, called Old Rail Spreader *because of its rigid non-articulated construction, has been rebuilt with a high hood, but clearly shows the jackshaft system for transferring power from the motor to the wheels. Left, middle: This is New York Central No. 277, a 2-B-B-2 "T-motor" locomotive with third rail pick-up, in the Bronx, New York, in 1936. General Electric produced thirty-six of the units between 1913 and 1926, and they were the standard power for all trains from Grand Central Terminal to the engine change points at Harmon and White Plains. Left, bottom: The Class O1 2-B-2 (0-4-0) box-cab electrics of the Pennsylvania Railroad resulted from a technological breakthrough that enabled small, powerful, axle-mounted, AC electric motors to be built, and ended the jackshaft era for the Pennsy. The first eight O1s, built in 1930 and 1931, were equipped with electrical equipment made by Westinghouse, General Electric, and Brown-Boveri; the power output varied between 500 and 625 hp.*

called a thyristor greatly simplifies the technology that allows DC motors to operate on AC current. The great electrified systems of modern Europe also allow for the operation of locomotives on all the various voltages of the AC and DC systems in use.

Ventilation problems in tunnels provided the impetus for many electrification projects. The Great Northern electrified the 2.6-mile (4.2 km) first Cascade Tunnel and its approaches in 1909, to relieve the smoke problems of steam locomotives operating in a confined space, and retained the system for the second Cascade Tunnel, at 7.77 miles (12.5 km) the longest in North America. The Simplon and St. Gotthard Tunnels in the Alps were also electrified soon after completion. The Great Northern, however, removed the electrification and converted to diesel-electric operations after improving the ventilation in 1956.

The Chicago, Milwaukee, St.Paul & Pacific Railroad (Milwaukee Road) took a more complete approach. They began to electrify their route between St. Paul and Seattle in 1914, eventually installing the 3,000-volt, overhead-wire DC system on 902 route miles (1,450 km). Hydroelectric generators supplied sufficient current to operate their 521,000-pound (236,000 kg) 3,840-hp locomotives, called Bi-polars, and the "Little Joes," named after Joseph Stalin because the engines were embargoed before shipment to Russia. After World War II, the Milwaukee Road dismantled the electrification in favor of diesel-electric locomotives.

The Pennsylvania Railroad, in keeping with its reputation as "the Standard Railroad of the World," was the most serious proponent of electrification in North America. Beginning in 1928, the Pennsy

The GG1 was the pride of Pennsylvania Railroad electrification. Here, a double-header led by No. 4887, in Penn Central livery, hauls a freight train on a snowy New Jersey day in 1978.

embarked on a massive project that installed a 25-cycle AC system, similar to the New Haven's, on 670 route miles (1,100 km) made up of 2,200 miles (3,500 km) of track over the following decade. Virtually their entire main line east of Harrisburg, Pennsylvania, was electrified for both freight and passenger traffic, and the legendary Raymond Loewy–styled GG1 locomotive was designed for use on this route—the last major electrification project in North America.

In the early 1960s, the Pennsy looked to General Electric for replacement of these 1930s-era electric units and bought sixty-six 5,000-hp units designated E44, but the GG1s toiled on anyway, side by side with the newcomers. The E44s were retired in 1984, when Pennsy successor Conrail abandoned freight electrification, but the venerable GG1s continued to roll under Amtrak.

Today, the New Haven to Boston to New York to Philadelphia to Washington route is operated by Amtrak as their

Northeast Corridor, a heavily traveled high-speed passenger line. The physical plant was substantially rebuilt beginning in the 1970s, and speeds of up to 120 mph (192 kph) were authorized. The adopted GG1s were joined by the new Metroliners, fast but visually straightforward self-propelled cars that could be assembled into trains as required. Amtrak soon experimented with other more conventional locomotives and train sets. GE delivered an order for twenty-six 6,000-hp E60s from 1972 to 1976, in two variations, for high-speed service on the Corridor. Tracking problems limited the E60s to 90 mph (144 kph), which Amtrak found unacceptable on this 120-mph (192 kph) line, so a number were sold.

Not content to stick with American products, Amtrak imported two locomotives for testing in 1977. The Swedish 80-ton (72 t) unit produced 6,000 hp, but was returned as being too light. The French unit was rated at 7,725 hp, but was also sent back when the tests were inconclusive. An order was placed for sixty-five AEM7 locomotives that were a variation of the Swedish ASEA unit, and were built in the United States under license to EMD.

The value of the Northeast Corridor electrification is well recognized, and great improvement in signaling and dispatching systems is currently under way. Unfortunately, the tremendous capital expenditure necessary has prevented further expansion in the United States or Canada outside of transit systems in urban areas. Extension of the former Pennsy's system, from Harris-

Above, left: General Electric built sixty-six C-C trucked 4,400-hp E44s for the Pennsylvania Railroad in 1960. The ignitron rectifier locomotives converted the AC power from the catenary to DC power for the traction motors, simplifying maintenance. Above, right: Despite an abundance of hydroelectric power, New Zealand has been slow to move toward heavy electrification. The commuter district around Wellington and the Otira Tunnel are the major exceptions.

burg, over the Alleghenies via Horseshoe Curve, to Pittsburgh has been studied many times but never initiated. Minor exceptions are coal mine–to–power plant railroads: the Muskingum Electric Railroad in Ohio; the Black Mesa & Lake Powell in Arizona; and the Deseret Western in Arizona are typical of such installations.

Much of the world, on the other hand, has embraced electrically powered mainline railroads. The Alpine tunnels inspired many of the early installations, in an effort to eliminate the smoke problems caused by steam locomotives. The Swiss Federal Railways experimented with main-line electrification as early as 1910 on the Berne to Lötschberg to Simplon Line and was completely electrified early on.

The rest of Europe proceeded in the same direction. In Holland, the entire rail system south and west of the Zuider Zee was rebuilt following World War II and electric power prevailed, with rather mundane self-propelled multiple-unit trains

providing efficiency in exchange for the wonderful diversity of steam power that prevailed before the war. The French were even more ambitious, having decided on a complete rebuilding of important junctions, including full remote control, as well as realignment of track in open country so that higher speeds would be possible. Prewar speeds had been limited to 75 mph (120 kph), but electrification, signaling, and control changes raised that to 90 mph (140 kph). In the 1980s, the Mistral was very impressive, covering the 98 miles (157 km) between Paris and Dijon in one hour, and many trains regularly ran at 125 mph (200 kph). The revolutionary TGV, running on a private right-of-way, has regularly operated at 125 mph (200 kph).

Britain made an early commitment to diesel power, and therefore was reluctant to embrace electrification, but considerable work has been done in dense traffic corridors. Many members of the former British Empire have gone further. India has electrified 3,000 route miles (4,800 km) since 1947, including both suburban service and mountain grades. South Africa, having plenty of coal, but little oil to encourage dieselization, has fully embraced electric power while retaining steam. Beginning in 1926, with 3,000-volt DC, the mileage under wire has grown to more than 3,500 (5,600 km), and the number of electric locomotives exceeds 1,700. Australia, New Zealand, and Canada have reserved electric railroads primarily for commuting and heavy corridor use, although British Columbia Railway built a new line from

Anzac, British Columbia, some 80 miles (128 km) inland, to serve new coal mines. This line was electrified at 50,000 volts, 60 cycles, and operated with 6,000-hp units built by GM of Canada with ASEA-licensed electrical equipment.

While the higher construction costs for electrification tend to relegate new installations to suburban commuter lines, heavily trafficked and relatively short corridors, or captive coal mine service, growing interest in high-speed service and fluctuating fuel prices mean that the situation is always in flux. It seems safe to say that locomotives drawing electricity from a distant power plant will share the load with those that generate their own power from on-board generators for the foreseeable future.

Electric locomotives are described, like the steam locomotive's Whyte System, by the arrangements of their wheels, counting axles rather than wheels and grouping them as they are mounted in a single swiveling unit:

unpowered axles	0,1,2
powered axles in a single truck	
2 axles	B
3 axles	C
4 axles	D

Groups of powered and unpowered axles mounted in a single swiveling or articulated unit (or truck) are separated by a plus sign (+).

Thus, a switcher with three powered axles that don't swivel would be described:

O–C–O. A switcher with a pair of swiveling trucks, each having two powered axles would be: B + B. A heavy-duty freight or passenger locomotive, like the GG1, with two articulated frames each supported by a pair of trucks having two unpowered axles or three powered axles is a 2–C + C–2. The Milwaukee Road Bi-polars were described as: 1–B + D + D + B–1 and their Class EF3, which was made up of three separate units semipermanently coupled together, was: (2–B + B) + (B + B) + (B + B–2). This system was not universal in the beginning— Pennsy preferred to call the GG1s 4-6-6-4, as in the Whyte System. Ultimately, the letter/number system came to describe diesel-electric locomotives as well.

EMD, the Electro-Motive Division of General Motors

The company that grew to be the largest diesel locomotive builder in the world evolved from three separate endeavors. The first was the tiny Electro-Motive Company (EMC), founded in Cleveland by H. L. Hamilton to produce gasoline-powered railcars for passenger service. The second was the Winton Engine Company, originally an automotive company turned successful manufacturer of four-cycle diesel engines for marine applications, whose engines were considered to be heavy, cumbersome, and sluggish. The key to the combine was Charles Kettering, who directed a project in the research facilities of General Motors that was experimenting with two-cycle diesels, and by 1930, had achieved the same horsepower in an engine 25 percent smaller and with a 20 percent weight reduction.

The low-cost, dependable, gasoline-powered railcars of EMC were popular with the railroads as they tried to stem the financial losses caused by passenger service on lightly traveled lines. Hamilton did not manufacture his own cars, but contracted to have them assembled from purchased components. Winton supplied the engines, other components came from the standard industry sources, and the parts were assembled by a car builder, such as St. Louis Car Company, at its own plant.

In the late 1920s, the rising price of gasoline and the demand for higher horsepower indicated the need for an improved diesel power plant, but the Winton Company, although profitable, was not big enough to commit the resources necessary for the development of a low-cost, lightweight, and efficient two-cycle power plant. GM needed a significant application for Kettering's new engine, so Winton, already a supplier to Electro-Motive, was acquired by GM. When the world slid into the Great Depression, EMC's business collapsed.

The Union Pacific M-10000 was a joint effort between Pullman Standard and General Motors and was the first "streamliner," completed in February 1934. Because of the brown and yellow unit's spark-ignition distillate engine, the Chicago, Burlington & Quincy's Zephyr, completed two months later, was credited as the first diesel-electric streamliner in the world.

As Winton's biggest customer and with experience in the application of internal-combustion engines to railroad products, EMC also became a target for acquisition by GM, and was purchased through a $1.2 million exchange of stock. The transformation of railroading in North America had begun.

The 1930s found GM establishing itself in the railroad industry. A Winton four-cycle power plant was installed in the Union Pacific's M-10000, the 1934 pioneer. As was typical of Burlington's Zephyr, Illinois Central's Green Diamond, and the other early attempts at Winton diesel-powered streamliners, the M-10000 was built as a fixed train set, with the power unit and individual cars articulated on shared trucks. This meant shop maintenance to any unit removed the entire train from operation, and these early power cars were not classified as locomotives.

This lack of flexibility, as well as the need to utilize the existing railroad passenger car fleets, encouraged GM to develop a pair of independent passenger road units, which were demonstrated in 1935. Producing 1,800 hp from their Winton engines and riding on four-wheel trucks with each axle powered, the locomotives impressed both the Santa Fe and Baltimore & Ohio enough for them to order some. These homely box cabs became the first high-speed, diesel-powered locomotives that could operate with any train.

While this example proved that the GM/Winton/EMC combination could deliver a functional product, many problems remained to be solved: the engines were still being built at the Winton plant for assembly by the supplier of the car bodies; the box cab packaging was inappropriate in the context of the streamlining mania of the 1930s; and no standardization had yet evolved.

The rakishly slanting boatlike nose of the Electro-Motive Division's early E Unit passenger diesel inspired a number of elegant "bow wave" paint schemes. Atlantic Coast Line's West Coast Champion roars across the St. John's River behind E3 No. 501, just a few minutes out of Jacksonville.

General Motors moved to solve these problems in 1935, giving stature (and the ability to raise expansion capital) to their locomotive business by establishing it as their Electro-Motive Division, or EMD, with consequences unanticipated by other builders. Manufacturing efficiency was improved with the establishment of a new plant, for both engines and car bodies, in La Grange, Illinois, a dozen miles (19 km) west of downtown Chicago; its first unit was completed in 1936.

Early business at La Grange consisted primarily of switch engines powered by eight- and twelve-cylinder Winton engines. The passenger locomotive designated TA, with its rakishly slanted nose, was built for the Rock Island in 1937; it was the first locomotive with the car body built by GM. Later in 1937, the stylish E Unit, although still Winton-powered, introduced GM's twin trademarks of distinctive styling and rigorous production standards to an industry that had previously relied on custom building.

GM was adamant that the standardization practiced in the automobile industry was the key to mass production and therefore the key to success with locomotives. A major railroad that had expressed an interest

Conrail has retained three EMD E8 A Units for use on official trains. The 2,250-hp units built by General Motors in 1951 represent the classic image of the diesel-electric passenger locomotive.

in a single locomotive of the new untried design arrived at the plant with a large roll of drawings detailing desired design changes. While this had been common in the old steam-loco tradition, the acceptance of any changes would legitimize the practice and make future standardization impossible. The order was canceled until GM offered to take the loco back if it failed.

This insistence on mass production efficiency through standardization (with add-on options) successfully initiated the concept for both EMD and the rest of the industry. Customizing an identifiable image for a railroad was accomplished with strong graphics and colorful paint schemes developed by GM's styling department. While steam locomotives had evolved to the point of being black with occasional color, and diesels of all manufacturers were multicolored with occasional black accents, the railroads of the coal regions often stood by tradition, opting for units in basic black.

By 1938, after years of exhaustive testing, La Grange was ready to produce GM's own two-cycle engine. GM was aware that road failures, particularly in highly publicized premium service, would destroy the image and acceptability of their new diesel engine. Corporate concern was strong enough that beds were installed in the engine rooms of early diesels so EMD mechanics could ride around the clock to ensure proper maintenance and handle emergency repairs.

Designated model 567 for the cubic-inch displacement of each cylinder, the sixteen-cylinder version of this engine, developing 1,650 hp, was installed in the first road freight prototype, model FT. The FTs differed from the E Units in that they were powered by a single engine and rode on four-wheel power trucks, while the earlier passenger loco had dual engines on six-wheel trucks.

GM readied the FT demonstrator for in-service testing in late 1939. The prototype was composed of two cab units semipermanently coupled to two cabless booster units (producing a total of 5,400 hp) dressed in dark green with buff trim and designated as a single locomotive, No. 103. The two cabs were blessed with the famous "bulldog" nose that was to become the La Grange image for the next twenty years, and both cabs and boosters carried four round portholes on their sides.

The demonstration tour was a magnificent success for GM. The FT hauled freight under all conditions on twenty railroads in thirty-five states. Santa Fe placed the first order and assigned their FTs to the "bad water" areas of the arid Southwest, while the Southern purchased the reconditioned demonstrator. The flexibility of the building-block approach that added horsepower by coupling on another booster made these new locomotives as useful for racing across the prairies as for struggling up mountain passes, which wasn't possible with specific-purpose steam locomotives.

The United States' entry into World War II helped solidify GM's position as the leader in the diesel locomotive field, as no other manufacturer built over-the-road freight diesels. Alco and Baldwin built only yard switchers; only Alco had gone so far as to design a road unit, but none was yet built. When the War Production Board assigned priorities, only GM was in a position to produce road diesels, but they were prohibited from building switchers. The wartime restrictions helped EMD's technological lead, which it maintained for almost forty years.

Following the war, all the builders scrambled to supply the railroads with new power. The extreme demands placed on both rolling stock and physical plants, already weakened by the depression, had hastened the further decline of the railroads. Baldwin, Lima, and Alco, still professing the superiority of steam, were introducing new models as late as 1946, badly misjudging the market. While there was little call for steam power, there were plenty of sales to be made in all categories of diesels—GM had booked F Unit orders with thirty railroads by the end of 1946.

GM promised increased horsepower, optional high-speed gearing for passenger service, and an improved electrical system. The interim successor to the FT was the F2, which was made for only five months before the F3 went into production at the rate of seventy units per month.

While the other builders emulated EMD, even producing comparable units

and, it could be argued, superior features, in most cases it was too late. EMD's established service organization with years of experience, and a system of factory branches and parts warehouses, meant that ordering from a different manufacturer was far riskier for both the executives involved and the railroad. Old alliances and offerings that filled particular market niches meant those risks were taken and business kept trickling in to Alco, Baldwin, Fairbanks-Morse, and Lima. But, in the early 1950s, the F7 swept the market.

GM ultimately sold approximately 7,100 freight-hauling F Units of all variations, 2,900 of them boosters (B Units) and 455 of the four-foot-longer passenger-hauling FPs (79 of them B Units). Additionally, the New Haven ordered sixty dual-power units, designated FL9, convertible between internally generated power and outside third rail. The final Fs were turned out of La Grange in 1960.

The F Units were so dominant that the established builders were mortally wounded. Congress was called upon to

The New Georgia Railroad operates two restored FP7 A Units obtained from the Southern Railway. The 1,500-hp locomotives were built in 1950 by EMD.

investigate whether GM had used illegal restraint of trade and unfair practices to create a monopoly. Hearings began in 1955, and testimony developed the theory that GM had used its position as the nation's largest shipper to force the railroads to buy EMD locomotives. It was alleged that GM was given an unfair advantage during World War II when it was the only builder allocated materials to construct road freight diesels, and therefore had been provided an insurmountable lead in the postwar marketplace.

The testimony against GM had been largely circumstantial and was refuted by somewhat vague statistics and equally circumstantial testimony, but the steam builders' postwar insistence on the superiority of steam combined with the inability of the other diesel builders to capitalize on their early lead in road-switcher sales was damning evidence. As the hearings droned on to the inevitable conclusion favoring GM, the F Unit was already obsolete, having been replaced by the road switcher.

To compete in the road-switcher niche, without obviously copying the competition, EMD introduced the lovable oddball BL1 (*B*ranch *L*ine) in February 1948. Offered in both freight and passenger versions, the production model was designated BL2, and was an F3 dressed up in a semi-

A trio of Pennsylvania Railroad F3s, in the classic A-B-A arrangement, highballs out of Enola Yard and along the Susquehanna River, near Harrisburg, Pennsylvania, in May 1950. What appear to be handrails on the roofs are actually induction train phone antennae.

streamlined car body for way freight use. The design provided front and rear-end platforms, a tapered engine compartment for rear visibility, and sloping notches in the sides so the engineer could easily see the brakemen working on the ground. Despite its heavy-shouldered, bulldoglike appearance, the BLs were thought to be attractive enough to serve on suburban and local passenger runs, as well as way freights, but only fifty-nine models were sold before production ended in May 1949.

After its competitors had pioneered the road-switcher concept, GM first dipped in a toe with the BL and then jumped into the market in 1949 with the GP7 (General Purpose), which shared the 1,500-hp 567 engine and other components with the F7. The Fs outsold the GPs until 1954, when the F9 and GP9 were introduced. The GP design featured a narrow hood over the engine compartment with an outside walk-way and a wide cab, so that visibility to the rear was greatly improved over the F, thus being more useful for switching cars at industries along the main line. The GP models, nicknamed "Geeps," became the universal loco the railroads were looking for. They pulled everything in sight—way freights, branch-line passenger, transfer drags, main-line passenger, commuter, main-line freight—whatever was needed.

In 1952, the SD7 (Special Duty), resembling a lengthened GP7 but with six-wheel C-C trucks, was introduced. The extra wheels provided lighter axle loading on branch lines, and the two extra-traction motors offered greater starting tractive effort as well as continuous tractive effort up to 12 mph (19 kph), an advantage in low-speed, heavy-drag, and transfer operations.

The GP and SD models were steadily improved with horsepower increases and such options as turbocharging, steam generators, oversize fuel tanks, and dynamic brakes. The SD40 of 1966 produced 3,000 hp from sixteen cylinders, and the SD45's twenty-cylinder prime movers turned out 3,600 hp. Both designs were produced in passenger hauling versions, and with the F45 (and passenger FP45) EMD returned to the cowl design—a sort of squared-off version of the bulldog nose.

Right: The Southern Pacific still rostered ninety-three of the EMD SD9s in 1992, almost 20 percent of the original production. The 16-cylinder 1,750-hp prime mover supplies power to six-wheel trucks. Below: Chicago Rail Link, one of the spinoffs of several major North American railroads, operates this GP7, the first EMD road switcher model (built from 1949 to 1954). The unit has been remodeled with a "chopped nose," which became a standard feature of later designs. Below, bottom: The 16-cylinder 567-series General Motors two-cycle diesel engine (prime mover) was originally built for the F3, but was the basis for power plants installed in EMD locomotives for fifteen years.

In January 1972, the Dash 2 line, which consisted of the earlier model designations with a "-2" added, was introduced. It had AC power produced by alternators, rather than the previous DC generators; modularized electrical cabinets; and a number of changes designed to enhance reliability.

While standardization as a way of life dominated thinking at La Grange, there was room for occasional diversity in the interest of experimentation and advancement. In 1956, GM produced a unique demonstrator—the turret-cabbed, lightweight Aerotrain, heralded as the passenger train of the future but very much a return to the early days of integrated train sets with power cars. Only one additional unit was built—the Rock Island Talgo Jet Rocket—but it was never mass-produced.

A 1951 experimental 340-hp industrial switcher was driven directly by means of Allison torque converters, and General Motors Diesel (Canada) produced the GMDH-1, a center-cab diesel-hydraulic industrial switcher. Thirteen of the MRS-1s were built for the U. S. Army, in 1952, with multi-gauge trucks, while the GA8 was produced for narrow-gauge lines in Mexico and Newfoundland.

Above, top: The merger of Southern Pacific and Denver & Rio Grande was accompanied by the adoption of a new logo, seen here on No. 7115, a 3,000-hp GP40M built in 1991 by the Electro-Motive Division of General Motors.

Above: A high-nosed SD7 with 1,500 hp exhibits the SP's former standard "bloody nose" paint scheme. A 1952 product of EMD, the unit was among twenty-eight survivors in 1992.

The Union Pacific was well known, in steam days, for its devotion to unusual, powerful, and often very large locomotives, and that reputation carried on in the diesel era. EMD designed the DD35, a thirty-two-cylinder, 5,000-hp, D-D trucked behemoth. More than 88 feet (26 m) long and with a rigid wheelbase exceeding 17 feet (5 m), longer by a foot (0.3 m) than the Baldwin Centipede, it was essentially two GP35s on a single frame and was called "the 5,000 horsepower track straightener" by trackside wits. UP's generous engineering standards allowed for such a monster, and management liked the idea of eliminating six- and eight-unit lash-ups on long, fast freights. UP bought forty-five of the units, and another forty-seven of the specially designed 6,600-hp DDA40X cowl units, called Centennials in honor of the one-hundredth anniversary of the golden spike ceremony at Promontory, Utah. Even these low-volume locomotives used standard components common to other high-production units, thus remaining consistent with the firm's basic philosophy.

The GM theories of mass production of standard models, with limited options turned into solid examples of the best of the locomotive builder's art, allowed EMD to dominate the North American locomotive market until 1983, when competitor General Electric, already well established in the worldwide market, suddenly jumped into the sales lead with their highly fuel-efficient Dash 8 models. The worldwide oil crisis drove up fuel prices.

On January 12, 1988, the unthinkable happened—GM announced that assembly of diesel locomotives at the sprawling La Grange plant would cease by 1991, and the facility that was EMD would be relegated to engine assembly, engineering, and a parts warehouse. Production of new locomotives would continue at the company's much smaller Canadian plant in London, Ontario.

It seemed impossible that the mighty giant that once had a virtual lock on the North American locomotive business had fallen victim to a combination of a depressed market and great technological advances evidenced by the products of rival General Electric. The situation remains in flux. The reliability of the GE locomotives has become suspect and production continues at La Grange. The future of EMD, the company that dieselized North America, remains to be seen.

End-of-Train Device (EOT)

With the costs of caboose maintenance and handling rising; computers, microwave communications, and radios reducing the need for on-train paperwork; and the advent of modern signaling systems, the romance and tradition of "the little red caboose" clattering along at the end of the train was becoming obsolete. The original purpose of the caboose—rolling office for the conductor; monitoring of air pressure continuity in the brake pipe; and a place to carry the marker lights and the rear end brakeman, both of which are needed for rear end protection from following trains—could be satisfied with less expensive alternatives.

Thus, the end-of-train device (EOT)—a portable unit hung on the rear coupler that flashes a warning light visible to a following train—was created. Also called FRED, an acronym for Flashing Rear End Device, it comes in both "smart" and "dumb" models, depending on the device's

The end-of-train device (EOT), along with computerized paperwork, has enabled railroads to eliminate the caboose on most trains.

capabilities. A dumb EOT is simply a battery-powered amber or red flashing warning light. It's designed to be easily attached to the coupler with an elastic strap, and will emit its steady flashing warning until it's turned off. A smart EOT, however, is a sophisticated electronic device similar only in its position on the last car and its use of the flashing warning light. A smart EOT also monitors train motion and brake pressure and is linked to the engineer in the locomotive cab by a self-contained radio.

The Trainlink EOT system, used by the Chicago & Northwestern and the Union Pacific, is typical of a smart unit. The system consists of four major parts: a combination sensor, transmitter, and rear marker unit; a battery box; a coupler mounting bracket; and a locomotive receiver. The battery pack is recharged between trips on a dedicated charger. A full battery charge is good for 120 hours at 70 degrees F (20° C) but it drops to 60 hours at 20 degrees below zero (–28° C).

A car inspector attaches the device to the rear coupler and attaches it to the air hose glad hand before departure from a terminal. The unit's discrete number code is reported to the engineer and is entered into the engine receiver. This numeric code restricts the radio link to the appropriate EOT device, so that the train crew reacts to the proper information.

The smart EOT transmits telemetry data such as: whether the last car is moving or stopped; whether the flasher is working; low battery charge (less than four hours); a radio break (no transmission in the previous five minutes); train line brake pressure on the last car; and a resettable odometer, so that the engineer can be assured that the last car has cleared a road crossing before stopping the train.

While the caboose still punctuates the end of the train in many countries, it has been fast disappearing on the main lines of North America. Through trains do not require major paperwork during the run, and the typical multiple locomotive power required provides adequate seating space for the operating crew and any others needed. FRED, the flashing end-of-train device, has proven to be a reliable tool in the search for railroad safety.

See also: *Caboose.*

power two sets of driving wheels. Most Fairlies were 0-4-4-0 or 0-6-6-0 types, and the largest was a 0-6-6-0 built for Mexico in 1911.

A single-boiler version was adapted by William Mason in the United States as the Mason-Fairlie type. A popular design for urban railroads, 148 were built in gauges from standard to 3 feet between 1871 and 1889, when manufacturing was taken over by the Taunton works and then Manchester. Alco built the final Mason-Fairlies at Schenectady in 1914, for the Boston, Revere Beach & Lynn Railroad, where

Above, top: **Merddin Emrys,** *of the narrow gauge Ffestiniog Railway, is a Fairlie locomotive built in 1879. The double-bogie, double-boiler design was an answer to the need for small, powerful, and flexible steam power on industrial railroads. Above: While Robert Fairlie is best known for his early articulated designs, he also produced other types. Ffestiniog No. 8, named* **Eryri,** *is a small tank locomotive now used for hauling tourists on the former Welsh slate quarry railroad.*

they remained in commuter service until electrification.

The 1-foot 11½-inch gauge Ffestiniog Railway in Wales continues to operate with three Fairlies, which were built in 1879, 1886, and 1979.

Falkland Islands Railroad

Just when the roughly 2-foot-gauge railway was built is not known, but the line connected Port Stanley with a radio signal station just 3 miles (4.8 km) inland. There was one small steam locomotive that monopolized traffic in one direction, but the other direction coincided with the prevailing winds, leading to a most unusual service. Sail-powered railcars provided informal, but more frequent, service in the downwind direction. The railroad is now abandoned.

Firth of Forth Bridge

The queen of England's railroad bridges is undoubtedly this triple cantilever spanning the great estuary that separates Celtic from Saxon Scotland. When completed, several hours were cut from the schedules.

Sir Thomas Bouch engineered the original design, which was for a twin-span suspension bridge, and construction contracts had been let when Bouch's great Tay Bridge collapsed during a storm. His reputation in tatters, the contract was canceled, and the promoters turned to Sir John Fowler and Sir Benjamin Baker for the design, with Sir William Arrol as contractor. They proposed a design composed of three cantilevered structures, with spans of 1,710 feet (513 m) each and a clearance of 157 feet (47 m). By comparison, the San Francisco-Oakland Bay Bridge spans 1,400 feet (420 m), and New York's Queensborough Bridge, 1,182 feet (355 m). Both are suspension bridges built fifty

years later. Each of the Forth main spans exceeds the single steel arch of Sydney Harbor Bridge at 1,650 feet (495 m).

The cantilever design allowed for a structure of great elegance, but the slender proportions of the members were due to steel, rather than the wrought iron then in common use. Hollow tubes, composed of hundreds of riveted plates, provide the primary structural support, while the stiffening elements are conventional laced girders.

The bridge was opened on March 4, 1890, by the Prince of Wales.

See also: *Tay Bridge Disaster; Sydney Harbor Bridge.*

Folsom Prison Railroad

One of the more unusual short lines was one that most folks preferred to ride just one way—out. The Folsom Prison Railroad was begun by private interests in 1867, to aid construction of a stone dam on the American River, near Sacramento, California, but the quarry provided both the location for a prison and the material to keep convicts occupied. The state took over the dam railroad and the quarry in 1868, and provided a specially outfitted coach for its passengers. Iron rings were firmly mounted in the floor for the attachment of leg chains.

The spectacular cantilevered bridge over the Firth of Forth, Scotland, is called the greatest railway bridge in the world. Opened in 1908, it is 8,298 feet (2,530 m) long and is built of steel riveted into tubular shapes.

Forney, Matthias Nace (1835–1908)

An American editor, inventor, and loco-motive builder, Forney was born in Hano-ver, Pennsylvania. At age seventeen, he was apprenticed to locomotive builder Ross Winans. After three years as a draftsman for the Baltimore & Ohio Railroad and a short term in business for himself, Forney entered the employ of the Illinois Central Railroad. In 1865, he was supervising loco construction at the Hinkley & Williams Works.

In 1860, Forney turned to the develop-ment of his ideas regarding locomotives to serve urban areas. Previous designs for this type had been designated as tank locomo-tives, because the attached coal bunker and the tank for water storage wrapped over the boiler, eliminating the tender. The resulting shorter length made for easier maneuverability and better visibility to the rear. The disadvantage was that as coal and water supplies were depleted, the weight on the drivers also decreased, with the end result being less tractive power. Forney's design set the water and coal above a trailing truck, his locomotive designated 0-4-4T (T for tank), so that the weight on the drivers was constant. The short wheelbase allowed for transit over the very sharp curves of city streets and elevated structures.

The Forney locomotive was not widely accepted until the 1870s, when an outbreak of equine distemper killed thousands of the horses that had powered city rail transit sys-tems. Forney, as editor and partial owner of the *Railroad Gazette*, had great influence on the railroad community, and he frequently editorialized in favor of his locomotive and against the then-popular narrow gauge. The Forney design was constructed by a number of builders and was adopted by both the Chicago and New York City elevated sys-tems and used on many railroads, including the New York Central and the New York, New Haven & Hartford.

Ill health forced Forney to give up the *Railroad Gazette*, but three years later, having recovered, he purchased the *American Railroad Journal* and *Van Nos-trand's Engineering Magazine*, which were combined into a new publication called *Railroad and Engineering Journal* until 1893. It was called *American Engineer and Railroad Journal* from 1893 until 1896, when the magazine was sold.

Forney also published the *Railway Gazette* and a book, *Catechism of the Loco-motive*. His other works included *The Car Builder's Dictionary* and *Memoirs of Horatio Allen*. Elected to honorary membership in

Below: A long way from the urban lines for which Forney designed his 0-4-4T, these rusting relics of the Council City & Solomon Railroad remind us of the gold rush days, mired in the tundra outside Nome, Alaska.

Below: Matthias Forney designed a rigid-frame locomotive that placed the fuel and water over an integral trailing truck rather than in a separate tender. Ariel, No. 26 of the New York & Harlem Railroad (Schenectady, 1876), was a heavy Forney intended for suburban commuter service.

the American Railway Master Mechanics' Association, Matthias Forney also helped to organize the American Society of Mechanical Engineers.

F Unit

The first diesel freight locomotive was not a General Motors F Unit, nor did the technology of its car body styling and relatively primitive engineering become the industry standard, but this timeless design was the first of its kind to be powerful enough, reliable enough, and versatile enough to perform to its owners' satisfaction on a daily basis. Over the previous decade, other designs were produced that could do the job sporadically, but the rugged dependability and attendant operating economy of the Fs forced North American railroads to reconsider their remaining commitment to steam and the traditional locomotive builders.

By 1938, the newly formed Electro-Motive Division (EMD) of GM had opened their brand-new plant at La Grange, Illinois, and was ready for production of GM's own two-cycle diesel engine, which was intended to supersede the four-cycle Winton diesel then in use, designated model 567 for the

cubic inch displacement of each cylinder. The sixteen-cylinder version of this engine, developing 1,350 hp, was installed in the first road freight prototype, model FT.

The FT differed from the earlier passenger-hauling E Units in that the freight locos were powered by a single engine and rode on four-wheel power trucks, while the passenger loco had dual engines on six-wheel trucks. Instead of the rakishly slanting nose that had been the hallmark of the E Unit, the FTs were blessed with the first of the soon-to-be-classic "bulldog" noses that were to become the signature of EMD locomotives for the next two decades. Rearrangements, variations, improvements, and options would evolve, but the F Unit was always a standard product of mass production.

By late 1939, the FT demonstrator, a pair of cab units spliced by a pair of booster units and designated as a single 5,400-hp locomotive numbered 103, was ready to embark on a barnstorming tour across America. Resplendent in dark green with buff trim and lettered *Electro-Motive*, No. 103 spent the next eleven months hauling freight on twenty Class 1 railroads in thirty-five states under all sorts of conditions. The tour was hailed as a grand suc-

cess, and the Santa Fe was the first to place an order, intending to assign them to their "bad water" routes in the Southwest. The Southern purchased the reconditioned 103, and was always proud to have the first F Unit ever built.

The onset of World War II had a major impact on the entire locomotive-building business. Only GM was building diesel road units, and the War Production Board was forced to assign the construction of all new units to them, leaving the switchers and steamers to the competition. This gave EMD a lead in technology and mass-production techniques that they would hold for forty years.

Following the close of hostilities, the scramble to replace the war-weary locomotive fleet began in earnest. By the end of

Originally built for the New York, New Haven & Hartford Railroad, the EMD FL9 was a unique locomotive that could switch from its own diesel-powered generator to third-rail power when it entered electrified territory. Metro North, the New York State–managed commuter system, now operates twenty-nine of these units.

1946, thirty roads had placed orders for F Units, which were to have higher horsepower, optional high-speed gearing for passenger train use, and an improved electrical system. The first postwar successor to the FT was the F2, built for only five months until the F3 went into production at the rate of seventy per month.

Other builders tried to copy the GM techniques and frequently improved on them, but it was more of a risk for officials to commit to other units over the well-proven Fs. Dependability combined with the established GM service organization backed with years of experience was too much to overcome, and the F7 model swept the marketplace in the early 1950s. There were 1,084 F Units on twenty-five railroads in January 1946, and in the next nine years some forty-six additional railroads invested in Fs.

In order to counter the competition's road switchers, EMD introduced the GP7 (General Purpose) in 1949, which shared the F7's 567 power plant and other components. While the F7 outsold the "Geep" 7 until introduction of the 1954 models F9 and GP9, the versatility of the road-switcher body won over the railroads and F Unit production wound down. The final units were dual-service FL9s, designed to run on both internally generated and overhead electricity, which were delivered to the New Haven in 1960.

Over 7,600 F Units had been built and the 567 power plant continued to be produced for new locomotives until 1966. F Units still serve on a number of railroads: in commuter service; on director's specials; and even rebuilt into road switchers such as the Santa Fe's CF7s, which would not be recognized by their original builders unless they looked in the engine compartment! Like the ubiquitous 4-4-0 Americans of the previous century, the pioneering F Units eventually found their way to virtually every depot in North America.

The EMD F Unit's obvious impact on railroad transportation entitles it to a place in history, ranking with the Concord coach, Conestoga wagon, Clipper ship, Model T Ford, and the DC-3 as a milestone in design.

See also: *Electrification; EMD; Diesel Locomotives.*

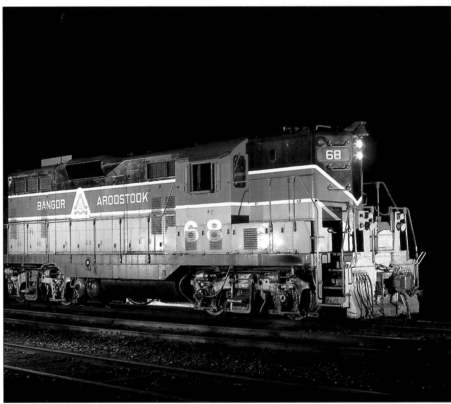

Above, top: The California State Railroad Museum includes a pair of EMD F Units in the exquisite Santa Fe "war bonnet" paint scheme. No. 347C is a 1,500-bp F7, while the trailing B Unit is a 1,350-bp F3; both were built by General Motors in 1949.

Above: Bangor & Aroostock GP7 No. 68 maintains the original design on the cab, where a short hood was placed flush with the roof. The GP7 road switchers produced 1,500 bp and were built by EMD from 1949 to 1954.

The New Haven operated the F7 in passenger service; No. 6691 carries the multicolor "billboard" paint scheme of the 1960s.

G

Gauge

The clear distance between the inside faces of the rails is called the "gauge," and agreement on this distance has been critical to the development of railroads throughout the world. Originally, when carts operating on primitive rails served only an individual mine, the gauge selected was simply a matter of local convenience, as long as there was room between the rails for the feet (either human or animal) of the propulsion system.

Once railroads developed the steam locomotive, engineering considerations became paramount and the need to balance the stability of a wider gauge with the lower construction costs of a narrower gauge caused considerable controversy. The great British engineer Isambard Kingdom Brunel firmly believed in the 7-foot gauge, while his countrymen had more or less settled on 4 feet 8½ inches as standard gauge, but 2 feet between the rails was common in Wales. The Irish preferred 5 feet 3 inches and the Australians were caught up in the controversy when both Irish and British engineers were hired to build railroads in

A tiny narrow-gauge rod locomotive works the slope of a bauxite mine in Arkansas. The short runs to the processing facility and the ever-present need to relocate track to the work sites made narrow-gauge economically advantageous in industrial and construction situations.

their own preferred gauges. The South Africans built at 3 feet 6 inches, and a number of other undeveloped countries preferred its economy.

Most of Europe accepted 4 feet 8½ inches as standard, but Spain still operates at 5 feet 6 inches. The first Russian railway was built by the czar at 6-foot gauge, but it went only, in the words of a cynic, "from the capital city to a tavern" and the country quickly adopted 5 feet as standard. There were also many isolated narrow-gauge lines constructed across the Continent where economic conditions or physical barriers warranted, but like everywhere else in the world, they were forced to accept the standard gauge of the systems around them, or they eventually withered.

The Americans generally agreed on 4 feet 8½ inches, but the Erie was begun with 5 feet and the southern railroads were a mixture. This inconsistency was to plague the Confederacy during the War Between the States, as the lack of easy interchange of

equipment between railroads of differing gauges meant that shipments needed to be unloaded and reloaded, at great cost in time and manpower. Much equipment was lost to raiders when rolling stock could not flee to safety on another line. The frugality ingrained in the "down east" Yankees of Maine led to an extensive system of lower-first-cost 2-foot-gauge railroads, while in the mineral-rich mountains of Colorado, Otto Mears, General Palmer, and the other rail barons forced a narrow gauge of 3 feet into the rough canyons of the Rocky Mountains.

The easy interchange of equipment was not a consideration in the early days of railroad building, so the construction engineers had a relatively free hand in the matter of gauge. As individual rail lines began to merge and connect into transportation systems, however, connecting lines of differing gauges were at a competitive disadvantage. Cargo had to be unloaded (usually by hand) from the cars of one gauge to the cars of another. Passengers had to disembark from their trains, often in the middle of the night, and reboard the next train. This was both inconvenient and costly. A line built in America's Allegheny Mountains, the East Broad Top (EBT), however, employed several unique solutions to "the break of gauge" problem. Although built to 3-foot gauge, it had

rather generous clearances, enabling it to haul standard-gauge cars except for the gauge differential. At their Mount Union, Pennsylvania, connection with the standard-gauge Pennsylvania Railroad, the EBT built a hoist straddling a section of trackage that had three rails, spaced so that the standard gauge used the outer rails and the narrow gauge an outer and the off-

Above: Dual-gauge trackage was inevitable at junctions where standard and narrow gauge met. The Prince Edward Island Railway used an unusual set of switch points to transfer the contact with the third rail (for narrow gauge) to the opposite side of the track in order to simplify trackwork on the switch, which is behind the photographer.

center third rail (dual gauge). A standard-gauge loaded car was moved under the hoist and lifted, allowing the trucks to be removed and narrow-gauge trucks installed. Adaptors for brake linkage and couplers allowed the standard-gauge car to be hauled to its destination on an EBT train. Upon the car's return to Mount Union, the reverse operation sent the car back to the Pennsy.

Since the EBT served numerous mines, a coal-cleaning plant accepted loads from the narrow-gauge hopper cars and then transferred the material into standard-gauge cars. Because of these unique conditions, the EBT continued commercial operations into the 1960s, long after the lack of interchange possibilities closed the other American narrow-gauge common carriers. The EBT is still operated today, carrying tourists, and is recognized as a significant historic landmark.

The problems of differing gauges ultimately was brought to a head in each country, sometimes with quite spectacular results. The Louisville & Nashville was encumbered with 1,500 route miles (2,400 km) of 5-foot gauge, when the prevailing American standard was 4 feet 8½ inches. In 1886, a massive effort converted the entire main line in a single day, by moving one of the flat-bottomed rails across the tie by 3½ inches. In Britain, Brunel's 7-foot gauge Great Western was generally converted piecemeal, a branch at a time, but the final 171 miles (273 km) of main line was changed over to the standard in a single weekend in May 1892. This required cutting the sleepers and moving the transoms over by 2 feet, a much more ambitious undertaking.

Australia was composed of relatively isolated states during the railroad boom. Each state made independent decisions on railroad gauge, heavily influenced by the nationality or personal preference of the engineers hired for construction. Therefore, the country suffered from having large amounts of trackage in three gauges: standard, 5 feet 3 inches, and 3 feet 6 inches. Unification of the gauges was first proposed in the 1880s and was discussed for years. Lord Kitchener pointed out the defense difficulties in 1911, and a Royal Commission proposed a solution in 1921. Unfortunately, the country itself was not fully unified, and agreement between the much separated state governments could not be reached. Several projects were done on a piecemeal basis, but an overall plan was always seen as too ambitious and costly. Finally, by the 1970s, enough of an interlocking system was in place to function, although still in multiple gauges, since the state-managed systems resist the federal government.

South Africa adopted 3-foot 6-inch gauge when Cecil Rhodes began to build from the coast to his diamond mines at Kimberley, and most of the other disconnected lines on his proposed Cape to Cairo railway have been built or converted to match, in anticipation of their eventual interconnection.

The matter of selection of gauge instigated many repercussions that would ultimately affect the finances of the fledgling empire builders and sometimes influenced the future and growth of the settlements along their lines. In the end, connection and interchange prevail—those railroads that can agree on a common standard may prosper, but a railroad isolated from its neighboring lines, unless in specialty service, cannot often survive. Despite these facts, an amazing variety of gauges remains in use.

Above, top: A section of track of standard North American and British gauge— 4 foot 8 1/2 inches. The steel rail is set on concrete ties (sleepers), which are beginning to replace the more common wood. Above: The chaos and delay caused by the break of gauge, as passengers and goods were transferred between trains, caused countries around the world to select a standard gauge and convert the nonstandard railroads.

GAUGE

The problems associated with the transfer of goods at the points of "break of gauge" were quite severe almost from the beginning. In England, a gauge differential between broad and standard gauge at Gloucester inspired a popular expression: "Lost at Gloucester" became the universal explanation of anything mislaid on the British rail system.

Geared Locomotives

The early days of logging by rail meant hauling the small log cars with a horse team, but inadequate brakes frequently failed on downhill grades—resulting in often-fatal collisions with the horses. The steep grades, tight curves, and often temporary nature of the track on logging railroads caused problems for conventional rod locomotives. The geared locomotive solved these problems by sitting a boiler on a frame that was supported on a pair of four-wheeled trucks (bogies). Through an arrangement of shafts, universal joints, and gears, the power from the cylinders was transmitted to all wheels. The combination of flexibility, offered by the swiveling trucks, and the all-wheel drive, enabling increased traction, meant a locomotive could climb steep grades hauling heavy loads without derailing on the rough track.

The first geared locomotive was built by Ephraim Shay, a Michigan logger, in his blacksmith shop. Shay's machine drew the interest of other loggers, but he was not interested in pursuing the locomotive business so he turned his design over to the Lima Machine Works of Lima, Ohio. As news of this successful locomotive spread, other manufacturers unveiled variations of the Shay design, but none achieved the popularity of the original. The closest variation was by the Willamette Works, of Portland, Oregon, which entered the market as Shay patents expired. The Willamette locomotive was popular in the

The Georgetown Loop Railroad operates excursion service in Georgetown, Colorado. Three-truck Shay No. 12 is photographed from the "wrong side," as the cylinders and drive shafts are on the engineer's side of the locomotive.

Pacific Northwest, and inspired Lima to improve its own designs and embark a protracted legal dispute with Willamette.

The locomotives could be built as a three-truck model by adding a separate water tank supported by the extra drive truck and could burn wood, coal, or oil. Over the years they grew into substantial locomotives weighing up to 162 tons (146 t). The roar from the exhaust, caused by the multiple strokes required for each revolution of the small-diameter drive wheels,

and the rapidly flailing drive gear give the impression of a swiftly moving locomotive, although it may be trundling along at only 10 mph (16 kph). Their success was to ensure the operation of geared locomotives in forests, mines, and quarries throughout the world, and many still operate. Baldwin, Vulcan, Dunkirk, and countless small machine shops built variations, adapted diesel engines to the running gear, or otherwise cobbled up locomotives and made modifications, but the three designs detailed below dominated the market.

Below: The Climax used an outboard crank to route the power to a gearbox centered with the drive shaft; the pairs of drivers were geared together. This is a stock 55-ton (49.5 t) class B from the company's 1904–1905 catalog.

Climax Locomotive. The earliest Climax design was more like a covered flatcar with a vertical steam engine and boiler driving the wheels through a gearbox and central drive shaft. It developed into a more traditional locomotive form that was unique in the placement of the pair of cylinders high along the smoke box sides and at a slope down to the rails, connecting the main rod to a transverse shaft and counterweight that drove a central longitudinal shaft via a gearbox. All the axles were powered through gearing to the shaft. The Climax was popular primarily in the eastern United States, and was built by the Climax Manufacturing Company, of Corry, Pennsylvania, from 1884 to 1930.

Heisler Locomotive. A type of geared locomotive used for both logging and industrial purposes, the first Heisler was built by the Stearns Manufacturing Company in Erie, Pennsylvania, and delivered to Mexico in 1894.

The company became the Heisler Locomotive Works in 1898, which was in business into the depression. The Heisler differed from the other geared designs in that the two cylinders were arranged in a V-2 formation, the power being fed, via a crankshaft, to a central longitudinal drive shaft that was geared to a pair of four-wheel trucks. One axle on each truck was driven through the gearing and the other pair of wheels was driven by connecting rods from the geared pair. A typical "modern" two-truck Heisler might have weighed about 60 tons (54 t) and had an enclosed cab.

Below: The Heisler differed from the Shay in having the crankshaft and drive run down the centerline to geared trucks, with pairs of drivers tied with connecting rods. Hetch Hetchy No. 2 was a three-truck, 75-ton (67.5 t) model built in February 1918.

Above: The Shay, "The Titan of the Timber," was the original geared locomotive design and the most common locomotive in logging areas around the world. It was unusual because the boiler was offset to the left to balance the exposed right-hand shaft drive.

Shay Locomotive. The original geared locomotive design, it was developed by Ephraim Shay (1839–1916), a Michigan logger who grew weary of the difficulties of skidding and floating logs to his sawmill. Tinkering in his workshop during the slow winter months, Shay built his first operating locomotive in 1880. It was basically a flatcar with adjacent vertical steam cylinders set along the right side; a vertical boiler was in the middle and a water barrel and fuel box occupied the opposite ends. A crankshaft drove a pair of geared trucks through a system of universal joints and drive shafts along the cylinder side.

In 1882, Shay assigned manufacturing rights to a small company that would grow into the giant Lima Locomotive Works. The design was refined and enlarged over the years; it was offered in models burning

A pair of three-truck Shays, led by Cass No. 3, pull a log train up Bald Knob in West Virginia in 1982. The state-owned Cass Scenic Railroad maintains a large collection of logging locomotives and equipment for excursion use.

wood, coal, and oil. This locomotive differed from the Climax and the Heisler by the side-mounted cylinders and running gear as well as the pronounced offset of the boiler, designed to balance the weight of the cylinders. Both two- and three-cylinder versions were offered as well as two-, three-, and four-truck models. A Shay might only go 12 mph (19 kph) on the level, but could climb grades of 6 to 14 percent.

The largest Shay operated was No. 12 of the logging line of the Greenbrier, Cheat &

Elk Railroad (GC&E), where the company-modified engine had four trucks (two under the separate water tank) and weighed about 400,000 pounds (180,900 kg) after modification. The largest Lima-built Shay is in dispute, but is generally considered to be the final one—a completely modern three-cylinder, three-truck unit built for the Western Maryland Railroad in 1945. It weighed 324,000 pounds (146,000 kg) and had a tractive effort rating of 59,700 pounds (25,865 kg). The giant No. 6 operated on the 9 percent grades of the Western Maryland's Chaffee Branch but was retired in 1953 and sent to the Baltimore & Ohio (B&O) Transportation Museum. In April 1980, No. 6 was removed from the B&O Museum and taken to Cass, West Virginia, for excursion service on the former GC&E and Mower Lumber Company logging line.

General Electric Company

GE was long noted in the rail industry as a supplier of electric traction components for street railways, interurbans, and other electrically powered equipment. The company originally entered the internal combustion traction business by supplying transmissions for gas-electric cars. The first American diesel locomotives were produced by GE in 1918. Three light switchers, including one armor-plated unit for the U.S. Army, powered by 200-hp V-8 engines were apparently not successful. A 1924 demonstrator, jointly produced with Ingersoll-Rand, operated on eleven eastern railroads and in two industrial plants, but was not sold.

From 1925 to 1928, GE furnished the electrical expertise in a partnership with engine builder Ingersoll-Rand and locomotive builder Alco, producing 300-hp and 600-hp box cab switchers. Alco dropped out of the consortium in 1929, when they acquired the McIntosh and Seymour engine works. A new line of its own locomotives was produced, continuing to use GE electrical components, but GE and Ingersoll-Rand marketed a separate line.

During the 1930s, GE sold a variety of small switching and industrial locomotives, using engines made by several suppliers. The earliest marketing successes were the 300-hp oil-battery and oil-electric-battery box cab switchers of 1930. The oil-battery (two-power) loco used a diesel engine and generator set, running at constant speed, to charge batteries that supplied the electricity for the traction motors. The oil-electric-battery (three-power) version

Above: Many U.S. locomotives extended their initial service lives outside the country. Ferrocarriles Nacionales de Mexico purchased large numbers of used locomotives, both steam and diesel, including General Electric U25B No. 7601. Its reprieve eventually ended, however, and No. 7601 was off the roster by 1992. Right: In 1978, when this photograph was taken, the Autotrain Corporation was still offering its rather unique services to the U.S. public. Here, two powerful General Electric U36B diesel-electrics can be seen hauling automobiles through Lorton, Virginia.

included third-rail shoes or pantographs for current pickup in electrified territory, so that more efficient outside power could be used to charge the batteries. Only five of the two-power units were produced, as the underpowered generators would barely keep the batteries charged for two hours of heavy work. These units were used by New York Central, Michigan Central, and Rock Island for light passenger switching in Chicago's La Salle Street and Central stations. The three-power units were used by Delaware, Lackawanna & Western, and the New York Central in electrified areas.

More conventional locomotives were produced during this time as well, and included units from 300 hp to 1,500 hp, in conventional rear-cab, box-cab, and center-cab designs. In 1954, an experimental 6,000-hp four-unit A-B-B-A test set was produced and numbered 750. The car-

body units operated on the Erie Railroad as a test bed until 1959, when they were sold to the Union Pacific.

In 1940, GE once again joined with Alco in actively marketing large freight locomotives, this time under the label Alco-GE. This partnership ended in 1953, and Alco assumed full responsibility for locomotive sales, with General Electric continuing as an electrical supplier. GE, however, began to develop its own line of heavy freight locomotives, incorporating significant design improvements, and introduced a 2,500-hp road switcher, designated U25B (Universal—2500 hp—B or four-wheel trucks), in 1960. Quickly dubbed "U-Boats" by rail fans, the design became the backbone of the GE fleet, slowly evolving to meet market needs; it constantly improved in reliability and fuel efficiency, and was occasionally modified for special needs, such as passenger service.

The excellence of these locomotives quickly propelled GE into the number two market position, surpassing Alco itself in just three years, and behind only General Motors' Electro-Motive Division (EMD). In 1983, General Electric's locomotive production exceeded GM's EMD, and GE became the world's sales leader. The sixteen-cylinder U series was superseded by the twelve-cylinder Dash 7 series (first unit designated B23-7) in 1984, as fuel efficiency gained in importance. The continuing horsepower race led to the Dash 8 series, with the 4,000-hp Dash 8-40C of 1987.

General Electric seemed always ready to innovate, but perhaps never as spectacularly as their experiments with turbine power. Two 2,500-hp steam-turbine cab units were built in 1939 and were tested on the Union Pacific, New York Central, and Northern Pacific before being scrapped in 1942. Westinghouse Electric was left to further steam-turbine technology, while GE moved on to gas turbines after World War II. The first unit was twin-cabbed demonstrator 101, producing 4,500 gross hp (3,900 at the rail) and operating on the Nickel Plate and the Pennsylvania before going to the Union Pacific.

Ten production turbines mechanically identical to the demonstrator, but with just one cab, were delivered to the Union

Pacific in 1952. Fifteen additional units were produced in 1954, differing only in the open "gallery" walkways along the sides. Thirty additional massive turbines of 8,500 hp were delivered between 1958 and 1961. The turbines were dependable, but could only be used on through trains since they used almost as much fuel at idle as they did at full throttle.

The development of high-horsepower diesels doomed the turbines, the final run being in December 1969. As they were retired, GE accepted them as trade-ins, and the running gear was used under the equally amazing 5,000-hp U50, basically two sixteen-cylinder U25 machinery sets mounted on a single chassis and riding on four four-wheel trucks with each pair connected by a span bolster. True to its well-earned reputation for buying anything with high horsepower, Union Pacific bought twenty-three U50s, while Southern Pacific had three. The U50C followed, still at 5,000 hp but derived from two twelve-cylinder engines riding on a pair of six-wheel trucks, and Union Pacific was again the purchaser.

Heavy electric locomotives remained a source of business for GE during this entire time. The company supplied both components and complete locomotives, and par-

ticipated in development and construction of the Pennsylvania Railroad's legendary GG1s and the Virginian's "Rectifiers" as well as other significant early developments. The growth of coal mining in the American West inspired a number of mine-to–power plant railroads that were appropriately electric powered. Seven 2,500-hp E25Bs were built for Texas Utilities, two 5,000-hp E50Cs for the Muskingum Electric, and six 6,000-hp E60s for several mining roads.

The Pennsy looked to GE for replacement of its 1930s-era electric units and bought sixty-six 5,000-hp E44s in the early 1960s, followed by Amtrak's order for twenty-six 6,000-hp E60CHs, in two variations, for their high-speed Northeast Corridor. Tracking problems limited the E60s to 90 mph (144 kph), which Amtrak found unacceptable on this 120 mph (192 kph) line, so a number were sold to New Jersey Transit and Navajo Mines. Other E60s went to the Deseret Western, another power plant line, and the National Railways of Mexico.

Locomotive production has always been based in GE's plant in Erie, Pennsylvania, with some of the smaller units having been built in the company's plant in Schenectady, New York. Over the years, the light

locomotives were powered by engines from numerous outside suppliers, including Caterpillar, Cummins, and Cooper-Bessemer. The U25B, their first heavy locomotive, used the Cooper-Bessemer FDL-16 engine, and the rights to the design were ultimately purchased by GE. The FDL design was put into production at Erie, and it has been used in all subsequent large locos, having been upgraded from 2,500 hp to 4,000 hp in twenty-eight years, often while reducing the number of cylinders and increasing fuel efficiency.

General Electric was always interested in the export market and developed small, light locomotives in a variety of gauges suited to the needs of many foreign railroads and opened foreign plants to better serve these markets. GE came to dominate the world's locomotive industry through careful marketing strategy, reliability, and the introduction of a more fuel-efficient unit at the precise time that railroads were reacting to the worldwide oil shortages of the 1980s. From those first tentative steps in 1918, through the various alliances of the 1930s and the spectacular experiments with turbines in the 1950s, to the current crop of high-tech Dash 8 locomotives, the company has dependably contributed to improved operations of the world's railroads.

Above: General Electric came to dominate locomotive sales during the 1980s, with the Dash B series of high-tech, fuel-efficient diesels, such as GE 809, seen here in Council Bluffs, Iowa.

Below: New York, Susquehanna & Western No. 4004, a 4,000-hp Dash 8 40B of 1987, and a pair of CP Rail diesels lead a mixed freight southbound at East Binghamton, New York.

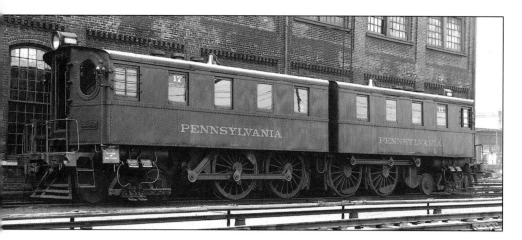

GG1 Electric Locomotive

The Pennsylvania Railroad, which had promoted itself as "the Standard Railroad of the World" and continued to pay dividends, was, nonetheless, hard hit by the economic stagnation of the 1930s. Despite the ravages of the depression, the Pennsy pressed ahead with the electrification of its eastern lines. This project, mammoth by any standard, was to encompass 2,677 miles (4,283 km) of trackage between New York's Penn Station and Washington, D.C., and represented 40 percent of the nation's electrification.

With an estimated cost of $175 million, the project encompassed far more than erecting catenary over the 224 route miles (358 km), as clearances necessary for the wire required raising tunnel roofs and bridges along the entire line. The track was upgraded with revised alignments, heavier rail, and new ballast. The right-of-way was expanded to six tracks in the Newark, New Jersey, area—the broadest spot in Pennsy's "Broad Way."

This vast construction project inspired the design of a new high-speed electric locomotive, but no new locomotive springs up

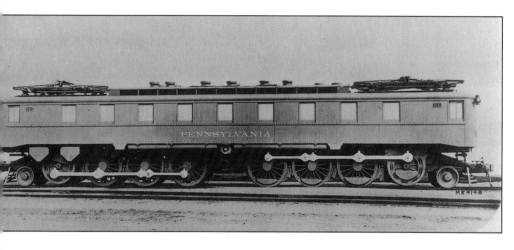

Left, top: Before the advent of axle-mounted traction motors, the designers depended on complex jack-shaft and side-rod "monkey-motion" machinery to transfer electric power to the drivers, as in the DD-1 2-B+B-2 of 1910. Built to replace steam for the trip under the Hudson River, they operated until 1933. Left, second from top: The 1-C+C-1 FF-1 of 1917 eliminated the connecting rod from the motors with direct gearing linked to a flexible spring wheel. "Big Liz" was simply too powerful and was not duplicated. Left, third from top: The L5 1-B-B-1 of 1925 continued the geared-drive- wheel design and developed 3,070 continuous hp, pulling trains at 70 mph (112 kph). The limitations of the side-rod design proved unsatisfactory. Left, bottom: By the 1930s, electric-motor designs had advanced enough to abandon the jack-shaft and side-rod drives. The L6 1-D-1, with 2,500 hp in its traction motors, proved too light, however, and a large number of partially completed units were scrapped.

magically. The steps leading to the prototype GG1 began with "Big Liz," the 1–C + C–1 design for the FF1 of 1917, a low-speed freight hauler with side rods, intended for the anticipated, but stillborn, electrification of the main line over the Alleghenies.

The next step in evolution came with the 1–B + B–1 L5, visualized in 1924 as the universal locomotive, suitable for both freight and passenger service with a simple gear change. The L5s, along with "Big Liz" and the third-rail-powered DD1 of 1910, were jack-shaft and side-rod powered, as electric motors small enough to fit on the axles, between the drivers, were not yet powerful enough for the heavy demands of mainline railroading.

In 1927, the Westinghouse Electric Company developed a suitable motor, and construction of prototypes for three locomotive classes began, all sharing the new motors and a number of interchangeable parts: the L6, a 1-D-1 2,500-hp freighter; the P5, a 3,750-hp 2-C-2 for heavy passenger service; and the O1, a 2,500-hp light passenger loco

in a 2-B-2 configuration. The most promising of these prototypes seemed to be the P5, and an order was placed for ninety production P5a's, with the box-cab body design common to all three versions. A 1934 grade-crossing accident that killed the engine crew caused the last twenty-eight P5a's to be built with a safer center-cab design that included the tapered nose and streamlining that became the hallmark of the future GG1.

Philadelphia to New York passenger service began in 1933 on the newly electrified line powered by the P5. Unfortunately, it proved to be underpowered and unstable, and had a habit of cracking driving axles.

The P5 2-C-2 began in 1931 as a box-cab design, as illustrated by this 1937 double-headed freight in Newark, New Jersey. The box cab style was abandoned after a crew was killed in a collision between a P5 and an apple truck. The design was modified to a center-mounted "steeple cab" in later construction, leading to the classic GG1.

To realize the high-speed benefits expected from the costly electrification project, the company had to continue its search.

Despite the Pennsy's tremendous research and development efforts of the previous seventeen years, it was a leased EP3a 2–C + C–2 box cab from the New Haven that pointed the way to the GG1. Brought to the new Claymont, Delaware, test track, the flexibility of the articulated 2–C + C–2 chassis, with the weight and horsepower spread over more axles, impressed the brass enough for a prototype GG1 to be ordered. At the same time, they also ordered the R1, a design that perpetuated Pennsy's undiminished faith in rigid frame locomotives, with a 2-D-2 chassis that used fewer driving wheels to carry the weight and horsepower.

When the two prototypes were delivered in August 1934, the proud PRR had assigned the class number 4800 to their own R1, while the "outsider" was assigned 4899. In a series of head-to-head trials at Claymont, the GG1 was clearly superior, so the R1 was not replicated, and the GG1,

now numbered 4800, was ultimately joined by 138 of its kind.

A $15 million order for the first fifty-seven units, financed through a Public Works Administration loan, was called "one of the largest locomotive orders in the history of American railroading" by *Railway Mechanical Engineer*. It was placed with a consortium of General Electric, Westinghouse, Baldwin Locomotive Works, and Pennsy's own Altoona Shops, all collaborators in the design. They were joined by Gibbs & Hill, engineers for the electrification project.

Serendipity entered the project when Raymond Loewy, a noted industrial designer, was added to the team. He had originally been retained by PRR management to redesign trash receptacles for New York's Penn Station; the GG1 project was his second for the railroad. Loewy's philosophy is probably best explained by the title of his autobiography, *Never Leave Well Enough Alone*, and that thinking was applied to the already satisfactorily engineered GG1.

Loewy's own words, as quoted by Karl Zimmerman, best describe the process: "They built one prototype of the GG1. It was entirely riveted, with overlapping metal sheets. So what I suggested right at the start was that they weld the entire body of the locomotive. I told them, 'Why build this when we can do it better,' so they gave me a chance." The presentation of a clay model and some renderings shocked the railroaders, since welding the entire shell was an automotive building technique, and not indigenous to the railroads. "Brute force can have a very sophisticated appearance, almost of great finesse, and at the same time be a monster of power. That's what I tried to do. The GG1 is almost an understatement." Ultimately, management was persuaded to try these new ideas and the design refinement continued.

To Loewy's advantage, he was starting with an already symmetrical center-cab design, based on the "safety cab" P5a's, that had been organically contoured in the interest of crew visibility. Those designers attempting to cope with the streamlining of steam locomotives were not so lucky! The most important of Loewy's changes

was the smoothly welded one-piece shell, unbroken by overlapping metal plates or rivets. But he also made subtle contour changes, modified the air-intake grilles and marker lights, eliminated the number board "bumps" atop the nose, and removed steps leading up the nose to the roof. In addition to the sleeker, more streamlined appearance, this smoothing of the shell resulted in better aerodynamics and reduced manufacturing and maintenance costs.

Turning to the paint, Loewy attacked the striping and lettering. The 4800, in the manner of its day, was lined along its panels, a pattern that was somewhat awkward and confused. In the interest of simplicity and smooth flow, this tangle of striping was replaced with an elegant band of five gold stripes that converged on each pilot in the now famous "cat whiskers." Loewy claimed a practical, as well as aesthetic, basis for his design: "I decided to put gold stripes in front in a noticeable pattern so people working on the tracks would see that gold on dark green, which would stand out very well in critical light situations." The lettering was stretched out so the word *Pennsylvania* ran across most of the side of the GG1, "to visually extend the length of the engine."

Except for the revolutionary welded shell, the changes were small, but in combination they were extraordinary. The streamlined Brunswick Green GG1 was ready for production, and none too soon. Its statistics were impressive: 4,620 continuous hp, with 8,000 available short term; a chassis weighing 460,000 pounds (207,000 kg); a length of 79 1/2 feet (24.2 m); articulated construction; driver diameter of 57 inches (142.5 cm); maximum starting effort of 72,800 pounds (32,760 kg); six pairs (one pair per driving axle) of twin traction motors; quill drive; 11,000-volt, 25-cycle, single-phase power; and gearing for 90 mph (144 kph).

On January 28, 1935, with the temperature hovering near zero, a Washington/New York round trip test run for government officials and dignitaries was made. The 134-mile (214 km) southbound run, including a Baltimore stop, took 110 minutes with the sprinting preproduction model, known as *Rivets*, No. 4800. The

average speed exceeded 73 mph (117 kph), but a portion of the run was timed at 102 mph (172 kph) without stretching the GG1's capabilities.

Regularly scheduled Washington to New York electrified passenger service was inaugurated on February 10, with the departure of the Congressional Limited behind GG1 4800 on the northbound run and P5a 4780 departing New York. By August 1935, all fifty-seven GG1s of the original order were in service and the P5a's were regeared for freight service. The GG1s were an unqualified success, cutting the time of the Congressional Limited from four and a quarter hours to three hours and forty-five minutes. By April 1936, it had been cut again to three hours and thirty-five minutes. These schedule reductions were possible because of the GG1's tremendous acceleration and its ability to storm up grades at no loss of speed, thanks to the short-term overload capacities of the electric motors.

The Pennsy's own pamphlet *Train Talks* described it correctly, if somewhat melodramatically: "Like flying shuttles of a giant loom, great engines harnessed to the magic force of electricity now flash between the nation's capital and its largest city over ribbons of shining steel."

The only significant failure of the GG1 happened in February 1958. Bitter-cold weather and high winds combined to create a snow so fine that it penetrated the French linen air filters, melted, and shorted out the traction motors, thereby eventually disabling almost the entire fleet. The Wilmington shops couldn't keep up with the losses and as many as seventy GG1s were out of service at once, causing the cancellation of numerous trains. This was the worst passenger service failure in the history of the PRR.

The P5s had not suffered from this freakish problem, and the railroad determined that the snow crystals formed at the same elevation as the GG1's air intakes, while the higher intakes of the P5 were immune. The problem was resolved with a modification to the ventilation that put the air intakes in a bulge on the roof, and forty units were redone. This solution worked, but was aesthetically unfortunate, and was the only major change, other than paint

Above: Old Rivets, *the original GG1, was built in a 1935 joint venture by Westinghouse and the Pennsylvania Railroad and was the model for the restyling by the noted industrial designer Raymond Loewy.*

Above: Loewy convinced the Pennsylvania Railroad management that welding the body was preferable to riveting, allowing for smoother edges and simpler construction. The GG1s survived in large numbers until environmental regulation and old age forced their retirement in 1983. A unit is preserved at the Pennsylvania Railroad Museum.

schemes, ever made to Loewy's original designs of the 1930s.

The GG1s served the Pennsylvania Railroad faithfully for many years, the first retirements not coming until March 1966; 75 percent of the roster still remained in 1976. Most outlived their master, surviving Penn Central and hauling trains for Conrail, NJDOT, and Amtrak. They appeared in many different paint schemes from black to red, white, and blue to silver over the years, some because of special occasions, sometimes in response to cost-saving measures as railroads struggled for survival, and ultimately because of changes in railroad ownership. They hauled crack passenger trains, football specials, and the funeral train of Robert Kennedy. But, like all mechanical things, their replacement eventually became necessary.

The age of the remaining GG1s began to show, particularly in fatigue and corrosion in the main frames. Amtrak ordered E60s from GE and Metroliners from Budd in the 1970s, but in a repeat of history, the E60s had tracking problems that limited speed to 85 mph (136 kph) and both succumbed to another siege of unusually cold weather in the winter of 1977,

> "Passenger service is like a male teat—neither functional nor ornamental."
> —*James J. Hill*

while the Gs rolled merrily along in their twilight years.

Suddenly no longer being taken for granted, GG1s were being preserved for historical purposes. Amtrak cooperated with a volunteer group called Friends of the GG1, with Raymond Loewy as honorary chairman, which raised funds and succeeded in restoring Loewy's original railroad triumph, Amtrak No. 4935, an unmodified GG1, back to its original Brunswick green-and-gold "cat whiskers" glory. Amtrak performed mechanical

Restored No. 4935, nicknamed Blackjack, *slips past Hunter Tower, New Jersey, looking as it did fresh out of the Altoona shops almost fifty years earlier.*

and electrical work, the sheet metal was repaired and painted, and the 4935 reappeared in its original form.

On May 15, 1977, with the designer on the rostrum at Washington Union Station, the GG1 was rededicated with a bottle of Pennsylvania champagne and the words: "To the Pennsylvania Railroad, 'The Standard Railroad of the World,' in honor of the men and women who worked for her and their service to the nation, I christen thee 'Pennsylvania 4935.'"

Shortly afterward, 4935 highballed north with the Murray Hill, looking and running every bit as superbly as it had on its inaugural run forty-two years before. The GG1 has been an exemplary locomotive and holds a very special place in railroad history. Its superb safety record is probably due to superior tracking characteristics. Fast, powerful, and rarely suffering breakdown, it was the first streamlined electric locomotive and ranks as one of the most handsome of any type. Loewy was to have this to say about his contribution to the GG1: "If we had to redesign it today, after forty years, I don't know what I would change. I probably wouldn't change anything."

Although it was his first major assignment, the GG1 outlasted everything else that Loewy designed for the railroads, but the last run was finally made when another restored GG1, New Jersey Transit Pennsylvania 4876, along with freshly repainted black 4882, and freshly retouched black 4879, hauled farewell specials on NJ Transit's Matawan-Newark line on October 29, 1983. Although several were saved in museums, the GG1 was gone from the main line after almost fifty years, and with it, the last of the Loewy designs for American railroads.

GG1

January 15, 1953, was not a good day in the history of the Pennsylvania Railroad's magnificent GG1 electric locomotives. The overnight Federal from Boston, hauled by 4876, was southbound and approaching Washington Union Station when its brakes failed. Running out of control, the GG1 punched through the station bumping post, rumbled through a newsstand and the stationmaster's office, and surprised travelers when it burst into the elegantly arched concourse and sank through the floor. There were no fatalities and the 4876 was cut into sections, hauled out of the basement, and sent to Altoona for rebuilding. The rebuilt unit served the PRR faithfully, finishing out its days hauling commuters for the New Jersey Department of Transportation.

The Strasburg Railroad, an eastern Pennsylvania short line known primarily for steam excursions, had a surprise visitor on December 14, 1976. Conrail's GG1 No. 4855 had burned an axle bearing on the main line at Parkersburg and was towed by the Strasburg's steamer, 2-6-0 No. 89, to their shop's drop table for repair.

Gooch, Daniel (1816–1889)

Born into a large Northumberland engineering family, Daniel Gooch was placed in charge of the locomotive department of the Great Western Railway (GWR) at a very young age. Taking advantage of the GWR's 7-foot broad gauge, he designed bold and simple yet much larger locomotives than his contemporaries.

Gooch's basic design was that of Stephenson's Patentees, with the Gothic Firebox of the early Stephenson Long-Boilers, but much enlarged. The large boilers, which provided a higher capacity for steam relative to the cylinders, the higher steam pressure, and Gooch link motion (for variable cutoffs), all combined to allow for more efficient use of steam—and, therefore, more power.

The Firefly class—sixty-two express locomotives with 7-foot (2.1 m) driving wheels, built between 1840 and 1842—featured an outside "sandwich" frame, a single pair of drivers, an open cab, and a pair of smaller wheels front and rear. One of these, *Actaeon*, ran for twenty-six years and even survived an 1856 boiler explosion.

From 1846 on, eight-wheeled express engines with 8-foot (2.4 m) driving wheels were the standard Gooch design, an example being *Lord of the Isles* of 1851. The design was so successful that similar, but slightly larger, engines were built to replace those that had worn out.

When the London Underground was opened, the fireless locomotive, *Ghost*,

Above: Sir Daniel Gooch, at the age of twenty-nine, poses with a model of his famed Firefly-class locomotive. Below: The broad gauge of the Great Western allowed Daniel Gooch to build larger, more powerful locomotives than his contemporaries could. The eight-wheeled Iron Duke, *with a single pair of 8-foot (2.4 m) drivers, typified the Gooch design after 1848; these fast locomotives lasted until the end of broad gauge in 1892.*

worth was hired as a foreman at the
Walbottle Colliery, but he was away from
locomotives for eight years. The development of the Hedley locomotive ceased with
Hackworth's departure from Wylam, and
further advancements were left to the hands
of George Stephenson at Killingworth
Collieries.

When Stephenson was awarded the
position of engineer for the Liverpool &
Manchester Railway, he was still involved
with construction of the Stockton &
Darlington and operating the Robert
Stephenson Locomotive Works at
Newcastle-upon-Tyne. Needing help
with locomotive construction, Stephenson
remembered the young enginewright from
Wylam, and appointed Hackworth as locomotive superintendent in May 1825.

Hackworth was involved with the
Stephensons in the construction of *Locomotion*, the world's first locomotive to operate
on a public railway. Quickly following
were *Hope*, *Black Diamond*, and *Diligence*,
all of the same basic design. The rigors of
regular service caused numerous difficulties, and Hackworth was kept busy with
maintenance and modifications. The use
of connecting rods between drivers is cred-

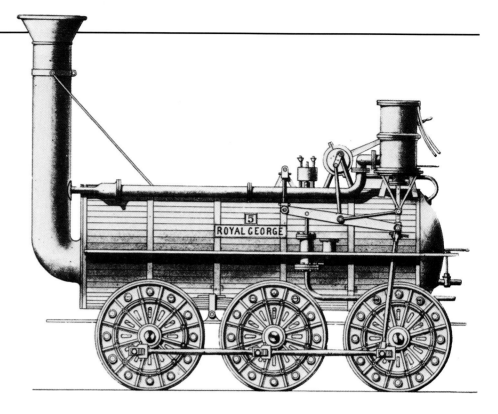

*Above: The 0-6-0 Royal George of the
Stockton & Darlington was the first six-
coupled locomotive. Timothy Hackworth's
successful design increased the boiler heating surfaces, eliminating the need to stop
along the line to build up steam pressure.
Below: The 0-4-0 Locomotion of the
Stockton & Darlington was the first locomotive built by the Stephenson Works. As
works superintendent, Hackworth devised
the "connecting rod" method of driving the
wheels, which eliminated the cumbersome
and undependable chain drives then in
common use.*

ited to him, as is the use of spherical coupling rod pins to allow lateral movement.

A major drawback to these locomotives
was their poor steaming characteristics,
and they had to stop frequently along the
line to build up adequate steam pressure.
To counteract this fault, Hackworth built
the first six-coupled locomotive, the *Royal
George*, for the Stockton & Darlington.
The longer wheel base could support a
larger boiler that had a U-shaped flue. The
firebox was at the front, with the fireman
and fuel tender, and the flue ran the length
of the boiler before bending around and
returning to a connection with the chimney, thus doubling the heating surface.
The driver remained at the rear, with a
water tender. Despite its unorthodox
appearance, *Royal George* was instru-
mental to the success of the Stockton &
Darlington.

At the 1829 Rainhill Trials, held to select
a locomotive design for the new Liverpool
& Manchester Railway, Hackworth
entered his own *Sans Pareil* and appeared
to be the chief competition to Stephenson's *Rocket*. Unfortunately, *Sans Pareil* was
much heavier than *Rocket*—too heavy for
the specified loading conditions. During
the trials, it also proved to be too slow; it
ran out of water and finally broke down.
Rocket won the competition, and the
Stephensons went on to fame and fortune.
Hackworth, although having responsibility

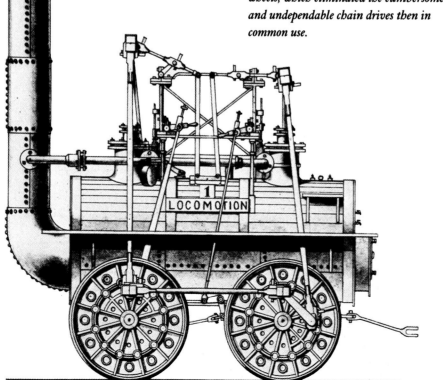

for many of the major advancements, never had the same success. A lay preacher when not locomotive building, he seemed to avoid the stresses that doomed other engineers and lived to the age of sixty-four.

Heavy Harry

Victorian Railways H220, a three-cylindered, 100-mph (160 kph) 4-8-4 emerged from the Newport Workshops in 1941. Two other 4-8-4s-in-progress were stillborn because of wartime shortages. This immense locomotive earned the nickname *Heavy Harry*, with a length of 90 feet (28 m), a height of 13 feet (4 m), and a weight of more than 260 tons (234 t). His tender carried 16,640 gallons (63,000 l) of water. Harry was the largest and heaviest steam locomotive in Australia.

Originally intended for heavy overnight trains between Adelaide and Melbourne, *Heavy Harry* was shifted to the north-eastern line to Albury when bridge-strengthening projects were delayed by the war. There he hauled fast goods, heavy troop trains, and occasionally even the crack *Spirit of Progress*.

After the war, bridge work was again deferred, and Harry rolled along the north-eastern line for seventeen more years, running more than 620,000 miles (1 million km). Dieselization began on the Adelaide line in 1952, and the need for big steam faded. In 1958, *Heavy Harry* was retired with honors to the Australian Historical Society Museum in Melbourne.

Hiawatha

In answer to the challenge of rival Burlington's stainless steel Zephyrs and Chicago & Northwestern's 400s, the Chicago, Milwaukee, St. Paul & Pacific—the Milwaukee Road—placed their new Hiawatha streamliners into Chicago to Minneapolis service in May 1935. Alco-built 4-4-2s, the first made in America since 1914, and the first streamlined steam locos manufactured new, were assigned Class A and numbered 1 through 4. They were truly a glorious sight, with their Otto Kuhler–designed "bathtub" shrouds resplendent in glossy maroon, orange, and gray, with a black roof and stainless steel winged symbol on the nose.

Patronage quickly outgrew the capacity of the original seven-car consists, so new trains of nine ribbed-side cars were placed behind the 4-4-2s after only sixteen months. In 1938, a second reequipping with class F7 4-6-4s 100–105, styled by the renowned Otto Kuhler, and with all-new consists, freed the original equipment for use on second sections, including the Midwest Hiawatha to Omaha, and runs to Mil-waukee and Madison. Both the As and the new F7s regularly exceeded 100 mph (160 kph) on the Minneapolis run, and Hiawatha was promoted as the "World's Most Popular Train."

The success of the Hiawathas inspired the Milwaukee Road to similarly convert two vintage 1900 ten-wheelers, in 1936, for a Hiawatha section to the northern Wisconsin resort areas. In 1941, elderly Pacifics 151 and 152 were streamlined in the Kuhler manner for the Chippewa, as were Pacifics 801 and 812 for service on the Sioux Falls section of the Midwest Hiawatha. No. 152 survived the earlier scrappings of Milwaukee Road steam, but went to the torch in 1954.

See also: *Hudson-type Locomotive; Kubler, Otto; Loewy, Raymond; Pacific-type Locomotive; Streamlined Steam Locomotives; Whyte System.*

The Milwaukee Road's streamlined 4-6-4 F7 class Hudsons, which were styled by Otto Kubler, were built to replace the line's overloaded Atlantics. The striking maroon, orange, and gray paint matched the new Hiawatha consist these locomotives regularly bauled at the "century mark" (104 mpb [167 kpb]) between Milwaukee and Minneapolis–St. Paul.

High-speed Rail Travel

Travel patterns began to change rapidly after World War II. The growth of the personal automobile and superhighway systems allowed travelers to set their own schedules and routes. The increased public perception of safety enhanced the flexibility and speed of air travel, which was not confined to a network of steel rails, and many people began to travel by airplane. Rail passenger service began a rapid decline, particularly in the United States, and even new streamlined equipment could not change the pattern. In Europe, where the population centers are relatively close together, the railroads turned to increased speed to retain patronage.

The French were the first to act when they made the decision to rebuild their war-damaged rail systems by conversion to electrical power. Revised right-of-way alignments, better signaling, and powerful electric locomotives all contributed to this new high-speed service. The best known of these postwar trains was the Paris-Lyons-Marseilles-Nice Mistral, which covered the 195-mile (312 km) route at an average speed of more than 80 mph (128 kph) but today regularly runs at up to 125 mph (200 kph). In 1955, a test was run on a special stretch of track near Bordeaux. A new 4,000-hp train, BB9004, shattered records with a top speed of 205.6 mph (329 kph).

Breaking the 200 mph (320 kph) barrier was a remarkable engineering feat, but it was accomplished under ideal conditions—it is still too fast for practical ground transportation. Yet it did encourage continued research on a system of scheduled trains that could exceed the century mark. It was the Japanese who first succeeded in this endeavor. In October 1964, the Japanese government opened the first of the Shinkansen (New Railways), the New Tokaido Line, running on a brand-new dedicated right-of-way between Tokyo and Osaka. Known worldwide as the Bullet Trains, these sleek electrically powered trains were carrying half a million passengers on eight round trips per day by 1969. The average speed was 101 mph (162 kph) and the top speed was 130 mph (208 kph). Although it was originally intended that freight trains would use the line at night, that plan was dropped when it became apparent that the line needed to be shut down each night for maintenance of track and catenary.

The Japanese success inspired President Lyndon Johnson to support the High Speed Ground Transportation Act, which provided funding for the development of high-speed passenger service between Washington, New York, and Boston. The

The first of the modern high-speed passenger trains were those of the Shinkansen of Japan. Known popularly as "Bullet Trains," they race along on a private right-of-way at speeds above 100 mph (160 kph) between Tokyo and Osaka.

high-density corridor, strung out along the East Coast, contains a major portion of the country's population, and presents transportation problems similar to those of Europe. Out of this came the Metroliners, self-propelled electrically powered passenger cars that could be coupled together into a train under the control of a single motorman. They were intended to operate at 160 mph (256 kph), but track conditions would not allow speeds that high. In fact, during a test run, the windows in a train of conventional multiple-unit equipment were shattered by the air blast of the passing Metroliner. Amtrak took over the start-up of this untested technology, and service began in 1971. Despite early problems, speeds of 90 mph (144 kph) were consistently achieved, and hopes for higher speeds were encouraged when Amtrak took over the entire right-of-way and began a complete rebuilding of track, signaling, and control in anticipation of future speed increases.

The French originated the high-speed research, and they responded with the TGV speedsters on the Paris to Lyons route. These trains operate efficiently at 125 mph (200 kph), but can exceed 160 mph (256 kph) and are among the world's most reliable high-speed trains.

Research on magnetic levitation (maglev), which eliminates wheel contact at speed using powerful magnetic forces to float the train a few inches above its guideway and propel it at speeds projected to be in the 300 mph (480 kph) range, is under way. Only time will tell if the planners and governments involved will be willing to spend the money and time necessary to develop this technology, but we can hope.

Right, top: Amtrak entered the high-speed passenger business in the northeast corridor (between Boston and Washington) with the multiple-unit Metroliners, but also used conventional trainsets. A General Electric E60 zips a string of Amfleet equipment across the Susquehanna River at Perryville, Maryland. Right: The French TGV trains (très grandes vitesse, or "very high speed") regularly operate above 125 mph (200 kph) on a private right-of-way between Paris and Lyons.

The handsome 4-6-4s of the New York Central were highly regarded among the classic steam locomotives. No. 5360, a class J3 Hudson, is taking on coal at the massive wharf at Harmon, New York.

Once the bathtub phase of streamlining ended, a number of quite handsome locomotives appeared on the U.S. railroads. The Henry Dreyfuss–styled 4-6-4 Hudsons of the New York Central were among the best and were assigned to the road's Twentieth Century Limited.

Hudson-type Locomotive

The 4-6-4 wheel arrangement was acclaimed by many as the epitome of passenger power. Developed for the New York Central at the American Locomotive Works in Schenectady, New York, it was named for the mighty river that made the New York Central's "Water Level Route" possible. The four-wheel trailing truck supported a large firebox, which made adequate steam to power large drivers at high speed. Frequently picking up water on the fly from water pans located between the tracks, the handsome Hudsons of Vanderbilt's railroad could power the Twentieth Century Limited at speeds of 85 mph (136 kph) and made the 960-mile (1,540 km) trip from New York to Chicago in sixteen hours. Henry Dreyfuss designed a handsome streamlined shroud for the NYC Hudsons that was applied to ten locomotives classed J3a. Other railroads adopted the design for their own high-speed limiteds, including the Milwaukee Road and Chesapeake & Ohio. The Hudson was built continuously between 1927 and 1948.

See also: *Atlantic-type Locomotive; Hiawatha; Loewy, Raymond; Pacific-type Locomotive; Streamlined Steam Locomotives; Whyte System.*

I

Ingalls Shipbuilding Company

Now a sophisticated builder of submarines for the U.S. Navy, Ingalls Shipbuilding of Pascagoula, Mississippi, entered the diesel locomotive market in 1945. It offered a substantial number of designs, ranging from a 660-hp switcher to a 2,000-hp A1A–A1A passenger unit. Ingalls built only one locomotive, model 4S, an intermediate unit of 1,500 hp riding on type-B trucks and powered by a Superior Diesel engine. Gulf, Mobile & Ohio purchased the turret-cabbed unit and numbered it 1900. It was traded in to the Electro-

Motive Division of General Motors in 1965 and scrapped.

The experience of Ingalls was typical of many companies that tried to enter the diesel locomotive market after World War II. Despite previous success with diesel engines, the major steam locomotive builders as well as the fledgling interlopers were forced out by the giant General Motors.

Irish Railways

The first railway in the Emerald Isle was opened on December 17, 1834, and ran between Dublin and Kingstown (now Dun Laoghaire). Further development continued in a piecemeal fashion, for with such a low population density there was little urgency. Gauges were selected at random until a royal commission chose a standard —by averaging the gauges then in use. Thus Irish standard gauge became 5 feet 3 inches, which Irish engineers proudly exported to other countries, especially Australia and New Zealand.

At the time of independence from Britain (1921), four major companies existed. The Midland & Great Western centered on Dublin and radiated to Sligo and Galway; the Dublin & South Eastern served Rosslare, Waterford, and Wexford; the Great Southern & Western ran to Cork and Killarney; and the Great Northern crossed the new border to serve Londonderry and Belfast.

Following the civil war (the Troubles) of 1923 to 1924, the government formed a new 2,200-mile (3,520 km) company, named the Great Southern Railways, from all the lines within its border including several smaller lines, some at 3-foot gauge.

The Irish railways retained a fascinating display of individuality until true nationalization in 1950. There were 143 locomotive types out of a fleet of 700, including modern Irish Queen 4-6-0s named *Maedh, Macha,* and *Tailte,* and ancient steam pots like the 2-2-2 single-drivers on the Waterford & Tramore line. The Londonderry & Loch Swilly rostered the only 4-8-4s in the British Isles—and they were 3-foot gauge! The GN's Fintona branch used horses to pull cars until the 1950s. The delightful Limerick Junction, where all trains had to reverse in order to pass through, was nowhere near Limerick, and the schedule of the narrow-gauge Tralee & Dingle was set at one train per month, coinciding with the cattle fairs.

Dieselization came to Ireland when lightweight railcars were put into service on the Great Northern's Donegal narrow-gauge lines in 1931. The London, Midland

A left-hand running Great Southern 0-6-2 tank engine passes under a warning sign written in both English and Gaelic at Killiney station in 1957. No. 673 was built in Inchicore in 1934 and retired in 1962.

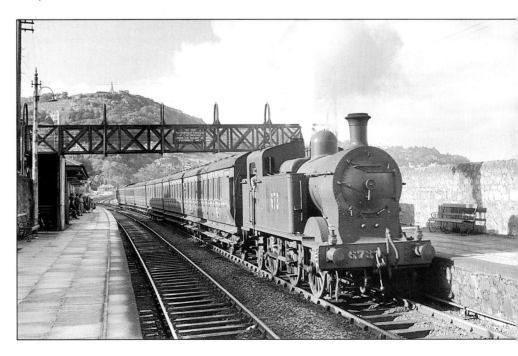

The Irish Mail, the first named train, began the run between London and Bangor on July 31, 1848. Since completion of the Brittania Tubular Bridge in 1850, the run ends in Holyhead in Anglesey, North Wales. A boat connection for Dun Laoghaire completes the crossing to Ireland.

& Scottish was half owner of the GN, and this cost-cutting move made the line, the other half owner of which was, ironically, the British government, as successors to the LM&S, the only profit-making railroad in Ireland.

Another uniquely Irish operation is the rail system of the Irish Peat Board. Truck operation is not satisfactory in the massive spongy peat bogs, so the peat that is dug for electric power plant fuel is handled on a 600-mile (920 km) system of 3-foot gauge

railway. The fleet of 250 diesel locomotives is larger than that of the national system, and the mileage exceeds the amount of public narrow gauge that ever existed in Ireland. While peat has been tried a number of times as fuel for locomotives, the results were never consistent enough for widespread use, except during the fuel shortages of World War II.

With the nationalization came integration with road and water transport and line closures—a 35-percent reduction in mileage —including all the narrow gauge. Modernization followed with replacement of steam (and horse) power with diesels. The Great Southern name changed in 1944, to the Coras Iompair Eireann (CIE), which now operates 221 diesel locomotives, 39 railcars, 528 passenger cars, 8,599 freight cars, and 3,500 highway vehicles. In 1974, it carried 190 million passengers and 5.4 million tons (4.8 million t) of goods.

J

Japanese Railways

The first railway in Japan connected the capital of the country with a port. The first train from Tokyo covered the 18 miles (29 km) to Yokohama on October 14, 1872, on a railroad built by an English engineer named H.N. Lay. He insisted that his Japanese assistants learn everything possible about the planning and building process so they would not be dependent on foreigners in the future.

The first trunk line ran through Tokyo, Osaka, and Kobe—the original Tokaido line. Completed in 1889, it established 3 feet 6 inches as the Japanese standard gauge. In 1906 the burgeoning system had spread to seventeen companies operating 2,800 miles (4,480 km) of track. These railways were then nationalized, adding to the 1,200 miles (1,920 km) that were already government-owned. Subsequent construction has raised the total to 12,500 miles (20,000 km) plus the Shinkansen high-speed line. Almost 4,000 miles (6,400 km) of private line still remain.

The Shinkansen (New Railways), featuring the "Bullet Train," have revolutionized rail travel forever. The first line opened in 1964, along the original Tokaido line to Osaka. High-speed electric trains operating on standard-gauge track run at start-to-stop average speeds of 100 mph (160 kph) several times per hour. The line has been extended to the western tip of Honshu (Japan's main island) and, via an undersea tunnel of 11.8 miles (18.8 km), to Fukuoka, on the island of Kyushu, 735 miles (1,200 km) from Tokyo.

The maximum speed of 120 mph (192 kph) was made possible only by engineering curves with a minimum radius of 2 1/2 miles (4 km). The 1975 extension has 139 route miles (222 km) in tunnels and 73 miles (117 km) on bridges. Only 35 miles (56 km) were built on grade. The 31-mile (50 km)-long Seikan Tunnel, the world's longest when built, bores under the sea to connect the northern island of Hokkaido and will accommodate 3-foot 6-inch-gauge trains as well.

The steam fleet once included 1,200 2-8-2s out of 4,800 total locomotives. The first of this wheel arrangement, they were named "Mikados" and the name was used around the world. Inevitably, the steam era ended—on December 14, 1975, with 400 steamers set aside for preservation. Steam

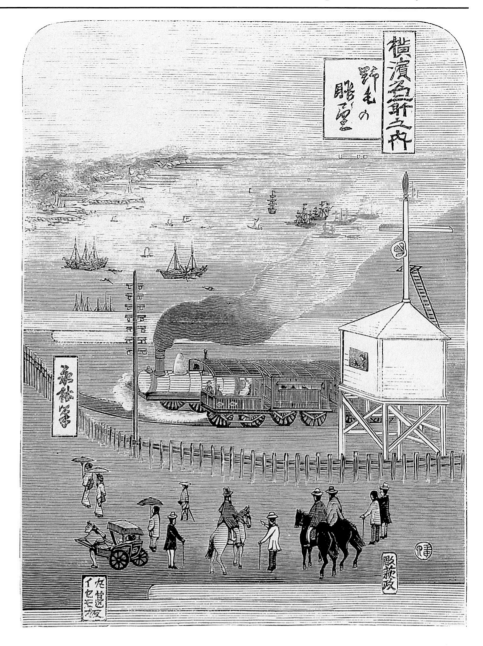

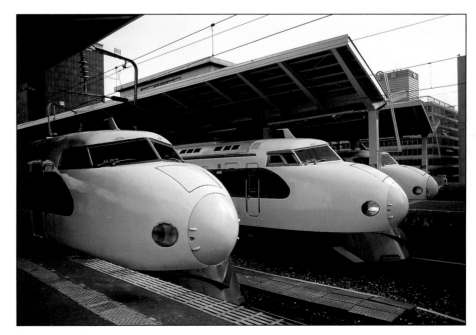

Above, right: Japan's first railway connected the port of Yokohama with Tokyo in 1872. It was built by local crews under the direction of a British engineer and adopted a gauge of 3 feet 6 inches. Right: In less than one hundred years, Japanese railroading has produced the Shinkansen and the "Bullet Train," which operates in service at average speeds of 100 mph (160 kph) on a line stretching 735 miles (1,176 km) from Tokyo.

Japanese National Railways built a new railroad from Tokyo to Osaka expressly for the high-speed electrically powered Shinkansen, allowing them the freedom to run above 100 mph (160 kph).

> "He was going down
> the hill at ninety
> miles an hour
> When the whistle
> broke into a scream—
> He was found in the
> wreck with his hand
> on the throttle
> And scalded to death
> by the steam."
> —*"Wreck of the Old 97"*

was always kept simple: articulateds, compounds, and multiple cylinders were rare on the coal-fired system, but there were Shays and other geared locomotives in the mountains. The most exotic rod-driven steamers were the C62 4-6-4s used on fast express trains, which were very straightforward locomotives just the same.

Conversion to electrical power began in 1925 using American equipment and now extends over 4,600 miles (7,400 km) and carries 75 percent of Japan's rail traffic. Newer electrification has been built at 25,000 volts AC instead of the original 1,500 volts DC.

Currently, the Japanese National Railways (JNR) rosters 2,050 electric locomotives and 2,134 diesels, including power for narrow-gauge expresses that operate at 75 mph (120 kph) on 3-foot 6-inch track. This fleet includes 29,000 coaches—12,000 of them are diesel or electric power cars— on the self-propelled system. A notable accomplishment was the conversion of all freight rolling stock (55,000 cars) from manual to automatic couplers on July 25, 1925, a feat that has never been matched.

See also: *Couplers; Electrification; High-speed Rail Travel.*

Jones, Casey (1864–1900)

John Luther "Casey" Jones began his railroad career in 1879, at the age of fifteen, when he was hired on the Mobile & Ohio as an apprentice telegrapher. Engine service was what he wanted, and he became a fireman three years later. In 1890, still firing, but now on the Illinois Central (IC), Casey passed his exam and realized his boyhood dream of being an engineer.

Illinois Central 2-8-0 No. 638, which had been exhibited at the Columbian Exposition, was assigned to Casey in the fall of 1893, becoming the most important thing in his life, next to his wife. While pulling freights with this loco, Casey fashioned the famous six-chime whistle, and his whippoorwill call readily identified the 638 and its engineer from Jackson, Tennessee, to Water Valley, Mississippi.

Casey gave up his beloved loco in 1899, when he was offered a regular passenger run—IC's flagship, the Chicago to New Orleans Cannonball, from Memphis to Canton, Mississippi. Within a few weeks, having memorized the route and the time card, Casey and his new fireman, Simm Webb, began the regular shuttle of the Cannonball from one end of the 190-mile (304 km) division to the other.

It was a matter of extreme pride to a good engineer that his train always arrive on time, and that's the way it was with Casey and the northbound Cannonball on April 29, 1900. Having arrived at the Poplar Street depot in Memphis, he was informed that the southbound Cannonball

had been delayed north of town, and the scheduled engineer had called in sick. Casey agreed to fill in, and whistled off at 12:50 A.M., an hour and thirty-five minutes late on a dark and foggy night. Casey called across the cab to Simm, "We're going to have a tough time going into Canton on time, but I think we can do it—barring accidents."

Memphis to Grenada was 100 miles (160 km) of straight and level track, and the scheduled running time was two hours and forty-five minutes, but Casey and the 382, whistle singing into the night, pulled out of Grenada having picked up a full hour. They were almost on time when they stopped at Durant, 55 miles (88 km) farther down the track, and picked up orders to meet the northbound Cannonball at Goodman. They "saw by" two freights sidetracked at Vaughan, 22 miles (35 km) south of Durant. Casey sped south at 70 mph (112 kph), intent on a timely arrival at Canton.

Murphy's Law was in effect that night, and the freights at Vaughan were already in trouble. A "saw by" was a common, if complicated, event on single-track railroads. The two freights had pulled into the long passing siding at Vaughan, but the combined length was too long to fit, leaving one end on the main line. This is normally not a problem, as the extra cars remain on the main line at the (south) end away from the approaching train, and once this train passes the clear (north) switch, the trains on the siding move to clear the south switch by allowing the north-end cars to occupy the main. The "sawing" motion of the train(s) on the siding provides the name for the maneuver.

This worked fine for the northbound Cannonball, which passed Casey at Goodman, but then another northbound passenger train, No. 26, arrived to take the other, shorter siding at Vaughan. While sawing north to allow No. 26 to reach the short siding, an air hose burst, leaving the caboose and three cars of the southbound freight fouling the main line, with Casey's Cannonball roaring toward it. Newberry, the flagman, raced up the track, clamped a torpedo on the rail, and had gone a half-mile (0.8 km) when he saw the headlight in the fog.

Casey passed the waving lantern at an unknown speed, but he was probably exceeding 70 mph (112 kph). The torpedo exploded as 382 rolled over it, and Simm watched Casey dump the air and then saw the glowing markers of the caboose just ahead. Shouting, "Look out! We're going to hit something!" he swung down the gangway and jumped, but Casey rode the engine into the caboose and two cars of the standing freight—and to his death.

No one knows what Casey Jones was thinking that night. He knew he

Casey Jones and fireman J.W. McKinnie pose with Casey's beloved 2-8-0 No. 638 in 1898, fresh out of the shops in Water Valley, Mississippi. The following year, Casey, while pulling the Cannonball with another Illinois Central locomotive, rode to his legendary doom.

had to make the "saw by" move, yet he approached Vaughan at high speed and ignored Newberry's frantically waving lantern. He did manage to substantially reduce speed before the collision, but Casey was the wreck's sole fatality. Simm Webb recovered from his injuries and was back to firing the same run in a few months, for Harry Norton, Casey's replacement.

Wallace Saunders, an engine wiper in the Canton shops, was responsible for the engineer's lasting legend when, upon hearing of his friend's death, he began to chant "Casey Jones—Casey Jones." It was picked up by others, and then heard by a professional songwriter who polished it, put it to music, and gave us perhaps the most famous railroad ballad in American folklore.

K

Kenya Railways

The future of the Uganda Railway was committed when George Whitehouse disembarked in Mombasa with an edict to build the 580-mile (928 km) British Government line, despite considerable opposition at home. Designed to help put an end to Arab slave trading and to stabilize the country by providing access to the interior, it succeeded on both counts.

Nairobi, the future capital, was then just a survey point when the railroad arrived in 1899, and the terminus, a landing on Lake Victoria called Port Florence, was attained in 1901. Entebbe could be reached via a 150-mile (240 km) steamer trip across the great lake, a source of the River Nile. In 1931, an extension across the Nile reached Kampala, leaving Port Florence, now called Kisumu, at the end of a 130-mile (208 km) branch line. A further extension

that took the railhead to Kasese, near the Zaire border and 1,080 miles (1,728 km) from Mombasa, was completed in 1956. Another branch of the railway stretches 315 miles (504 km) to within 100 miles (160 km) of the Sudanese border.

In 1926, the name was changed to the Kenya-Uganda Railway and then, when the Tanzanian lines were included in the system in 1948, changed once again to the East African Railways & Harbours Administration.

Construction problems were many, including not only the normal disease, terrain alternating between arid desert and thorny bush, and supply difficulties, but also marauding lions and hostile natives. At the beginning, several inclined planes were used to carry equipment up such obstacles as the Mau Escarpment. The critical choice of gauge was influenced by the availability of Indian meter-gauge locomotives and rolling stock from "across the bay." Its difference from British Africa standard of 3 feet 6 inches would be regretted much later. A force of 32,000 Indians was imported for the difficult construction, but unfortunately 2,500 of them did not survive.

Until the coming of the articulated Beyer-Garratt locomotives in 1926, operations were difficult, despite the easing of four grades with spirals, as the rails climbed to more than 9,000 feet (2,736 m) in eleva-

tion. By 1957, there were 129 Garratts in a total fleet of 450 locomotives. The first Garratts were basically two of the road's standard 4-8-0s joined together as 4-8-2 + 2-8-4s. Sharing the 10-ton (9 t) axle loadings of their predecessors, they could operate on the light 50-pound-per-yard (24 kg/m) rail. With the Garratts, coal superseded eucalyptus wood as a fuel (except in remote areas) until the switch to fuel oil after World War II. The last Garratts delivered were the magnificent "59" class of 1954: 4-8-2 + 2-8-4; 104 feet (31 m) long; and having an axle loading (on new 75-pound [34 kg] rail) of 21 tons (19 t)—and once the most powerful steam locomotives still operating in the world. Their ability to handle 1,200-ton (1,080 t) trains with ease, between Mombasa and Nairobi, helped to fend off the diesels until the 1970s. New "61" class Garratts, the largest ever designed, were proposed as successors, with a length of 125 feet (38 m) and a 25-ton (22.5 t) axle load. But these plans were dropped in favor of dieselization, which was virtually complete by 1980.

In 1977, the East African administration was dissolved and operations were turned back to the three countries: Kenya, Uganda, and Tanzania. In 1978, Kenya Railways operated 130 diesel locomotives, 513 passenger cars, and 6,637 freight cars, still on meter gauge and still an important barrier to a Cape to Cairo railroad.

CONSTRUCTION ON THE CAPE TO CAIRO

Kenya Railways requires that all trains stop for several minutes before crossing a dam in the southern part of this African country. The practice was adopted on the advice of local residents after several mysterious derailments on the Mwatate Dam were blamed on the evil spirits that inhabit the reservoir. Townsfolk claimed that the spirits were angered when the trains moved across the dam without first appeasing them by stopping in tribute.

Among the difficulties encountered in the building of the Uganda Railway (later Kenya Railway) were the dangerous marauding lions of the Athi Plains. One report from the construction site stated: "Progress has been seriously impeded by man-eating lions. Twenty-eight men have been killed by the lions."

The image of railroading in the former British colonies of Africa is forever linked with the legendary Beyer-Garratt articulated locomotives. The light rail and steep grades caused serious operational difficulties until the arrival of the powerful but lightly treading locomotives that were used in both passenger and freight service. Nos. 5916 (opposite page) and 5509 (above) are shown in their daily work, while No. 5709 (above, top) rests at the Nairobi engine shed.

Key West Railroad

One of the more amazing railroad endeavors in the United States was "the railroad that went to sea"—the Key West Extension of the Florida East Coast Railway. Conceived by the flamboyant magnate Henry M. Flagler, this glorious folly crossed the sea for 114 miles (180 km). Completed in 1912, the line was not built to reach a destination, but to shorten the sea passage for the heavy rail traffic between Florida and Cuba.

The Florida Keys are a series of exposed coral reefs, some inhabited, that trail off the southern tip of Florida into the Caribbean. Flagler strung these low-lying islands together with 20 miles (32 km) of embankment in the shallow water, 17 miles (27 km) of bridging, much of it trestles, and several movable spans to clear navigation. Riding on this line was like skimming over the waves, and the land was often out of sight.

In 1936, a hurricane knocked out much of the line, trapping trains and severing the railway forever. Financially unable to rebuild, the Florida East Coast abandoned the Key West extension, but the bridges and fills were ultimately repaired and the right-of-way was converted into a highway.

Krauss-Maffei Diesel Hydraulics

Between 1961 and 1963, Krauss-Maffei, the noted builder from Munich, Germany, exported twenty-one diesel-hydraulic locomotives to the United States. They were operated on a number of American railroads to test the hydraulic transmission under mainline conditions. The 1961 units had a turret cab, and the 1963 units were of a road-switcher design, but all had (2) Maybach engines, C-C trucks, and Voith transmissions. Breathing difficulties in tunnels caused modifications consisting of adding large ducts to draw air from near the tracks. All were retired.

Kuhler, Otto (1894–1976)

Born in Remscheid, Germany, in the heart of the industrialized Ruhr Valley, Kuhler moved to the United States in 1923 and settled in Pittsburgh. He earned a reputation as a watercolorist, using the heavy

industry similar to Remscheid's as his subject matter. He later turned to etchings and resettled in New York.

Kuhler's industrial art brought him to the attention of the railroad managements, and his work—which had a rather "Buck Rogers rocket ship"–like quality, with sharp-edged fins and chrome strips—contributed to the 1930s mania for streamlining steam locomotives. The Lehigh Valley applied Kuhler designs to a number of Pacifics used on such passenger trains as resplendent Cornell red-and-black John Wilkes. The Baltimore & Ohio had Kuhler shroud the *President Monroe* for the brand-new blue-and-gold Royal Blue in 1935, and the Southern hired him to streamline their Tennessean. The classic orange, gray, maroon, and black bathtub shroud on the Milwaukee Road's Hiawathas ranks among the classic streamlined steam designs.

There is great controversy among American purists regarding the appropriateness of streamlining a machine as straightforward as a steam locomotive, although in Europe, elegant paint over pure, simple lines hiding plumbing and appliances was the norm. Many would agree, though, that Kuhler's restrained design for the Mountaineer of the New York, Ontario & Western was perhaps his best. The NYO&W was in dire financial straits in 1936 and the limited $10,000 budget he had to work with produced a completely renovated train in maroon enamel with thin multiple striping in orange. The Mountain-type (4-8-2) locomotive was austere, with a smooth "bib" above the pilot and a smooth skirt along the running-board edges.

In the 1930s Otto Kuhler became a consultant to the American Locomotive Works, where he contributed to its styling department and was responsible for the appearance of the DL-109 diesel locomotive of 1940, his final assignment.

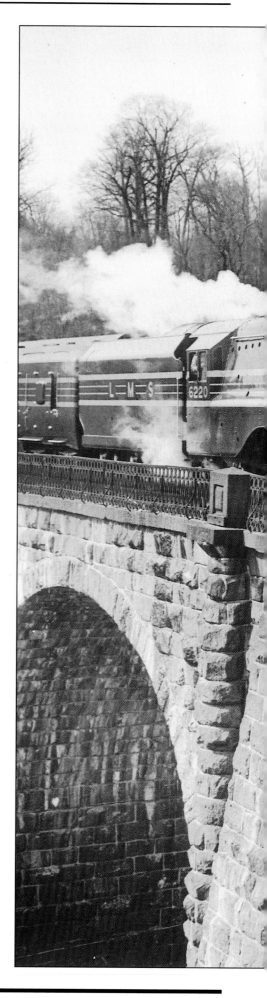

The touring British train Coronation Scot (on the left) poses alongside the Baltimore & Ohio's Royal Blue, similar in streamlining and paint, on the famous Thomas Viaduct, March 18, 1939. The size disparity is due primarily to the limitations of track clearances (loading gauge) established in the early days of British railroading.

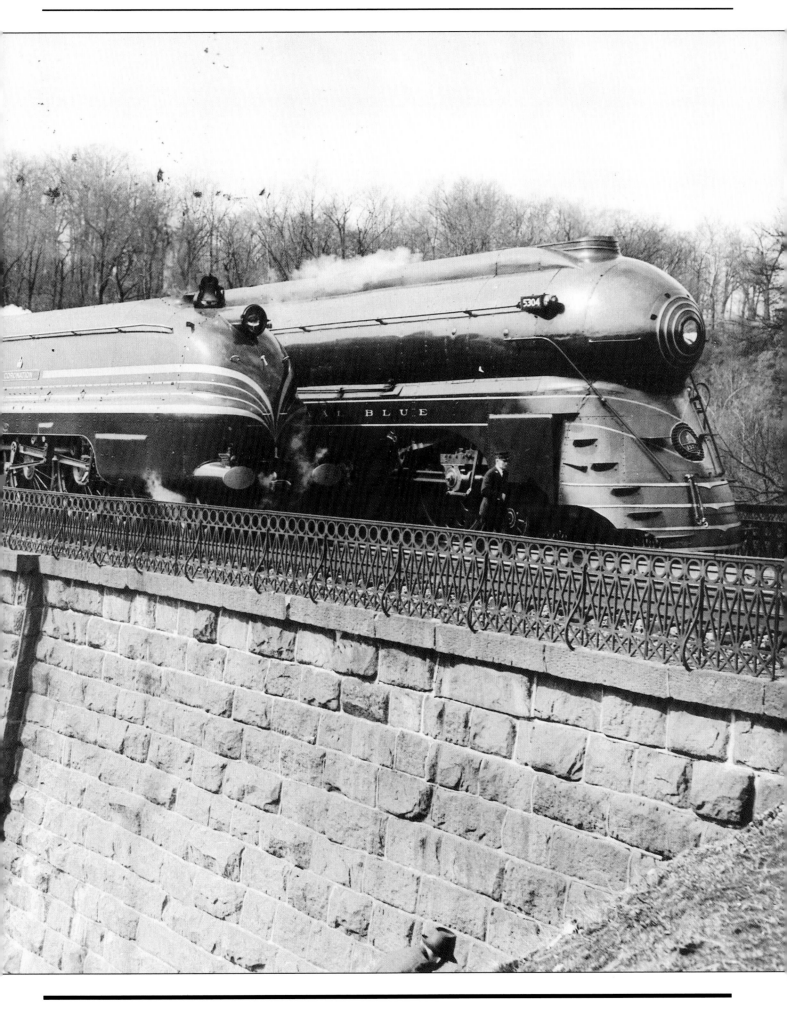

Kuhler retired to Santa Fe, New Mexico, where his interests in painting and railroads continued until his death in 1976.

L

Lima-Hamilton

Generally referred to as Lima (LIE-mah, not Lee-mah), the Lima-Hamilton diesel business never really developed. The Lima Locomotive Works, of Lima, Ohio, was one of the premier steam locomotive builders in the world, and the Super Power designs from the end of the steam era were second to none. But by the end of World War II, it was obvious that steam power was dying on the railroads, so Lima dipped its toe into the diesel market in 1947, teaming up with engine builder Hamilton, of nearby Hamilton, Ohio, and turned out a switcher in 1949. A year later, Lima merged with Baldwin, another giant of the steam era—and equally desperate—but the Lima diesel designs were not carried over to the Baldwin catalog. There was little to distinguish the Lima products, either visually or mechanically. The four switcher models, one road switcher, and a twin-engined center-cab model did not get an opportunity for fine tuning. Not exactly bestsellers, no Limas were sold west of Kansas City. They can be found only on a few short lines and in museums today.

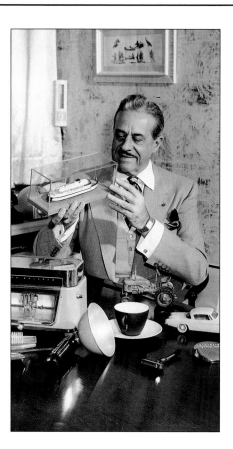

Above: Noted industrial designer Raymond Loewy examines a model of a streamlined ferry in 1953. He was responsible for its design, along with the design of the other items on his desk. His work for the Pennsylvania Railroad ranged from depot trash containers to the T-1 locomotive. Below: Before the full development of their legendary Berkshires, Lima built smaller 2-8-4s for the Illinois Central. An example of the Class L-63, formerly numbered 7013, is shown here after a later rebuilding and renumbering, to 8015.

Loewy, Raymond (1893–1986)

The man who may well be the best-known nonrailroader in the railroad world has also left his mark on almost every area of product design, from postage stamps to NASA's Skylab, and has been credited with helping to found the profession of industrial design.

Born in Paris in 1893, Loewy's first design was for a model airplane when he was fifteen years old. He patented the design, formed a company, the Ayrel Corporation, to manufacture it, and hired a salesman. He then turned to boats, and designed an award-winning three-foot (0.9 m)-long speedboat model. In 1919, after serving with distinction in the French army and emigrating to New York, he was hired to design a store window for Macy's. The spare, clean, and uncluttered window enraged his employer and, preferring not to be fired, Loewy resigned.

He had a varied career in advertising, illustration for department stores and magazines, and costume design for Florenz Ziegfeld, but was dissatisfied enough to consider returning to France. Instead he committed himself to a "one-man industrial crusade under the aegis of good taste" and became an American citizen in 1938.

After designs for Gestetner duplicating machines and the Hupmobile helped to solidify his philosophy and reputation, Loewy continued to be obsessed with transportation designs. Interestingly, his railroad career began with the redesign of the lowly trash cans in Pennsylvania

Station, New York. Legend has it that Loewy was such a pest in the offices of the mighty Pennsylvania Railroad that he was given the task just to get rid of him. Having successfully completed that assignment, he was invited to submit a proposal for the styling of the newly engineered GG1.

The presentation of a clay model and some renderings shocked the Pennsy staff, since welding the entire shell was an automotive building technique, and not indigenous to the railroads. But the combination of the sleek streamlined body and the extremely elegant five-stripe "cat whisker" paint scheme of gold on Brunswick green carried the day, resulting in one of the truly great locomotive designs.

The design for the GG1 was followed by streamlining that was applied to an already operational steam locomotive, the famous

Above, top: Baldwin built the first T-1 4-4-4-4 Duplex for the Pennsylvania Railroad in 1942. The original Loewy streamlined styling was much simplified when fifty more, including No. 5533, were added in 1946. The controversial and short-lived 100-mph (160 kph) passenger locomotives were capable of up to 6,000 hp. Above: The Loewy-styled Pennsylvania Railroad No. 6100 (Altoona 1939) was the only S-1 6-4-4-6 Duplex built and was displayed under steam at the New York World's Fair, with its 7-foot (2.1 m) drivers slowly turning on rollers. After the fair, its use was limited to passenger service between Chicago and Crestline, Ohio. The massive 140-foot (43 m), 304-ton (274 t) locomotive was too large to make the final curve into the Pittsburgh Station. It was finally scrapped in 1949.

K-4 Pacific, and by Loewy's styling of Pennsy's brand-new streamlined S-1 Duplex (6-4-4-6) steam locomotive. Extensive wind tunnel testing helped achieve a striking aerodynamic design that deflected smoke away from the train, and the S-1 became the largest and fastest high-speed steam locomotive placed in service in the United States.

Loewy's relationship with the Pennsylvania Railroad Company went on for many years, and included designs for the Baldwin-built shark-nosed T-1 steam locomotive and a complete redesign of the railroad's flagship passenger trains—the celebrated 1938 "Fleet of Modernism," which matched Loewy and the Pennsy against both of their archrivals, Henry Dreyfuss and the New York Central's Twentieth Century Limited.

Diesel locomotives received the Loewy touch as well, with notable visual successes such as the Baldwin shark-nosed freight and passenger units and the Fairbanks-Morse H-10-44 switchers. His career ultimately moved on to designs for ships, Studebaker and the Avanti cars, Air Force One and other aircraft, and NASA products.

See also: *Baldwin, Matthias William; Fairbanks-Morse; GG1 Electric Locomotive; Streamlined Steam Locomotives.*

The Lucin Cutoff

When the builders of the Central Pacific and Union Pacific Railroads raced toward each other across the Utah desert, one last great obstacle remained in their path: the Great Salt Lake. The line detoured around the north shore of the lake, climbing 680 feet (204 m) over the Promontory Mountains as it did so. The operational difficulties and extra distance involved caused the railroad, by then known as the Southern Pacific, to engineer a shortcut across the shallow lake.

This approach was examined by the original engineers, but was rejected as information on the lake bottom was inadequate, the permanent water level of the lake was uncertain, and the costs were projected to be high. Thirty-three years after the golden spike was driven, a bypass was completed that proceeded almost directly east from

Lucin through the Great Salt Desert and crossed the middle of the lake on 16 miles (26 km) of rock-filled causeway. It boasted a 12-mile (19 km)-long wooden trestle, using 27,000 pilings, and included a mid-lake depot. The 32-mile (51 km) Lucin Cutoff reduced the distance to Ogden by 44 miles (70 km) and was completed in 1903 at a cost of $8.4 million. Ironically, the bypass reduced Promontory, the site of the Golden Spike Ceremony, to a minor spot at the end of a long siding, and finally even that trackage was pulled up during World War II.

The wooden trestle had its share of maintenance problems, and in 1959, the Southern Pacific rerouted trains to a $53 million rock fill parallel to the fifty-six-year-old trestle, and it was abandoned to the Great Salt Lake. Rising water levels in the lake created new problems for the cutoff in the 1980s, with storm-whipped waves frequently washing across the tracks. A program of lowering the lake level combined with raising the track promises to keep the Lucin Cutoff in operation well into the future.

Northern Pacific called these 2-8-8-4s Yellowstones in honor of the national park in the area they served. The extremely long firebox was designed to burn lignite, a slow-burning hard coal. No 5002 was made by the Baldwin Locomotive Works in 1930.

Mallet, Anatole (1837–1919)

A French engineer, Mallet was responsible for developing the first successful compound locomotive and, in 1884, patented the first compound articulated locomotive, which bears his name. In this design, exhaust steam with depleted pressure is reused in larger, low-pressure cylinders on an additional set of driving wheels that pivot independently of the main frame and boiler.

The first Mallet was built in 1887 by Ateliers Metallurgiques at Tubize, Belgium. The 0-4-4-0 had a gauge of 1 foot 11½ inches and could produce higher tractive effort while maintaining lower axle loading for light track and flexibility on tight curves. The concept was introduced on European main lines in 1890, and in 1903 the concept was imported by the Americans, who developed the design to its limits.

Alco built the first American Mallet, an 0-6-6-0 for the Baltimore & Ohio in 1903, followed by five Baldwin 2-6-6-2s for the Great Northern in 1906. The Virginian Railroad, in 1918, employed a 2-10-10-2 with 48-inch (1.2 m)-diameter low-pressure cylinders, the largest ever used. They also tried a "triplex" design—a 2-8-8-8-4—

which added a third set of powered drivers, also low pressure, under the tender. The Erie tried the triplex, building three 2-8-8-8-2s in 1914, but the difficulty of maintaining adequate steam at anything above starting speed doomed the triplex, and most were rebuilt to other configurations.

The introduction of the superheater rendered the Mallet concept of steam reuse in the cylinders unnecessary and further large locomotive development was in "simple" articulated locomotives. The Chesapeake & Ohio 2-6-6-6 Allegheny, Northern Pacific 2-8-8-4s, and the Union Pacific's Big Boy 4-8-8-4s, all simple, each weighed over 500 tons (450 t).

The last active simple-expansion articulateds, although not true Mallets, were

built by Baldwin as 2-6-6-2s between 1941 and 1949. They operated on Brazil's Teresa Cristina Railway until the 1970s.

Mikado

The original 2-8-2 engines were Baldwin-built in 1897 for the 3-foot 6-inch-gauge Japanese Railways. This gave the name Mikado to the type, which was quickly shortened to Mike in North America. During World War II, there was an effort made to change the name to MacArthur, but it did not take. The first American Mikados were built for the Bismarck, Washburn & Great Falls Railway.

While visually spectacular, the 2-8-8-8-2 triplex Matt Shay, a 1914 Baldwin product, was not particularly successful in mechanical terms. The three sets of drivers and cylinders were a maintenance headache, the engine under the tender tended to slip as the weight of fuel and water lessened during operation, and the boiler could not produce sufficient steam to meet the demand.

Mogul

The first 2-6-0 was the *Pawnee* of the Philadelphia and Reading. Built by James Milholland in 1850, this was a rigid wheelbase locomotive. The first true Mogul, with a swiveling pilot truck, was built by Baldwin Locomotive Works for the Louisville & Nashville in 1860. The name Mogul has been attributed to the Central of New Jersey locomotive built by Taunton in 1866, but the name came into general use with the *Master Mechanic's Association Report for 1872*.

Mountain-type Locomotive

The 4-8-2 type became the most popular locomotive design in North America, where about 2,400 were in service. Introduced on the Chesapeake & Ohio in 1911, the first were built to help on their mountainous divisions, thereby providing the name. Able to do the work of double-headed Pacifics, the 4-8-2 quickly earned a place as a fast freight or passenger hauler. Over 2,000 Mountains were rostered on American railroads, half of them on the New York Central and the Pennsylvania. The great French engineer André Chapelon chose the wheel arrangement for his 241Ps of 1948, which continued in service until 1970.

A few Mountains have been preserved for display—by the Spokane, Portland & Seattle, Canadian National, and Northern Pacific. St. Louis-San Francisco (Frisco) No. 1522 and CM 6060, known as *Bullet Nose Betty*, have been restored for excursion service.

Below: The 4-8-2 Mountain was a workhorse when it came to hauling freight and passengers. Pennsylvania Railroad No. 6707 is a Baldwin product of 1930. Note the prominent bulge in the boiler in front of the cab. This "Belpaire" design was preferred by the Pennsylvania but virtually ignored by the other U.S. railroads.

Above: The fireman provides a fine smoke plume for the photographer as restored Frisco 4-8-2 No. 1522 storms by with an excursion train.

N

Newcomen, Thomas (1663–1729)

At the beginning of the eighteenth century, an Englishman named Newcomen responded to the need for pumping water out of coal mines by building a successful piston pump powered by steam. He solved the pumping problem by attaching the pumping piston directly to the steam piston, so that they moved simultaneously as steam was intermittently allowed into the steam cylinder.

Newcomen's first pumping station, a two-story oak, iron, and brick "atmospheric engine," was built in 1705. Opening a valve allowed steam into a vertical cylinder with a large piston at the top that was connected to the pumping piston by a walking beam. With the steam cylinder full, the valve was closed and the operator opened a second valve, allowing cold water to flow over the outside of the heated cylinder and cool it, thereby condensing the steam and creating a vacuum. Outside air pressure then forced the steam piston down, which raised the opposite end of the walking beam and thus the pumping piston, lifting the water out of the mine shaft below.

An inventive young man named Humphrey Potter was hired to operate the pump, and he quickly grew weary of the tedium of opening and closing the valves every fifteen seconds. He devised a system of ropes attached to the walking beam that automatically opened and closed the proper valves, thereby eliminating his own job!

Newcomen had begun full operation of his pump when a most fortunate mishap occurred. A valve broke, allowing the cooling water to flow directly into the cylinder, with the happy result that the steam condensed more quickly and the engine operated at a cycle of ten seconds instead of fifteen. A modification made the situation permanent, and Newcomen's pumps were widely built in Britain and Europe. It was up to James Watt, another Englishman, to take the next big step.

See also: *Aeolipile; Branca, Giovanni.*

The first locomotive to arrive in Alaska was this small narrow-gauge Mogul, photographed in Skagway on July 20, 1898. The crew appears to be filling the boiler with a hose, as the tender is not yet present.

FIRST LOCOMOTIVE IN ALASKA - SKAGWAY, JULY 20, 1898.

New Zealand Railways

With a total north-to-south length of 1,500 miles (2,400 km) and a total east-to-west length of 100 miles (160 km), the two islands of New Zealand make for a primarily linear railroad system. The spine of the Southern Alps keeps the major line of South Island along the east coast, with only scattered and disconnected lines on the west coast. The more populous North Island is dominated by three central volcanic peaks, and the rail lines circle the high elevations by skirting the coast where possible, although major construction was necessary to penetrate the interior. The largest area of flat land is the 200-mile (320 km)-long and less-than-30-mile (48 km)-wide area around Christchurch on the South Island.

The combination of a small population and terrain obstacles kept railroads from developing in New Zealand until fairly late. Political fragmentation into five provinces by 1870 meant that, as in Australia, the provincial governments were left to establish railroads on their own. The first line was opened in 1863, built to Irish standard gauge of 5 feet 3 inches, from Christchurch to Ferrymeade, in Canterbury. A connection to nearby Lyttleton was critical, as it was the port of entry for many immigrants and it served the larger Christchurch, but it was separated by a ring of hills 1,600 feet (486 m) high. An ailing Robert Stephenson was approached about building the line, but he turned the project over to his cousin George Robert. The connection was made via a tunnel of 1.75 miles (2.8 km) on a 6-mile (9.6 km) railroad that opened in 1867.

Then the province of Southland opened lines in two gauges: Invercargill to Bluff, in 4-foot 8½-inch gauge; and Dunedin to Port Chalmers, with 3 feet 6 inches. On the North Island, the Wellington to Hutt Valley Line stayed with 3 feet 6 inches, but standard gauge was picked for the line from Auckland to Drury.

At this point, the New Zealand government took action to avoid the Australian

The "long boiler" heritage of Robert Stephenson is evident in this 2-4-0 inside-cylinder tank engine, known as a "Pilgrim" locomotive, of the New Zealand Railways.

gauge debacle. In 1870, 3 feet 6 inches was established as New Zealand standard gauge along with the authority for future construction and the raising of foreign capital. From then, construction proceeded more slowly: 370 miles (592 km) from Christchurch south to Dunedin and Invercargill were completed in 1879; Wellington to Auckland in 1909; Christchurch to Greymouth in 1923; and, finally, Christchurch was linked to Picton in 1946.

A well-integrated coastal shipping industry meant that, in such a compact island nation, development of a full web of rail links was less essential, but it also meant that isolated sections of railroad connecting with ports could have de facto connection with the rest of New Zealand; a number of these lines were developed, and six were still operating until 1930. Closure of underused branches has reduced the total rail network by 15 percent from the 1950s high of 3,500 miles (5,600 km).

Perhaps surprisingly for a small country, there are three tunnels more than 5 miles (8 km) long. The 1923 Otira Tunnel between Christchurch and Greymouth is 5.3 miles (8.5 km) long. The 5.5-mile (8.8 km) Rimutaka Tunnel, built in 1955 on the Wellington to Masterton line to replace a very steep (1-in-15), 3-mile (4.8 km)-long

Above: Nubaka Viaduct, on New Zealand's North Island, is one of the most spectacular of the many bridges on the railway; it is 908 feet (277 m) in length and 318 feet (97 m) above the river. Left: The line to the Otira Tunnel was electrified to eliminate smoke problems in the tunnel. A pair of steam locomotives have paused on a newly constructed bridge with a set of electric locomotives that are being hauled to the electrified section.

incline, worked on the Fell principle of using a central rail gripped by horizontal driving wheels on specially constructed locomotives. A normal train needed four of these steamers. Rimutaka was the longest-operating and most significant installation to use this principle. The equally long Kaimai Tunnel opened in 1978 on the new line from Hamilton to Tauranga.

The rugged country also made bridges—spidery wooden trestles and tall steel viaducts—necessary. Nuhaka Viaduct on the North Island is the most impressive. Built on the line between Napier and Gisborne, the steel viaduct is 908 feet (276 m) long and towers 318 feet (97 m).

The great variety of the country's locomotive fleet is out of proportion to its small size. Virtually every steam locomotive type was given a trial (one notable exception being the steam turbine). There was one unsuccessful class of Beyer-Garratts; a single Mallet; and Shays, Climaxes, and Heislers on the logging lines. A locomotive destined for Australia was diverted to New Zealand when traffic on the Melbourne & Essendon did not live up to expectations. Thus, the balloon-stacked *Pilgrim*, built by Slaughter, Gruning & Co. of Bristol, became No. 1 on the Canterbury Provincial Railways and was followed by a series of small tank engines. Larger locomotives became the norm, and both British- and American-built 2-6-2s and 4-6-0s worked side by side until the turn of the century. By then, it was obvious that the American products were better suited to the local conditions, and the mostly

Left: The rugged mountains that form a spine down the islands caused an abundance of spectacular engineering projects. This concrete viaduct carries the electrified line to Otira Tunnel, although it is a steam locomotive hauling the passengers in this photograph. Inset: The 3-foot 6-inch gauge of the New Zealand Railways supported a wide variety of steam locomotives of British and American influence. No. 1234 appears to be a Ja Class 4-8-2 built by the North British Locomotive Co. in 1951. The Ja Class could pull a 400-ton (360 t) train at 50 mph (80 kph) on the 3-foot 6-inch-gauge track.

domestically built designs followed American practice from then until the end of steam in 1957. Walschaerts valve gear and superheating became an early standard as well as the 4-6-2, 4-8-4, and 4-8-2 wheel arrangements that allowed speeds of 60 mph (96 kph) on the narrow gauge.

The country's diesels, in contrast, are very straightforward, with the early British designs being discarded in favor of American and Japanese types. Limited electrification has been installed at 1,500 volts DC, but it has been confined to the Otira Tunnel and the Wellington suburban service, despite abundant hydro-electric power.

As many other countries have been doing, the NZR has been phasing out passenger service, although an estimated 284 million passenger miles (458 million km) were run in 1990. The Silver Star, an all-sleeping-car express from Auckland to Wellington, fulfilled the requirements of a first-rate train. Locomotive-hauled trains from Wellington to Napier and Christchurch to Invercargill also provide important service. Secondary routes are handled by railcar. Freight traffic is still important, with increasing amounts moving in containers for export and import. A train ferry links the two islands between Wellington and Picton.

NZR is typically single track, with CTC and color lights replacing the old British-style electric-tablet and semaphore signaling. One unusual advantage the railway maintains is an ordinance prohibiting road hauling of freight (except livestock) on routes paralleling rail lines, therefore strengthening the market for rail freight and improving the future of railways in New Zealand.

"If any man has invented a mechanism with just fifty percent of the steam locomotive's solid spiritual satisfaction, he hasn't applied for a patent yet."
—David P. Morgan

Northern-type Locomotive

The 4-8-4 wheel arrangement was known by many names. The Northern Pacific pioneered the type in 1926, so Northern is generally accepted, but they were also named after important features on their owners' lines, such as: Confederation, Canadian National; Dixie (region) Nashville, Chattanooga & St Louis; GS—Golden State (California) and General Service, Southern Pacific; Greenbrier (river), Chesapeake & Ohio; Niagara (river, falls), New York Central; Pocono (mountains), Lackawanna; Potomac (river), Western Maryland; and Wyoming (local county), Lehigh Valley.

The four-wheeled trailing truck supported a larger firebox, giving the 4-8-4 an advantage over the 4-8-2 Mountain. Most North American railroads owned a fleet of 4-8-4s for dual use in freight and passenger service. There were 900 Northerns built between 1926 and 1950, many having boosters, roller bearings, and the latest refinements of steam technology. The last commercially built American steam locomotive was Lima's Greenbrier No. 614 for the C&O, which retired after only eight years in service. Now restored, 614 operates in excursion service, along with Cotton Belt No. 819, Union Pacific 8444, Norfolk & Western 611, and Southern Pacific 4449.

Above: Southern Pacific No. 4449, a restored 4-8-4, speeds through the California farm country with an excursion train. All equipment is painted in the colors of the legendary "Daylight" from the classic era of passenger service.

Below: Reading Railroad's No. 2100 was the first of a fleet of handsome Northerns that were converted from 2-8-0s by company forces in 1945; several survived to serve in excursion service. The 2101 gained further fame as the American Freedom Train No. 1 during the Bicentennial tour as well as the Chessie Steam Special from 1978 to 1979; it is now in the Baltimore & Ohio Museum in Baltimore.

O

The Orient Express (The Wagons-Lits Company)

A visit to America in 1868 exposed Belgian banking heir Georges Nagelmackers to the luxurious elegance of the sleeping cars operated by the Pullman Company. Such amenities were unheard of in Europe, where the early experiments with primitive bunk cars made long-distance travel an unpleasant and uncomfortable experience.

Nagelmackers saw at once that the Pullman Palace Car concept could be successfully implemented in Europe, but upon his return home, he failed to interest financial backers in his own ideas for practical sleeping cars. He was able to convert a few cars into Pullman-like sleepers, using his own money, and began operating his service on trains between Ostend and Cologne. Despite modest success, his underfinanced operation was facing bankruptcy and failure when he met Colonel William d'Alton Mann, of the U.S. Army Engineers.

Mann, who was wary of entering the sleeping-car business in the United States and thereby competing with Pullman, had made an unsuccessful attempt to enter the British market. So he joined Nagelmackers, and the two entrepreneurs began building the Mann Boudoir Sleeping Cars in Continental Europe.

A long-term contract with the French Railway system and Nagelmackers' persuading the Prince of Wales to use a Mann Boudoir car for a highly publicized trip through Russia helped the fledgling company's credibility, and it began to prosper. Mann was bought out in 1876, and Nagelmackers formed the Compagnie Internationale des Wagons-Lits et des Grands Express Européens, more commonly known as the Wagons-Lits Company. Realizing the important relationship between food and travel, Nagelmackers added an elegant dining car that served first-class meals, and 500 Wagons-Lits diners and sleepers were in service on 90,000 miles (144,000 km) of line by the turn of the century.

The Pullman Company began with converted coaches but was building its own sleeping cars by 1865. This example of an early car, reportedly the first Pullman-built sleeper, shows how the curtains were rigged to provide privacy for the berths.

Above: The famous Orient Express became the standard of elegant rail travel in Europe, its luxurious cars providing a mysterious setting for novels and movies. Right: Georges Nagelmackers was the guiding force behind European sleeping-car service and the visionary entrepreneur responsible for the Orient Express.

Further rail history was made with the 1883 introduction of the Orient Express, the European *train de luxe*, which operated across the Continent to Constantinople exclusively with Wagons-Lits equipment.

The train became an almost instant legend, the epitome of the elegance and romance of travel by train. The first Orient Express included three coaches, with partitions carved and inlaid using teak, walnut, and mahogany; silk bed sheets; and gold plumbing on marble sinks.

An elegant car that included a men's smoking compartment, a library, and a

ladies' lounge followed the coaches, but the dining car was the most opulent. Carved wood was a sumptuous background to crystal chandeliers and paintings; linen-covered tables were adorned with fine china, sterling silver, and crystal. It was common for the aristocratic passengers to dine in full evening dress and to be entertained with live music. The vast quantity of food, wine, champagne, and brandy required for the long journey was carried in its own separate car.

This grand traveling hotel became the backdrop for hundreds of stories. Agatha Christie had Hercule Poirot riding the train in *Murder on the Orient Express*. The Orient Express came to symbolize mystery and intrigue, opulence and luxury. But the realities of a changing world ultimately caught up with Wagons-Lits.

The company merged with the European Pullman Company, after the deaths of both Georges Nagelmackers and George Pullman, and dominated travel on the Continent for another forty years. Ultimately, however, even the rich abandoned their trains, preferring the sanitized speed of air travel to the leisurely luxury of the Orient Express. When the service was abandoned in 1977, the age of the luxury train was dead, and with it much of the romance and allure of travel by train.

The service was resurrected in the 1980s as the Nostalgic Orient Express, restoring some of the equipment from the 1920s and operating from Zurich to Istanbul. A new generation has learned to appreciate fine travel, and the service has been successful enough to warrant a second train. The Orient Express began operating from Singapore to Bangkok in 1992. The twenty-two car train makes the run from Malaysia to Thailand in forty-one hours, continuing a tradition that is over a century old.

The luxurious image of the Orient Express was well deserved, as illustrated by the sumptuous interior of the Piano Bar car.

THE CAR THAT SAW TWO TREATIES

At the end of World War I, the armistice between France and Germany was signed in a railroad car, Wagons-Lits car 2419, which has been called one of the most historic railroad cars of all time. On a railroad siding at the Forest of Compiègne, about twenty-five miles (40km) outside of Paris, Marshal Foch of the French armed forces acknowledged the German surrender on November 11, 1918.

More than thirty years later, when Germany overran France during World War II, Hitler ordered car 2419 taken from its place in a museum and hauled to the spot where the treaty had been signed in 1918. It was in car 2419, on June 22, 1940, that Hitler received France's surrender.

Today, car 2419 is no more. In 1945, knowing that the end of World War II was imminent and that Germany faced certain defeat, the Nazis blew it up. They didn't want to sit in it for a third treaty, which would certainly have resembled more closely the document of 1918 than that of 1940.

A triumphant Adolph Hitler exits Wagons-Lits car No. 2419 after accepting France's formal surrender in 1940.

P

The 4-6-2 Pacific-type became the standard passenger locomotive on many railroads. Minneapolis, St. Paul & Saulte Ste. Marie No. 2702 was turned out by American Locomotive Works' Schenectady plant in 1910.

Pacific-type Locomotive

The first 4-6-2 was built by the Vulcan Iron Works, Wilkes-Barre, Pennsylvania, in 1886 and went into service on the Lehigh Valley Railroad. The earliest "classic" 4-6-2, as an enlargement of the 4-4-2 Atlantic with a larger firebox, was built in 1901 by the Baldwin Works for export to New Zealand (NZ "Q" Class). In 1902, Brooks built some 4-6-2s for the Missouri Pacific, and it is not known which of these two orders christened the type "Pacific."

Prairie-type Locomotive

The 2-6-2 wheel arrangement was developed to answer the need for more power, both in the larger boiler and as applied to the rails. The first Prairies were built by the Baldwin Locomotive Works in 1885 for shipment to New Zealand. Many others were built for both passenger and freight work in the American Midwest, thus the name. This type never achieved wide popularity in the United States, but was somewhat popular with logging and branch lines as the trailing track provided stability while backing up, a necessity on lines with no turning facilities.

The final American 2-6-2 was built in 1910, but the wheel arrangement remained popular on many Eastern European lines and in Britain. Sir Nigel Gresley's famous V2 was introduced on the London & North Eastern Railway in 1936 and the first of these, No. 4771, *Green Arrow*, is preserved at the National Railway Museum, York.

Puffing Billy

In 1813, Christopher Blackett and William Hedley built a steam locomotive based on the best features of several earlier designs. They combined an improved version of Trevithic's boiler; the two cylinders (thus eliminating the flywheel) of Murdoch and Cugnot; a rocking-beam driving arrangement from Murdoch's tricycle; and a complex gear drive that spread the power and load over four driving wheels (therefore reducing stress on the rails). Blackett and Hedley produced a locomotive that succeeded in its intended use as power for the Wylam Colliery, but the complex gearing and long piston stroke restricted speed and the design was impractical for long-haul freight or fast passenger service.

Despite these shortcomings, the locomotive proved Trevithic's theory that adhesion alone was sufficient for propulsion and that the much more expensive cogwheels and rail were unnecessary. Additional historic significance is attributed to its influence on two future locomotive builders. A Wylam Colliery blacksmith named Timothy Hackworth was assigned to maintenance and used this experience to produce more advanced designs. George Stephenson, called the father of the modern railway, was born alongside the colliery railway and was inspired by his daily contact with the locomotive to pursue a mechanical trade, which led to a distinguished career as a railroad builder.

The unofficial nickname—*Puffing Billy* —ultimately became the engine's historic name. The locomotive is preserved at the Science Museum, London, and is the world's oldest existing steam locomotive.

See also: *Stephenson, George; Hackworth, Timothy.*

Above: The trailing wheels under the Prairie-type allowed for both a larger firebox and a locomotive that operated well in reverse. Baldwin built this 2-6-2 for export to New Zealand in 1885. Below: Puffing Billy earned its name honestly. It was one of the earliest locos to have the steam exhausted through the smoke stack, increasing the draft for the fire and creating a pronounced "chuffing" noise, described at the time as a "blast." The Billy *was built by William Hedley.*

Pullman, George Mortimer (1831–1897)

Born in Brocton, New York, Pullman's early trade was as a cabinetmaker, but he moved to Chicago in 1855 and began a construction business. Aware of the uncomfortable bunk-type sleeping cars then in use, he contracted with the Chicago & Alton Railroad to convert two coaches into comfortable sleeping cars, which entered service in 1859.

In 1854, Pullman and his friend Benjamin Field were granted a patent for a folding upper berth. They constructed their first new car, The *Pioneer*, a sleeper that added another patented concept—facing seats that extended and slid together, making a comfortable lower berth. The *Pioneer* was first displayed in 1865 and garnered much publicity when it was used by Mrs. Abraham Lincoln in the president's funeral train. The enthusiastic reception encouraged the builders, and the Pullman's

Above: **Pioneer,** *the first newly constructed Pullman car, was assigned to the Lincoln funeral train. It was used by Mrs. Lincoln when she accompanied the slain president back to Springfield, Illinois, and the exposure secured the future of the Pullman Company.*

Below: *The basic concept of the Pullman sleeping car changed little over the years. The overhead compartments folded down and the seats slid together to make upper and lower berths for overnight travel.*

(later Pullman) Palace Car Co. was incorporated in 1867. By 1875, Pullman was producing the majority of the sleeping cars in the United States.

In 1880, Pullman's paternalism led to the founding of the model company town of Pullman, Illinois, just south of Chicago. His hopes of creating an ideal worker's society were dashed when, in reaction to an 1894 wage decrease along with raised rents, his employees went on strike. When Eugene Debs' American Railway Union boycotted the handling of Pullman cars, a general railway strike ensued, paralyzing the western railroads and seriously affecting the rest. There were many acts of violence to both sides, and federal troops were finally called out to guarantee the delivery of the mails and to protect interstate commerce. Debs was jailed and the strike collapsed.

Pullman's business approach was to reduce the railroads' involvement in the production of first-class travel accommodations (sleeping cars and, to some extent, dining and parlor cars) and encourage them to haul his cars in their trains. The cars, their maintenance and staffing, the linens, and other luxuries were the responsibility of the Pullman Co., whose name came to symbolize all sleeping-car service in North America, to the extent that it became customary for passengers to address all Pullman porters as "George."

By the 1920s, Pullman operated almost 10,000 passenger cars in the United States, Canada, and Mexico, and was building freight cars as well. Its market dominance led to antitrust action in 1947, which separated car building from operation. The falloff in passenger traffic eventually led to the demise of Pullman sleeping-car operations, but the freight-car building business is still very active.

It seems unlikely that a single standardized form of transportation will ever dominate the travel business as the Pullman sleeper did in the first half of the twentieth century.

Q

Quebec Bridge

The world's longest cantilever span crosses over the St. Lawrence River with a main span of 1,800 feet (548 m) and shore spans of 562 feet 6 inches (171 m). The central suspended span was replaced after it collapsed while being lifted into position during construction. Completed on December 3, 1917, by the Canadian Pacific, it is an important link south to New York. The first attempt to bridge this site ended in failure on August 29, 1907, when the south cantilever, being erected by the Phoenix Bridge Company, collapsed and killed seventy-five workers.

R

Railbox (RBOX)

Traditionally, rolling stock was owned by the individual railroads with a few types (primarily tank cars and refrigerator cars) privately owned by nonrail companies, usually a shipper. The cars were freely interchanged between railroads under agreements that specified per diem charges to be paid to the home road (owner) for the time the car was off the home rails. When a load originating on railroad A was delivered to a customer on railroad B (both railroads sharing in the shipping charges), railroad B was obligated to return the empty car to railroad A as quickly as possible. The ideal situation was if a load could be found for delivery on railroad A, but typically, the car was returned empty, costing money to haul but earning no income.

This system worked relatively well for many years in the United States, but in the late 1960s the rail industry's fleet of general-service boxcars was both diminishing in size and deteriorating in quality. The Trailer Train company had been formed

earlier, by a consortium of railroads, to solve the problem of providing cars for the growing intermodal (piggyback) business. Railbox (RBOX), a wholly owned subsidiary of Trailer Train, was created on January 14, 1974, expressly to provide a fleet of free-running general-service boxcars that would alleviate the shortage.

RBOX was financed by a series of leveraged leases guaranteed by twelve financially strong railroads that held stock in Trailer Train. This acquisition was the largest financial transaction ever undertaken for freight car equipment, and was financed by General Electric Credit Corporation.

The initial order of 10,000 cars was built by ACF Industries, Pullman-Standard, Berwick Forge & Fabricating, Paccar, and FMC. The first RBOX car was delivered on October 15, 1974, and the 10,000th on June 9, 1976. The order was subsequently increased by 500 cars. The Railbox pooling agreement signed by 137 railroads provided for access to high-quality cars that could be routed virtually anywhere in North America and were free of the requirement to return the car to the home road. The bright yellow cars carried the appropriate slogan on their sides: "Next Load—Any Road." This increased utilization of the cars, and therefore their profitability, since they could be sent where needed, rather than arbitrarily to the home road.

Between 1976 and 1980, RBOX had 15,000 additional cars built, some (ABOX) with a 6-foot (1.8 m) plug door beside the 10-foot (3 m) sliding door, which provided a wider opening for lumber loading. The recession of 1981 ended twenty-five years of expansion for Trailer Train, as a substantial drop in rail traffic, particularly in items requiring boxcars, resulted in RBOX being unable to meet financial obligations on January 1, 1983. A debt restructuring, and the assignment of both cars and financial obligations to the railroads that guaranteed the debt, stabilized RBOX. Direct sale of 1,600 cars to the Canadian National helped to reduce the RBOX fleet to 13,000 cars by 1986. The railroads were encouraged to retire 11,000 of their older general-service cars by offering incentives for using RBOX cars, and the company returned to profitability by 1987.

The yellow RBOX cars still ply the rail lines of North America, providing "the nation's boxcar pool" with safe, clean, and free-running cars.

Railgon

The same shortages that plagued the boxcar fleet of the American railroads in the early 1970s were spreading to the industry's gondola fleet by the late 1970s. Railgon was formed, as a subsidiary of Trailer Train, on May 24, 1979, and operated in the same manner as Railbox, with the gondola fleet free-running and no requirement to return empty cars to the point of origin.

The initial fleet of 4,000 cars was built by Berwick Forge & Fabricating, Bethlehem Steel, Greenville Steel Car, Pullman-Standard, and Thrall Car. Research data from railroads, shippers, and Trailer Train's own engineers contributed to the final design. The reinforced ends are attached to the sides with vertical steel pins, allowing the ends to flex under impact. Beaver-tail connectors join the sides and the frame. Half the fleet was riveted, and the other half was welded.

The cars were delivered in 1981, just as a growing recession began to affect the steel pipe and scrap industries. This virtual shutdown of the very market the cars were intended to serve was disastrous. Many of the cars went right into storage upon delivery. As in the case of Railbox, debt was restructured. CSX leased 2,000 gondolas directly from the creditors and Railgon leased 800 more cars to Denver & Rio Grande Western, Kansas City Southern, and Chicago & Northwestern. Car utilization dropped to its lowest point in 1983, but the slow recovery of the steel industry combined with fleet reductions increased utilization to 92 percent by 1989.

Railgon was begun with much promise to fulfill a real need, but as throughout the history of railroading, the vagaries of the economic climate have spoiled many good ideas. Despite these setbacks, Railgon has been able to continue in its role as the "nationwide gondola pool."

Railway Express Agency (REA)

In 1839, young William Harnden, an ambitious and enterprising conductor on the Boston & Worcester Railroad, audaciously promoted a new package delivery service between New York and Boston. In advertisements placed in Boston's major newspapers, Harnden claimed he was operating an express car with a messenger to Providence, where steamboat connections would complete the four-times-weekly journey.

On March 4 of that year, Harnden boarded the Providence train with a carpetbag full of packages, the initial step on what was to become the road to the pre-

The Railgon pool of gondola cars was created in response to an ongoing car shortage. The carefully researched design was successful in answering a need that quickly faded away.

mier package-delivery service in North America, with agents in virtually every hamlet large enough to have a railroad station, long strings of railroad cars, and a fleet of dark green delivery trucks that was one of the largest in the world.

The business flourished as word of the reliable young man spread. Within months, several messengers had been hired, new offices had been opened along the route, and expansion included New York to Philadelphia and Boston to Albany services. But competition also flourished.

Harnden became more interested in business affairs in Europe, as he became disenchanted by his express business. Henry Wells, his agent in Albany, was encouraged to establish his own separate service through to Chicago, as Harnden believed the venture too risky. Wells joined with George Pomeroy, another expressman, to initiate the first leg of operations, despite the need to combine train travel with stagecoach as through rail connections were lacking. Pomeroy left the business and Wells was joined by William C. Fargo, a railroad freight agent, marking the beginning of Wells & Company, predecessor to REA.

Consolidation began in 1850. John Butterfield, of Butterfield-Wasson Express, joined with Wells and Fargo to form American Express Company, which organized another company to serve the booming California Gold Rush trade, and the legendary Wells Fargo & Company was born. With a reputation for security well established, and contracts with steamship, stage, and riverboat lines across the West, Wells Fargo became the standard for shipping precious metals and eventually entered the banking business.

Recognizing the need for faster and more reliable mail service to the far West, Wells Fargo and the post office cooperated to form Southern Overland Mail Company (subsequently the Butterfield Line) to carry mail and passengers from the Mississippi River to San Francisco. The run took twenty days on a once-a-week schedule.

The Civil War disrupted mail service, which had to be rerouted to avoid the Confederate States, so the Southern Overland was sold to Majors Russell and

Waddell, who moved the line to their own Overland Route and operated it in conjunction with their Pony Express. The Pony Express riders cut the route time to seven days, but for heavily loaded stagecoaches, fourteen days was necessary. The coming of the transcontinental railroad and the adjacent telegraph line doomed the Pony Express, and stage lines gradually succumbed to the trains, while the express companies expanded and garnered great success.

When World War I began, the number of major express companies had dwindled to just seven, but they operated the largest fleet of horse-drawn vehicles in the United States, and employed 150,000 people and 30,000 delivery horses in 30,000 offices nationwide. Through the United States Railroad Administration, control of the industry passed to the government, which formed American Railway Express Company to administer the express business, beginning July 1, 1918.

Following the war, the federal government was obligated to return the business to its owners, but many offices had been closed and duplicate services eliminated. Employees had been transferred, accounting systems standardized, and like Humpty Dumpty, it couldn't be put together again, as it was before nationalization. Congress passed the Transportation Act of 1920, returning the American Railway Express Company to private ownership intact and serving the entire railroad industry through uniform contracts.

The railroads quickly realized it was to their advantage to control the express business, so on March 1, 1929, the assets of the company were purchased and the name changed to Railway Express Agency. The ubiquitous red-enameled diamond-shaped sign became a symbol of the standard of service to which other companies aspired —it was the UPS of its day.

As early as the 1920s, experiments had been made with air service for priority deliveries, and American Airway Express was formed as a division of American Railway Express. By the eve of World War II, 12,000 route miles (19,200 km) were in operation on six of the most important air routes in the country, serving eighty-five cities daily. Second-day service was guaranteed from New York to San Francisco and

Express business was very important to the railroads, and a common sight for many years was the express truck parked next to a baggage or express car for transfer of local packages so that the train could resume its journey quickly.

Los Angeles, as was overnight service to Chicago. Air Express was operated as a premium extra-fare service and it was common to see the familiar green REA truck plying the same route, just ahead or behind the Air Express truck, since the high prices charged for the service justified the duplication.

The economic surge of the 1950s kept the business profitable, but like the railroads, REA was not glamorous. It failed to attract the savvy young executives, and the fortunes of the company suffered as a result. By the 1960s, an increasing amount of express mail was being shipped in REA piggyback trailers, and a decreasing number of passenger trains was creating service gaps. The system was unraveling, and the onset of Amtrak in 1971, which eliminated

express service from all passenger runs, was the final blow, although the company managed to limp on for four more years.

REA sold off the railroad equipment, and the expanding United Parcel Service absorbed the express traffic. Amtrak's modern "material handling" (package express) cars run on the original trucks of the dismantled REA refrigerator cars. Many of the piggyback trailers continued to operate under the REA reporting marks *REAX* and *REAZ* for the Transamerica Corporation. REA, REALCO, Adams Express, American Express, and Wells Fargo continued in business for many years in various forms.

Thus the company that, in its heyday, operated over 190,000 miles (304,000 km) of railroad, 14,000 miles (22,400 km) of shipping lines, and 91,000 miles (145,600 km) of air routes with 17,000 trucks handling 300,000 daily shipments slipped into history. Whether it was perishable items like flowers, zoo animals, racehorses, pets, clothing, or very fragile and flammable nitrate-based movie film, Railway Express was the only reliable method of shipment. Until 1975, REA did it all and did it best!

Railway Post Office (RPO)

Transportation of the mail was once an important component of the operation of passenger trains, and in some countries it still is. The following details are based on practices in the United States, but the principles apply to railway mail handling around the world.

Congressional legislation of July 7, 1838, decreed that every railroad was a postal route. Railway mail cars were introduced in 1840, and by 1859, mail was being sorted en route in early railway post-office cars. All-steel mail cars were first built in 1888, and by 1891, the government had formulated regulations governing the design of postal cars, and all railroads were required to provide cars meeting the specifications of the United States Post Office.

RPO cars were in common use on most passenger trains by the early 1900s, and routes with heavy mail traffic, such as New York to Chicago, were plied by fast locomotives hauling solid trains of postal cars. Long-haul mainline trains usually included a full-length railway post-office car, where postal clerks sorted mail, and perhaps several more sealed cars devoted to storing presorted mail. Secondary trains frequently carried combination mail-baggage cars, with smaller railway post-office compartments.

Regulations demanded top priority for the mails, with heavy fines levied for violators of such rules as:

Mail was to be carried on the first section of all trains.

Mail was to be transferred first in the event of a wreck or other service interruption.

Mail was to be loaded first at all stations, before baggage, even if other head-end traffic was left behind for lack of space.

Mail was to be distributed and dispatched from terminals within eight hours of arrival, and delays were to be reported to the government.

Storage mail was moved in either regular baggage cars or special boxcars modified for passenger service. These cars were loaded, locked, sealed, and moved to their designated destinations, while RPO cars were literally a "post office on wheels."

The elements of a Railway Post Office changed little following the building of this early Chicago, Burlington & Quincy car. The pigeon-hole rack for sorting letters is on the rear wall; there is a stand-up desk at the right and heating stove on the left. The pipe running across the ceiling is to help support the clerks as they move around in the swaying car.

Mail was collected, canceled, and sorted on the moving train. At stations where the train stopped, customers could deposit mail in a slot on the car side.

At smaller stations, where the train didn't stop, picking up mail on the fly became possible with the invention of the standardized mail crane, which worked in conjunction with a car-mounted catcher. The mail was placed in a specially designed leather pouch, carefully arranged for equal weight in the two ends. A leather strap tightened around the middle forced the pouch into an hour-glass shape and the pouch was hung on the trackside mail crane. As the train approached, going as fast as 80 mph (128 kph), the mail clerk opened the sliding RPO door and extended out a long, side-mounted, U-shaped hook. When the hook impacted the mail pouch right on the leather strap, the combination of weight and momentum forced the pouch to fold over the hook and slide to a loop by the door, where the clerk could retrieve it. The mail sack to be dispatched for local delivery was simultaneously thrown or kicked from the car. Bystanders had to be careful to remain clear of the dispatch area, and the mail clerk had to make sure the sack was not sucked under the train and destroyed. The clerk then closed the door so work could begin again.

Safely aboard, the pouch was opened, and the contents checked for items destined for nearby towns. They were handled immediately. After stamping the cancellations, the items were sorted into the pouches or letter cases designated for their various destinations.

Security regulations required the postal cars to be locked at all times, and even the train crews did not have access. Therefore,

the RPO was usually the first occupied car after the locomotive, and postal clerks were required to carry firearms. The train's working baggage car usually followed the RPO, train crews needing access, and express refrigerators and mail storage cars were carried ahead of it since accessibility was not required.

Following World War II, the railroads began to modernize their crack passenger trains with new streamlined equipment. This meant putting the traditional regulation RPO appointments into car bodies matching the rest of the train. The new trains, unfortunately, were not enough to

Below, left: The postal clerk on a fast mail train had to be both sharp-eyed and agile. As the train roared past a mail station, he had to drop or kick the inbound mail sack onto the platform and simultaneously manipulate the side-mounted hook so as to pluck the outbound sack suspended from the trackside mail crane. Below: The design of the RPO car continued to develop into the era of the heavyweight passenger cars. Each sack in the racks is destined for a particular location, and it was the postal clerk's job to get the letters and packages sorted into the proper sacks as the car rocked and swayed at high speed.

The Railway Post Office (RPO) was important to the efficient delivery of the mail. The windows indicate the compartment where the clerks worked sorting letters. The right-hand door has a mail book for the retrieval of mail sacks on the fly.

save the passenger train in North America, and as passenger service declined, the post office began to transfer mail traffic to trucks and planes. While Amtrak and Via still carry a modest amount of postal traffic, even to the point of ordering new cars, the en route handling of the mail is no longer efficient, since much of the work is now heavily computerized and automated. The final American RPO run was carried by the Penn Central, itself created as a result of failure, on a New York to Washington trip, June 30, 1977.

RDC, the Budd Rail Diesel Car

The decline of the American passenger train was clear in the late 1940s. Attempts by several railroads to establish new premium passenger services were stillborn and an alternative to the traditional new train sets was necessary. The Budd Company, of Philadelphia, applied its passenger car construction experience to the old railroad standby, the "Doodle-bug," or self-propelled passenger car, which had been taking over on lightly traveled lines for several decades.

Budd sold the first RDC to New York Central on April 19, 1950. The design was made possible because of the advancements in diesel engines fostered by the war. General Motors had built 275-hp engines for use in tanks, and its layout was a relatively flat, 20-degree V, thus fitting nicely below the car floor. Maintenance was easily accomplished by switching in a new engine (in ninety minutes) and then making repairs on the old one.

The lightweight, fluted stainless steel RDCs were designed for a top speed of 83 mph (130 kph) and accelerated from 0 to 60 (96 kph) in two minutes. On a 1 percent grade, the top speed was 55 mph (88 kph), 40 mph (64 kph) at 2 percent, and 25 mph (40 kph) at 3 percent. The units were designed for a two-man crew: one operator, with a dead-man switch for emergencies, and a conductor. They looked very much like a Budd lightweight passenger car, with a large bulge (containing the cooling radiators) on the roof.

Slow initial sales were met with a heavy marketing effort by the Budd representa-

tives, who customized their approach for each railroad. The results were RDC services sporting such unique names as B-Liners, High Liners, Day Liners, Speed Liners, Shore Liners, and even Zephyrettes. The units were offered in five versions: RDC-1, the most popular, was a ninety-seat coach; RDC-2, a coach-baggage combination; RDC-3 offered a coach-baggage-railway post-office combination; RDC-4, the least popular model, was a combination baggage section and RPO, with no provision for passengers. The RDC-9, which was powered but had no controls, had to be coupled with another unit. This concept of multiple units with a single operator was an operational advantage and it was not uncommon to see "trains" of RDCs on more heavily traveled routes.

The units cost from $118,000 to $122,000 at first, with operation adding fifty-six cents per mile with a two-man crew. By 1956, however, the price of an RDC-1 was $151,950, a result of improvements such as larger wheels and an increase in horsepower to 300.

There were several experimental variations, including the Hot Rod, a five-unit train for the New Haven, with an F Unit streamlined nose and a top speed of 110 mph (166 kph). New York Central also experimented with high speed, mounting a streamlined pod containing two J47 jet engines on the roof of a single RDC and

adding a smooth shovel nose for lowered wind drag. Operating on a long straight section of track, the train reached speeds of 185 mph (296 kph), although further development was abandoned.

The final batch of twelve RDCs was delivered to the Reading Railroad in December 1962. These units were still in service on the British Columbia Railway in 1991. The waning of rail passenger service in the United States finally caught up with Budd, and the RDC merely prolonged the life of the passenger train, rather than save it. Many RDCs earned a second chance when they were sold to Cuba, Brazil, Saudi Arabia, and Australia.

RDCs sped passengers from Baltimore to Washington and Pittsburgh on the Baltimore & Ohio's Speed Liners, carried boxes of baby chicks to farmers in Arkansas on the Rock Island, or, crammed with commuters, rumbled into Boston on the Boston & Maine. They carried mail and packages to countless small communities across the country and the world. Once numbering 398, there are now just a dozen.

See also: *Budd Company; EMD; F Unit.*

The Budd Company took advantage of its experience building railroad passenger cars when it later built its highly successful RDCs. The self-propelled rail car, shown here crossing the Knife River in Minnesota, was typically used on lightly traveled lines.

One of the advantages of the RDCs was that they could be strung together in a train if traffic density warranted. A diesel engine in each unit meant that the power output was always matched to the load.

Simplon Tunnel

The first tunnel between Brig, Switzerland, and Iselle, Italy, was completed June 1, 1906, and was christened Simplon. It became the world's longest at 12 miles 537 yards (20 km), exceeding St. Gotthard Tunnel's 9 miles 562 yards (15 km), although it was only single-track. In 1922, the second Simplon bore was completed, at 22 yards (20 m) longer, providing for a second track. To avoid the exhaust problems of Gotthard, electric traction power was installed early on.

Below: An electrically powered train of the Swiss Federal Railways emerges from the second Simplon Tunnel. Opened in 1922, it paralleled the first bore (1906) and provided for a second track through the 12.5-mile (20 km) tunnel.

Stephenson, George (1781–1848)

Although he clearly did not invent the steam locomotive, Stephenson has been called "the Father of the Locomotive" because of the innovations developed under his direction. The son of an engineman at Wylam Colliery, Northumberland, George Stephenson went to work as a "plugman," tending the mine's steam pump and going to night school, a background very different from most of the well-to-do engineers of the day. He was entirely self-taught, but his character, perseverance, vision, attention to detail, and ability to make and keep friends helped earn him a reputation as a solid mechanic and colliery enginewright and were invaluable as his ideas matured.

In 1813, William Hedley's celebrated *Puffing Billy* came to Wylam, and

Above: George Stephenson, a steam-pump tender in his youth, parlayed a nightschool education and a natural mechanical aptitude into a career as a master engineer of railways that earned him the title "the Father of the Locomotive."

Stephenson saw a future for steam power that extended far beyond the trundling coal wagons along the Tyne. Having come to the attention of his first patron, Lord Ravenswood, owner of the Killingworth Colliery, Stephenson was given the financial backing necessary to build his first locomotive.

Blucher, built in 1814, was similar to *Puffing Billy* in that it was gear-driven and ran on smooth rail. It was named after the Prussian general who figured so prominently in the Battle of Waterloo just a year later. *Blucher* was not an outstanding success, but it helped Stephenson understand the complexities of a steam locomotive, and inspired his process of simplification and improvement a step at a time.

Stephenson was dissatisfied with *Blucher*'s noisy and unreliable gear drive, and, along with Ralph Dodds, a fellow Killingworth employee, he took out a patent on a gearless drive. Two cylinders drove separate axles through crankpins set 90 degrees apart, the axles being connected by a chain-and-sprocket arrangement. This became known as the Killingworth-type locomotive.

Further experimentation showed that a narrow chimney produced more draft and a hotter fire. Mounting the cylinders on top of the boiler simplified the drive, lessening the power loss. Connecting the driving wheels with connecting rods and crankpins became the standard until the end of steam. Stephenson also turned his attention to the rails, inventing the Stephenson and Losh rail, which had a half-lap joint, eliminating the wear and tear caused by butt joints.

A Quaker financier named Robert Pease was impressed by Stephenson and appointed him to the post of engineer for the Stockton & Darlington Railway, newly authorized by an act of Parliament. In this position, George was responsible for the complete construction of the world's first public railway. He managed the grading and track work, built the first iron railroad bridge and several stationary steam engines to rope-haul the carriages over two steep ridges, and generally performed in a manner far more sophisticated than his background or education would have indicated.

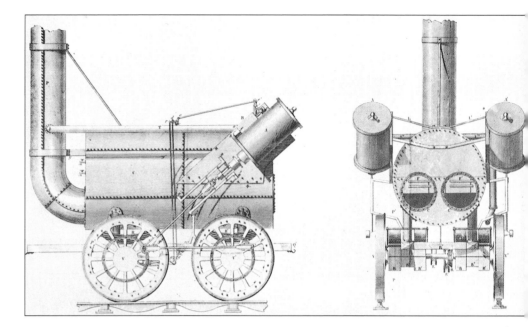

Above, top: The 0-4-0 Lancashire Witch, *built in 1829 for the Bolton & Leigh Railway by the Stephenson Works, advanced locomotive design by including two fireboxes with converging flues and inclined cylinders mounted high on the boiler.*

Above: Stephenson's Planet *continued the advance of steam locomotive design. The cylinders were placed under the smokebox and drove a cranked axle. The first Planet was built in 1830, and was still working on the Liverpool & Manchester ten years later. The name came to designate the locomotive type and many more were built, both as four-coupled and single-driver types, including* Pioneer, *shipped in 1836 to the Bangor & Piscataquis, in the United States.*

Above, top: Stephenson's locomotives continually evolved as new ideas developed. This 0-4-0 Planet, which was built for the Glasgow & Garnkirk Railway, used a wood and iron sandwich frame along with inclined inside cylinders that allowed the piston to clear the front axle as it drove the rear axle. *Above: Three of these 0-4-2 goods locomotives were built for the Stanhope & Tyne Railway in 1834. The sandwich frame was used once again, but the rear wheels provided support for a larger firebox, which in turn could provide more steam and therefore greater power.*

While Stephenson was building the Stockton & Darlington, Pease financed the Robert Stephenson Locomotive Works, at Newcastle-upon-Tyne, which was named for George's son and partner. Their first locomotive was *Locomotion*, which opened the Stockton & Darlington in 1825 and was a significant improvement over *Blucher*. Three additional locomotives for the railway followed: *Hope*, *Black Diamond*, and *Diligence*. They had several deficiencies, but Timothy Hackworth, appointed locomotive superintendent by his friend Stephenson, was a talented mechanic who made the necessary adjustments and repairs, and ultimately spurred many modifications and improvements.

Hackworth's assistance with the locomotives allowed Stephenson to pursue a much more difficult and ambitious project: the engineering of the 35-mile (56 km) Liverpool & Manchester Railway, a post to which professional engineers of the highest status had unsuccessfully aspired. The Rainhill Trials were established to select, by competition, the best locomotive design possible. Hackworth entered his own, *Sans Pareil*, formidable competition for Stephenson, but *Rocket* performed flawlessly and won the competition.

Many other locomotives came out of the works at Newcastle-upon-Tyne: the *Lancashire Witch* of 1829 moved the cylinders to the outside and inclined them; the *Northumbrian* of 1830 included a smoke box, with the stack on top of the boiler, an internal firebox with a fire-tube boiler, and a proper tender tank instead of a barrel over the coal pile; the *Planet* moved the cylinders inboard, under the boiler, and drove a cranked axle; the four-coupled Planet-type *Samson* was developed in 1831; and the single-driver Planet-type *Pioneer* of 1836 was exported to the Bangor & Piscataquis in the United States.

A major advance in locomotive design was the Liverpool & Manchester's 1834 *Patentee*, an elongated, single-driving-axle Planet-type, which had rigid leading and trailing wheels and horizontal inside cylinders. The wooden frame was now strengthened by iron plates—the sandwich frame—which was to persist, particularly on the Great Western Railway, for fifty years. The support of the trailing wheel allowed for a larger, more adequate firebox for better steaming. Thousands of the Patentee-types were built, many for export to Europe. *Der Adler* (Eagle) was built in 1835, for the first German public railway, which ran from Nürnberg to Fürth. Other Patentees were sent to the Netherlands, Russia, and Italy. The locomotives continued to evolve, and the Stephenson Works prospered for more than a century.

George Stephenson continued to consult on railway construction around the world, pioneering techniques in tunneling, bridges, and viaducts. The Liverpool & Manchester needed to cross Chat Moss, a 30-foot (9 m)-deep bog. Stephenson devised a floating raft of brush and heather to carry the track across. Another bog was filled with a thousand tons of rock and dirt. The cut through Olive Mount was 70 feet (21 m) deep in solid sandstone, and the Sankey Valley was spanned with a nine-arch masonry viaduct, the longest ever built at the time.

His hard work and organizational skills served Stephenson well until his death. He was the first of an emerging breed of millionaire-engineer, and was one of the instigators of the Industrial Revolution.

Stockton & Darlington Railway

The first public railway in the world was authorized by an act of Parliament and received the Royal Assent on April 19, 1821. The Stockton & Darlington was to be constructed in northeast England, between Stockton, Darlington, and the Bishop Auckland coalfields, in County Durham. It did not result from the concepts of a single man but was the culmination of experimental trial and error over many years: Ralph Allen's horse-drawn wooden rail tramway in 1733, Newcomen's steam-powered pumps, William Jessop's edge rail of 1789 laid on stone sleepers, James Watt's improvements in steam consumption, Richard Trevithic's

use of high pressure steam, and William Hedley's two-cylindered and geared *Puffing Billy* all contributed to the mix that was blended by George Stephenson.

Stephenson was a humble colliery mechanic, a background very much different from the upper-class experimenters of the day. His many skills brought him to the attention of Lord Ravensworth and Edward Pease. Lord Ravensworth, owner of the Killingworth colliery, was seeking greater efficiency in the coal mines to

North Eastern 1115, formerly Stockton & Darlington No. 115, is an example of Stephenson's "long-boiler" development in the 1850s. The short wheel base under such a long boiler resulted in an unsteady ride at high speed, but the inside-cylinder locomotive exhibits the beginnings of a rudimentary cab. Furthermore, the elegant wheel coverings and smooth styling resulted in what would become the hallmark of British steam.

afford him an alternative to farming his vast landholdings, and he provided the money for Stephenson's first locomotive. Nicholas Wood was an influential mining engineer who introduced Stephenson to Edward Pease, head of the Quaker coal barons of Darlington, who were contemplating the building of a railway.

Pease and Stephenson met on the very day the Darlington Railway Act was approved. The young engineer's vision and enthusiasm convinced Pease to hire him, and to accept the recommendations that at least a portion of the railway use steam locomotives, rather than the horses that had been decided upon earlier, and that iron rails replace the planned wooden tramway. More important, Pease agreed to finance the Robert Stephenson Locomotive Works, at Newcastle-upon-Tyne, named after George's son and partner.

The Stockton & Darlington Railway was conceived from the beginning as a coal hauler—passenger conveyance was included in the act, but was a minor point. The Old Etherly Colliery, just northwest

of Bishop Auckland, was 25 miles (40 km) from tidewater at Cottage Row, Stockton. Although the first 20 miles (32 km) inland were relatively level, two major ridges— the Etherly and the Brusselton—had to be crossed. The investors had planned a canal, which was determined to be too expensive. The grades over the two ridges were thought to be too steep for locomotives but not for stationary steam-engine-powered, rope-hauled, inclined planes, with the remainder of the line powered by horses.

As engineer, Stephenson inherited a completed survey, but it was his responsibility to verify the survey, carry out the construction of cuts, fills, bridges, drainage, and structures, and construct the loco-

The Locomotion *was an immediate success, its vertical cylinders and connecting rod–coupled wheels permitting a maximum speed of 12 mph (19.2 kph). Originally,* Locomotion *hauled coal trains.*

motives. Near St. Helens Auckland, across the river Gaunless, he built the world's first iron railway bridge—four elegant wrought-iron fishbelly girders, the sophistication of which belied his humble background. A portion of this Gaunless Viaduct survives on display at the National Railway Museum at York. The river Skerne was spanned by a massive single masonry arch, with graceful wing walls. Rather than use his own Stephenson and Losh patented half-lap joint rail, which would have been personally profitable, he specified the much longer rolled rail from Bedlington Ironworks, using his own rail for making up short lengths and at switch points.

Stephenson had anticipated locomotive power to be used for the level portion of the line, but when the Stockton & Darlington opened for business on September 27, 1825, only *Locomotion*, a variation of his own Killingworth-type, was available. Nonetheless, driven by George Stephenson, *Locomotion* was a triumph. A newspaper account of the grand opening reported: "The engine started off, drawing

six loaded wagons, a passenger carriage, and twenty-one trucks fitted with seats. Such was the velocity that in some parts the speed was twelve miles per hour [19 kph]. The number of passengers was counted to be 450, which with coals and other things, would amount to nearly thirty tons [27 t]. The engine and its load did the first journey of 8.75 miles [14 km] in five minutes over an hour."

Locomotion provided sufficient power for the coal traffic, but passengers were relegated to modified stagecoaches mounted on flanged wheels and pulled down the tracks by horses. Passenger coaches were leased to outside contractors, who supplied their own horses and paid tolls for track use. The steep grades were handled with the originally planned stationary steam engines and rope haulage.

To eliminate the troublesome chain and sprocket connection that kept the pairs of wheels in the proper relationship, Timothy Hackworth, a talented mechanic appointed locomotive superintendent by his friend Stephenson, connected the wheels on each side with a simple connecting rod; that device, which was first applied to *Locomotion*, became standard for the duration of steam power. Hackworth's main concern, however, was in the steaming qualities. The boilers produced insufficient steam for continuous running, and trains frequently had to stop and build up pressure.

Hackworth built a much larger locomotive, with three pairs of wheels coupled together and a boiler with a U-shaped flue; the firebox was at the front, along with the fireman and coal tender. The driver remained in the rear with a water tender. The Royal George went into service in November 1827. A great success, it saved the day for the Stockton & Darlington, which became quite profitable and attracted attention from investors in Europe and America.

George Stephenson's association with the first public steam railway in the world assured his place in history, and sent him to the much more ambitious Liverpool & Manchester Railway to continue his work. The era of modern transportation had begun.

See also: *Hackworth, Timothy; Stephenson, George.*

Above, top: In the nineteenth century, laying the tracks for a new railway was a gala event, and a large crowd has gathered to celebrate the beginning of operations on Stephenson's Stockton & Darlington in

Stockton-on-Tees in 1825. In the early days of the locomotive, passengers were carried in horse drawn carriages that were fitted with flanged wheels.

Stoney Creek Bridge

The Canadian Pacific Railway encountered the gorge of Stoney Creek 4 miles (6.4 km) east of Connaught Tunnel, in the Rocky Mountains. Two wooden Howe trusses with 200-foot (60 m) spans and a single one of 100 feet (30 m) supported by tall wooden towers were constructed in 1886 to accommodate what would be the tallest wooden bridge in the world.

In 1893, the bridge was replaced with a steel arch span, designed by H. E. Vautelet and erected by the Hamilton (Ontario) Bridge Company, without stopping traffic. Similar to Alexandre Gustave Eiffel's great Garabit Viaduct in France, it was a parallel double-chorded arch, although it differed in having the hinge pins in the bottom chord. The bridge was reinforced in 1929, with an additional set of arches on the sides and new girders. The bridge deck rises 307 feet (93.6 m) above the gorge.

Streamlined Steam Locomotives

The 1930s saw a revolution in principles of industrial design. Previous ideas regarding applied ornamentation and historical influence were pushed aside, and the age of spare clean lines, "form follows function" —streamlining—was born, influencing the aesthetic of all kinds of vehicles, including steam locomotives. While English builders had, from the earliest days, taken the visual aspects of all machinery design far beyond functionalism, American locomotives had been simply a tool. The basic form had to accommodate the horizontal cylinder of the boiler perched atop the wheels; a pilot or footboards on the front, a cab to keep the crew dry, and a container for carrying fuel and water; air pumps, steam dome, sand box, and piping hung on the boiler at appropriate locations. The headlight

was perched at the front. The only real aesthetic decisions were which side of the boiler to hang the air pumps; whether to put the headlight up high on the boiler, or centered on the smoke box; and how many windows to give the cab. The color, of course, was black.

The color scheme began to change when the Pennsylvania Railroad hired a young designer named Raymond Loewy to clean up the design of their new GG1 electric locomotive. Loewy smoothed the contours and convinced the skeptical Pennsy to weld the bodies, eliminating the rivets. His paint design used five thin gold "cat whisker" stripes to accent the sleek, almost black, Brunswick green lines of the elegant locomotive.

In early 1934, the Union Pacific sent its brand-new streamliner M-10000 diesel train set on tour and, in May, the Burlington's Pioneer Zephyr made its non-stop demonstration run from Denver to the Century of Progress Exhibition in Chicago. The Age of Streamlining had arrived for the railroads of North America, and the railroads looked at their investment in steam power and knew they had to act.

The New York Central acted first, sending three-year-old Alco J-1e Hudson to their West Albany shops. The 4-6-4 emerged in December 1934 as the Commodore Vanderbilt, America's first streamlined steam locomotive. Cleveland's Case School of Science, under the guidance of Norman F. Zapf, designed the jet black with silver trim shroud inspired by the Burlington's diesel-powered Zephyr.

Immediately following Commodore Vanderbilt, the New York Central looked to another designer, Henry Dreyfuss, to modernize one of two 4-6-2 Pacifics for service on their Cleveland-Detroit Mercury. He applied a somewhat similar "bathtub" shroud, but included "white-wall tires" on the drivers. Now in a race with the Pennsylvania Railroad for passengers on the highly competitive New York to Chicago route, the New York Central again commissioned Dreyfuss to design new equipment for the Twentieth Century Limited, and he produced one of the finest complete trains yet seen and set the direction for later designs. Its "bullet" nose, smooth skyline casing, rounded edges on the tenders, and elegant two-tone gray

The Commodore Vanderbilt *became America's first streamlined steam locomotive, when the newly shrouded New York Central 4-6-4 Hudson was unveiled on November 24, 1934. Named for the railroad's founder, the locomotive was expected to use less fuel because of lowered wind resistance.*

Above: The conservative management of the Pennsylvania, "The Standard Railroad of the World," was most reluctant to join the streamlining club. Pennsylvania relented with No. 3768, a K-4 Pacific used on the redesigned Broadway Limited of 1938. Industrial designer Raymond Loewy was responsible for the "rocket ship" styling; but when four more K-4s were shrouded in 1940, the design had been simplified.

Above: The penchant for streamlining during the 1930s was by no means limited to the United States; this English 4-6-0, the King Henry VII, was streamlined secretly by the Great Western Railway at their Swindon works and unveiled in 1935.

with silver striping paint scheme was an instant success.

Rival Pennsy returned to its favorite designer (and Dreyfuss' arch rival), Raymond Loewy, for its remodeled Broadway Limited, the flagship of its highly touted "Fleet of Modernism." Often playing second fiddle to the New York Central, it had to supplement some new equipment with renovated cars. Loewy had shrouded one of the Pennsy's faithful K-4 Pacifics in 1936. It was given a skyline casing, a bullet nose, a skirt that ran from the running boards down so low the bottom was aligned with the lower tender edge, and the old reliable "Buck Rogers" fins.

While Loewy's style was considered to be much improved on the brand-new "shark-nosed" T-1 of 1942, and Dreyfuss returned to the "inverted bathtub" with the *James Whitcomb Riley*, Otto Kuhler, who originally styled the Milwaukee road Hiawathas in the "bathtub" style, switched to the "Buck Rogers" motif for the Lehigh Valley. Miss Olive Dennis, the first female civil engineer on the Baltimore & Ohio staff,

Above: Southern Pacific's Daylight, as represented by restored GS-4 4449, has been called "the world's most beautiful train." The simply shrouded 4-8-4s were streamlined for the San Francisco to Los

Angeles Daylight, a lightweight passenger train that made the trip in the daytime. An alternate train, the Lark (painted gray), made the trip at night.

provided a shroud of restrained elegance for the P-7d Pacifics used to power the Cincinnatian, but many railroads' homegrown designs bordered on the ludicrous. The sheet metal wings running from nose to cab along the running boards of several classes of Lackawanna power are generally looked upon as an embarrassment today.

European-style "elephant ear" smoke deflectors were tried by the Union Pacific and the Delaware & Hudson, but most railroads that made the attempt went for the "inverted bathtub" or the "bullet nose," skyline casing and running-board skirts. The magnificent orange, red, and black Daylight 4-8-4s of the Southern Pacific and the glossy-black-with-red-band locomotives of the Norfolk & Western are generally considered to be among the most handsome examples. Some other railroads preferred to finish the locomotives with fluted stainless steel, which matched their new lightweight consists.

Streamlined steam was not unique to North America. German railways experimented with streamlining, beginning with smoke deflectors. German State Railways 05.001, one of two experimental high-speed 4-6-4s built by Borsig of Berlin in 1935, was completely enclosed in a smooth sheet metal shroud, from the top

Below: The Lehigh Valley's Black Diamond rolls through Easton, Pennsylvania, behind the "Buck Rogers"–styled 4-6-2 Pacific No. 2089 in the summer of 1941. Despite the effort to unify the differing car styles with paint in this "low-budget streamliner," the second car is clearly an interloper.

Above: The Germans took streamlining very seriously, as evidenced by No. 031010, photographed just before the outbreak of World War II. Not satisfied with simply smoothing over the appliances, the designers made several changes: the bathtub shroud flares over the walkway; the headlights have been moved to the pilot; and the unusual smoke lifters are graded into the boiler.

of the boiler to a few inches above the rail; they were three-cylinder simple, with 7-foot 6 1/2-inch (2.3 m) drivers and a boiler pressure of 284 pounds per square inch. With a light test train that included a dynamometer car, the 05.001 reached a speed of 125 1/2 mph (200.8 kph), a world speed record for steam.

The British, despite the simple elegance of their traditional locomotive design, built the Coronation Scot with full shrouding, and it hit 114 mph (182 kph). The Silver Fox of 1935 had an "inverted bathtub" shroud; the Bullied-designed Pacifics of 1941 were given the full treatment, includ-

ing smoke lifters and skyline casing; but by the time *Evening Star*, the final British steamer, was built, styling was simplified to smoke lifters and a light running board skirt. Australia produced a number of handsome designs, a fine example being a 5-foot 3-inch-gauge 4-8-4, the shark-nosed *Sir Malcom Barclay-Harvey* of the South Australia Railways.

Applied streamlining generally disappeared during World War II, as difficulties with maintenance access combined with scrap drives relegated extraneous pieces of sheet metal to the war effort. The controversy surrounding the entire concept of

covering an honest piece of machinery with visually appealing "clothing" remains to this day, although the streamlining did contribute to several speed records. The coming of the diesel to the named passenger trains in the United States and the electrification of European trains ended the experiment, although single examples of both Norfolk & Western and Southern Pacific 4-8-4s are currently operating in limited excursion service in the United States, and a Canadian Pacific Royal Hudson still runs on special occasions in Canada. Many other examples have been preserved in museums around the world.

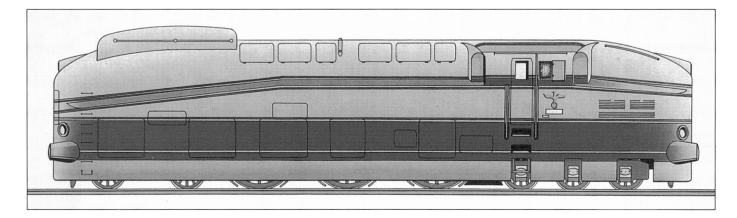

Above: In 1938, von Henschel & Sohn built a streamlined 4-6-6 (2-C-3) three-cylinder steam locomotive intended for high-speed passenger service on the Deutsche Reichsbahn. The driving-wheel diameter of almost 7 feet 6 inches (2.3 m) made speeds of 105 mph (168 kph) possible.

Above: British designers had always been more inclined toward smooth lines and modest ornamentation than toward functional form, and they too fell victim to the streamlining craze. W.A. Stanier of the LMS produced the blue and silver

Coronation Scot for the London to Glasgow route—401 miles (642 km) in six and a half hours. Below: The Alco PA, painted in Santa Fe's red, yellow, and silver "war bonnet" scheme, is generally acknowledged as the high point of diesel locomotive

aesthetics. Here, a classic A-B-B-A matched set of PAs leads one of the AT&SF's first-class passenger trains across Arroyo Seco trestle, near Pasadena, California, a few minutes out of Los Angeles.

Sydney Harbor Bridge

While not strictly a railroad structure, the world's longest steel arch has a span of 1,650 feet (503 m). Two railway tracks (originally four) are carried in addition to a highway, a footway, and cycle paths. Opened in New South Wales, Australia, in 1932, the bridge is 170 feet (52 m) above the water.

Tay Bridge Disaster

As the growing rail system stretched north into Scotland, two great barriers, the wide estuaries of the Firth of Forth and the Firth of Tay, 40 miles (64 km) farther north, blocked the direct route from Edinburgh to Dundee and Aberdeen. The Forth was first bridged at Stirling, where it narrowed to a river, but a long detour west was required before the Tay and Forth could be crossed.

A great competition was brewing between the east and west coast routes to the popular vacation destinations of the Scottish Highlands, and the Tay detour via Perth was causing enough delay to negate the otherwise inherent advantage of the eastern line—and in the growing competition for holiday traffic, speed was everything. Ferries transferred passengers across the firths for a time, but to the North British Railway, it was obvious that the Tay would have to be bridged.

Engineer Thomas Bouch produced a design for a very tall and slender cast- and wrought-iron viaduct that would carry the North British Line directly into Dundee. The 2-mile (3.2 km)-long bridge was completed by the contractor, Hopkins, Gilkes

Right, top: Sydney Harbor Bridge, the largest steel arch ever built, dominates the harbor as it soars over the fleet of sailboats and the concrete sails of the landmark opera house. Right: This is a view of the north end of the Tay Bridge following the collapse.

and Company, and opened for passenger traffic on June 1, 1878. Queen Victoria rode over the Tay Bridge on her way to Balmoral, and shortly after, she knighted Thomas Bouch.

Unfortunately, the design was not particularly skillful—in fact, Bouch calculated the lateral wind loading at just 10 pounds per square foot, which was hopelessly inadequate. To compound matters, the workmanship was poor, and the quality of the cast-iron columns was deplorable.

On the night of December 28, 1879, during a fierce gale, the North British Railway Edinburgh Mail from Burntisland to Dundee crept slowly across the firth behind 4-4-0 No. 224. The high girders forming the center of the bridge swayed and then began to tear apart. The entire train, carrying seventy-five passengers, plunged into the stormy water. There were no survivors of the first railway disaster.

A long inquiry led to the discovery of the design and construction inadequacies, and Sir Thomas Bouch was disgraced. He had already produced a twin-span suspension design for the Forth bridge, and construction contracts had been signed. These contracts were immediately canceled, the design responsibility was transferred to John Fowler, and Bouch—his reputation in as great a ruin as his bridge—went into seclusion. Mentally and physically broken, Sir Thomas Bouch died in 1880.

Stirling of Kippendavie, chairman of the North British Railway, exhibited great courage in immediately contracting the engineers W. H. Barlow and his son Crawford to redesign the bridge. Their admirably solid two-track structure was completed in 1887 and still carries fast trains to the Highlands.

See also: *Firth of Forth Bridge; Stoney Creek Bridge; Sydney Harbor Bridge.*

Divers search the wreckage of the Tay Bridge for the submerged passenger train that was lost in the previous night's collapse. The spindly towers and faulty cast-iron columns were no match for the severe winds that destroyed the bridge.

TAY BRIDGE

Patrick Matthew, known as "the seer of Gourdie," is credited with predicting the disaster when he said:

"In the case of accident with a heavy train on the bridge, the whole of the passengers will be killed. The eels will come out to gloat over in delight the horrible wreck and banquet."

Ten-wheeler-type Locomotive

The first 4-6-0 (ten-wheeler) was built by the Norris Brothers and delivered to the Philadelphia & Reading Railroad in 1847. Named *Chesapeake*, this locomotive was matched by the Boston & Maine's *New Hampshire*, completed almost at the same time by Holmes Hinkley (1793–1866).

Thomas Viaduct

The oldest stone viaduct in the United States, the Thomas Viaduct's eight arches carry the Baltimore & Ohio across the Patapsco River in Maryland. It was completed on July 4, 1835. Each granite elliptical arch spans 58 feet (17.7 m), for a total

of 617 feet (188 m), rising 60 feet (18.3 m) above the river. Designed by Benjamin Henry Latrobe (1806–1878), architect of the Capitol, it is still used by CSX.

Below: The magnificent Thomas Viaduct, located near Relay, Maryland, still carries the heavy traffic of CSX Transportation into Washington, D.C., even though the stone structure is over 150 years old. Below, bottom: Great Northern No. 650 exhibits the characteristic bulge in front of the cab of the Belpaire boiler that was more commonly associated with the Pennsylvania Railroad. This stylish ten-wheeler passenger locomotive was a product of the Brooks Works.

Thurmond, West Virginia

Typical of many towns around the world that grew to prominence in conjunction with an adjacent railroad, was Thurmond, West Virginia. The town was founded by a Confederate officer named Thurmond, who returned home after the Civil War to find that his neighbors had been so offended by his allegiance to the South that they had burned down his house. When he rebuilt, it was burned again. With considerable bitterness, he moved to land he had obtained alongside the bottom of the isolated deep gorge formed by the New River.

When the Chesapeake & Ohio (C&O) Railroad came through, he founded the town of Thurmond, where alcohol and gambling were prohibited, and access was only by rail. The town grew into an important rail center, the locus of numerous important coal branches. The immense amount of coal coming into the marshaling yard and sent east meant that Thurmond shipped more tonnage than either Cincinnati, Ohio, or Richmond, Virginia; three banks faced the C&O main line, which substituted for a street.

Because of the Thurmond prohibition, headquarters for drinking and gambling were in Glen Jean, just across the C&O bridge over the New River. The Glen Jean Hotel became famous as a resort destination, and was the site of the longest continuous poker game, which ran for fourteen years, as shift workers rotated into the chairs. Many a winner did not make it back across the bridge after midnight. A body was found floating in the river one

morning, and the town sheriff, having discovered a pistol and fifty dollars in the unfortunate victim's pockets, quickly judged the man guilty of carrying an illegal weapon, fined him fifty dollars, confiscated both the money and the pistol, and had the body buried at county expense.

Today, the coal mines are closed and Thurmond is all but a ghost town, with only the rafters running the New River rapids, and C&O Railroad maintenance workers regularly visiting. The Glen Jean Hotel burned down before the depression, and all of the businesses are gone. A few houses are still occupied on the hill above town and a narrow winding road connects Thurmond with civilization at the top of the gorge. The gorge has been included in a new federal reserve, and there are plans to preserve Thurmond as a historical resource.

Trans-Australia Railway

In 1905, when Sir John Forrest, the Western Australian member for Swan in the five-year-old Commonwealth government, first raised the suggestion of a railway connection between Western Australia and the eastern states, the local populace was skeptical. "What's a million?" was his reply to a heckler's estimate of the cost.

Forrest was one of the few men in the new country to fully understand what was involved in crossing nearly 1,060 miles (1,700 km) of desert between Kalgoorlie and Port Augusta, South Australia. In 1854, during his days as an explorer, he and six others spent five months walking across the continent. As premier of Western Australia, he led the colony into the new nation on the promise of a railway connection, and now he wanted the promise fulfilled—whatever the cost.

The concept of one-point perspective is clearly illustrated on the Nullarbor Plains. The world's longest stretch of straight track runs 285 miles (456 km) on the Port Augusta to Kalgoorlie Line, east of Cook, West Australia.

Work started in 1908 when two survey parties began a year-long project to define the route, one party leaving from Port Augusta and the other from Kalgoorlie. The ease of working in open country was more than offset by the inhospitable desert —there were no running streams along the entire route, and no potable water outside of a few wells in the easternmost 250 miles (400 km).

Construction did not present any major engineering obstacles, but the supply problems were immense. There was no timber

for sleepers (ties) and no water, game, or shelter for the workers, who had to be brought in, as there was no local labor. Camels were used to carry the supplies from the two end points to the work sites, and some wells were successfully drilled, which minimized water hauling.

Once construction began, the line advanced quickly until material shortages caused by World War I slowed progress in 1914. Not having much in the way of mechanized earth-moving equipment, an army of navvies worked with pick and shovel, wheelbarrows, and horse-drawn scoops to push the line across the vast, dry plain. There was an occasional steam shovel for the major works and a few motorized tractors later on; then, for the first time in Australia, track-laying machines were used to put down 2 1/2 miles (4 km) of track per day.

The navvies lived in tents, and the quarters moved with the railhead. For those who brought their families, a tea and sugar train carried supplies for their use, and if it arrived in the night, a whistle blast startled the families into scurrying for their supply allotment. The single men lived commu-

Left, top: The early days of railroad construction required great physical effort. On the Trans-Australia, the navvies struggled with primitive tools to build the roadbed, which had to not only closely match the designed grades and curves, but be stable enough to carry the weight of loaded trains and drain water away. Left, middle: The rough wooden ties (sleepers) were placed by hand on the graded roadbed, then the steel rails were set on the ties and gauged, and finally the spikes driven in by men with heavy mauls. Left, bottom: The line ran through the desolate wilderness of the Australian outback, where there were no trees, game, or water to be found along much of the route. Everything needed by the navvies had to be brought in at great expense. Construction materials, food, and water were hauled great distances, and where the railroad was not complete enough for train use, camels were pressed into service.

nally in canvas boardinghouses, boozing, brawling, and gambling their way across the desert.

The job involved 2½ million sleepers and 140,000 tons (126,000 t) of 80-pound (36 kg) rail, and maintained a ruling grade of 1 in 100, with a short stretch of 1 in 80. The line included the world's longest stretch of straight track, 285 miles (475 km); from a point between Ooldea and Watson to a point between Loongana and Nurina, there is not the slightest bend. Fortunately, standard gauge of 4 feet 8½ inches was chosen for this railway, which was not the case in many parts of Australia.

The rails from the east and the west were joined on October 17, 1917, but the ongoing war eliminated any formal ceremony. Sir John Forrest rode the first train over the line, crossing the desert in three days, rather than the five months it had taken him on foot. The cost, however, was well in excess of the million at which he scoffed, the final tally being more than over £5 million.

Transcontinental Railroad (USA)

It was not long after the initial operations of the early American railroads along the eastern seaboard that talk began of a rail link to the Pacific Ocean. In 1832, Dr. Hartwell Carver, of Rochester, New York, began advocating a line to run west from Lake Michigan to Oregon. The wilderness west of the Mississippi seemed like an overwhelming obstacle at the time.

In 1844, a New York merchant in the China trade named Asa Whitney promoted the idea of selling government land to pay for a railroad. His proposed sale of 77,952,000 acres (31.5 million ha) of land at sixteen cents per acre would finance a line on a similar route. His extensive travels and persistence convinced legislatures in seventeen states to support this scheme, but Senator Thomas Hart Benton, of Missouri (a key state), was opposed. Benton preferred a government-owned line with an eastern terminus in St. Louis, on the Mississippi, and used his influence in

The original inhabitants of the Great Plains were concerned by the intrusion of the "iron horse" and the white hunters who gathered the vast amounts of wild game needed to feed the construction workers. The railroaders and soldiers here are fighting off one of the frequent attacks.

Congress to back railroad experts, who attacked the Whitney plan as not feasible. Congress tabled the proposal, and the promoter turned his attentions north to a Canadian transcontinental proposal, another unsuccessful venture.

Whitney did succeed in creating excitement about the idea of a Pacific railway, and other plans evolved. Benton arranged for a survey to ascertain the western topography. John C. Fremont ("the Pathfinder"), a renowned scout who was married to Benton's daughter, was chosen to lead the expedition. Fremont left St. Louis in 1848, following a route along the 38th parallel toward San Francisco. The expedition ended in disaster, with no definitive data and the deaths of ten men. Benton was convinced of this route and proposed that Congress set aside a 100-mile (160 km) strip of land along the 38th parallel for a government-owned "central national highway." Other routes were also proposed. The army favored a route along the Southern Trail to facilitate quick troop movements between Texas and California. Some favored the well-known covered wagon route, the Emigrant Trail, that passed through the Platte Valley and crossed the Continental Divide at South Pass, before splitting to Oregon or California.

With support growing, Congress authorized a survey of the most likely routes for a Pacific railroad in 1853. Responsibility was assigned to Jefferson Davis, secretary of war, who quite naturally favored a southern route, but eliminated it from the list of surveys in an attempt to conceal his preference. He hoped that the other routes would prove unfeasible, leaving only the Southern Trail as a viable alternative. Skeptics insisted, so the final survey assignment was as follows:

Great Lakes to Puget Sound, between the 49th and 47th parallels (the Northern Trail)—Isaac S. Stevens.

West from Omaha, through the Platte Valley (Emigrant Trail)—Grenville M. Dodge.

St. Louis westward, along the 38th parallel (Benton's Buffalo Trail)—John W. Gunnison.

Fort Smith, Arkansas, west, along the 35th parallel to Albuquerque, then through the Mojave Desert to California—Ameil Whipple.

El Paso west, along the Mexican border breaking south of the Gila River (Southern Trail)—John Pope and J. G. Parke.

Only ten months were allowed for the work, not enough for anything but a rough survey, but Davis received the reports in time. Even though much of the southern route passed through Mexican territory, it was no surprise that Davis selected it. James Gadsden was sent to Mexico to buy the land needed for the route (the Gadsden Purchase), but the outbreak of the Civil War doomed the Southern Trail route.

An early map of the Overland Route promotes the tourist value of train travel along what was the first transcontinental railroad (although it began at the Missouri River). The Central Pacific became the Southern Pacific and built another line across the southern states, the Sunset Route. *The transcontinental lines of other railroads have been conveniently omitted by the SP and Union Pacific. In addition to the obligatory reference to "cowboys and Indians," the other native resident of the Great Plains, the buffalo (bison), is featured. Major scenic treats, such as the Buttes, Devil's Slide, and Pulpit Rock of western Wyoming; Ogden Canyon and the Great Salt Lake of Utah; and Lake Tahoe in California, are natural attractions along the route. Man-made points of interest include the rail crossing of the Great Salt Lake and the Truckee-Carson Dam, as well as the cities that can be visited along the line. Attracting patronage with this type of advertising was common during the golden era of passenger trains, as was the habit of omitting alternate routes and connections that might divert business to competing railroads.*

Meanwhile, in 1854, a surveyor for the Sacramento Valley Railroad was laying out a 22-mile (35 km) line east from Sacramento to the western slope of the Sierra Nevadas. Theodore Judah was convinced that this line could become a leg of the transcontinental railroad and published a pamphlet, *A Practical Plan for Building the Pacific Railroad*, which was very critical of earlier surveys. Judah made several trips east to lobby for his plan, but the government's attention was focused on the impending war. Judah returned west, and with the help of Daniel (Doc) Strong, a Dutch Flat Pharmacist, spent the early 1860s verifying the potential routes through the Sierras. They made maps, drew up articles of association, and sought investors for their Pacific railroad. The prominent Sacramento merchants Leland Stanford, Mark Hopkins, Collis P. Huntington, and Charles Crocker, known collectively as "The Big Four," formed the core of the group committed to Judah's plan.

Back in Washington, concern grew that California, isolated from the east, might be lost to the Confederacy, and the matter of a transcontinental rail link became very important to the Union. The Pacific Railroad Act of 1862 was passed by Congress to provide critical financing for the project's continuation. With Jefferson Davis gone to the Confederacy, a northern passage became prudent, and the Emigrant Trail route, surveyed by Grenville Dodge, was chosen as the way west from the Mississippi. The act provided that two railroads would proceed with the construction. The Union Pacific, under Thomas Durant of the Rock Island, would begin at Omaha and build west—the Central Pacific and the Big Four would build east from Sacramento. Land grants of alternate sections 10 miles (16 km) wide along the right-of-way were to be deeded to the railroads for each mile of track built. A loan of $16,000 was to be granted for each completed mile on the plains; $32,000 and $48,000 for each mile on the Great Basin and the mountains (both Rockies and Sierras), respectively. This money proved totally inadequate.

Judah became frustrated when the Big Four decided to stop construction in Nevada until there were sufficient customers to provide some traffic and income. He traveled east to seek financial backing to buy out his investors, but contracted a fever crossing Panama and died.

Grenville Dodge had his own problems with the Union Pacific. Having resigned from the army to become the Union Pacific's chief engineer, he found that management wanted to complete as much track as possible, no matter how far it deviated from a direct route or how poorly engineered, to maximize the government funding. Dodge insisted that the line be built more slowly, substantially, and directly so as to be more efficient and long-lasting. General Ulysses S. Grant sided with Dodge, ending the dispute.

Both railroads were in serious financial difficulty from the beginning, as the venture was much too speculative for most potential investors. Why risk capital in the Pacific Railroad when so much fast and easy profit could be made at little risk from war contracts? The Big Four had to pay for the ground breaking out of their own pockets before the California legislature could be persuaded to grant $10,000 per mile for track laid within the state. An initial grant of $600,000 was delayed when it became embroiled in litigation. A carefully crafted geological report that set the base of the Sierras much closer to Sacramento than what might normally have been assumed was used to secure an extra $1 million in federal funds.

The Union Pacific suffered similarly. Charter provisions made it necessary to raise $2 million from stock sales before construction could begin, a problem that was not solved until Durant offered to put up 10 percent of the cost as a loan to any buyer. But money remained in short supply.

Huntington and Durant traveled to Washington and managed to cajole, lobby, and bribe their way to a revision to the Railway Act of 1862. The Railway Act of 1864 doubled the land grants to 20 square miles (52 sq km) in alternate sections for each mile of track, and allowed for two-thirds of the cash loans to be granted in advance of construction.

The Central Pacific had built 31 miles (50 km) toward the east by June of 1864, but the Union Pacific was still within the city limits of Omaha. President Lincoln grew increasingly frustrated by the lack of progress and turned to millionaire Congressman Oakes Ames for help. Ames and some of his wealthy Bostonian friends invested over $1 million into Credit Mobilier, a company formed by Durant and wily financier Charles Francis Train. The supposed purpose of the new company was to sell the stock and award materials and labor contracts for the Union Pacific, but Credit Mobilier became a corrupt base for a few individuals to accumulate great wealth through the contracts, kickbacks, and other schemes, even as it provided the thrust for the Union Pacific to begin moving west. The Central Pacific created the Contract and Finance Company to serve a similar purpose (in both senses), making the Big Four and their close associates very wealthy men.

This camp of the Central Pacific, at Victory, Utah, is along the section where workers completed 10 miles (16 km) of track in a single day. The bearded man on the flat car is J. H. Strobridge, superintendent of the crew that accomplished the feat—a construction record that still stands.

"The Devil must have combed Hell to find them and to Hell they will, of course, return after graduating from Cheyenne!"
—*Comments of a visitor to Cheyenne after Hell on Wheels— Union Pacific's mobile track headquarters—had arrived in the newly created Wyoming town.*

Once begun, the Union Pacific made quick progress across the plains, despite Indian resistance to the intrusion into their ancestral hunting grounds. The track gangs, recruited from Irish immigrants, Civil War veterans from both sides, and former convicts, managed to complete 105 miles (165 km) in 1866; 240 miles (384 km) in 1867; 275 miles (440 km) in 1868; and 380 miles (608 km) in 1869. Scarcity of labor in the West caused Crocker to import Chinese immigrants, and by 1867, some 6,000 were toiling in the Sierras. Despite severe engineering and construction difficulties, the crews were through the mountains and racing across the Nevada desert by 1868.

The rivalry for both prestige and the distance-based subsidies meant that both sides raced to maximize their own mileage, actually grading miles of parallel lines a hundred feet (30 m) apart in opposite directions. On April 10, 1869, a compromise meeting point was established by Congress at Promontory, Utah.

On April 18, 1869, in the barren desert of Utah, the Central Pacific laid 10 miles (16 km) of track in a single day, setting a record that was never broken. A crew of eight men, rejecting a relief crew at noon, handled 3,500 lengths of 56-pound (25 kg) rail, weighing a total of 1,000 tons (900 t). Other members of the crew placed 25,800 ties, 55,000 spikes, 7,040 line poles, and 14,080 bolts—4,362,000 pounds (1,975,000 kg) in all. The actual measured distance, verified by officials of the rival Union Pacific, was 10 miles 200 feet (16

The driving of the final spike in the transcontinental railroad was an event of such importance that it was covered by photographers and telegraphers. The two locomotives are touching pilots to the cheers of crews from both the Central Pacific and the Union Pacific. Note the bottle passing between hands in the center; the officers of the Central Pacific were so offended by this scene that they commissioned a large but inaccurate painting that depicted ladies with parasols and a parson in the assembly.

km). The attempt was timed for when the two railheads were too close together for the UP to break the record, allowing Charles Crocker to collect on a $10,000 bet with Thomas C. Durant.

A great celebration was held on May 10, 1869, when the Union Pacific's No. 119 approached from the east, and *Jupiter*, of the Central Pacific, steamed in from the west. Brief remarks were made by Leland Stanford, now governor of California, and General Dodge. The final tie, of polished California laurel bearing an engraved silver plate, was placed under the rails and four spikes—two of silver and two of gold—were presented. Stanford stood on the north side and Durant on the south and drove the last spikes with silver hammers. The telegrapher signaled "done" and the two locomotives moved forward until the pilots touched. The transcontinental railroad was complete, setting off wild celebrations from San Francisco to New York. The Union Pacific had been credited with 1,038 miles (1,660 km) and the Central Pacific 742 miles (1,187 km).

*The locomotive **Jupiter** of the Central Pacific is a replica built for the centennial of the golden spike.*

The workers quickly dispersed, some joining the railroads' work forces, others moving on to new projects as the other proposed routes were also eventually covered by rail. A concrete monument marks the spot at Promontory, but the trains of the Southern Pacific now bypass the spot following construction of the Lucin Cutoff across the Great Salt Lake. The National Park Service has built replicas of the historic locomotives and operates them for tourists.

Trans-Europe Express (TEE)

One of the more amazing European railway accomplishments, the result of magic as much political as technical, are the border-crossing TEE trains of western Europe. Although some TEEs operate entirely in one country, many are international, overcoming electric power and gauge changes at borders and offering fast first-class service between important population centers on a schedule that competes with air travel. The umbrella rail organization Union Interna-

tional des Chemins de Fer, to which any European railway may belong, has been important in maintaining physical compatibility and political practicality throughout the European rail system.

TEE trains may be diesel-electric powered or draw electricity from an overhead wire, but several tricks were required to allow electric locomotives to draw power from the various supply systems across the continent. The power in Germany and Switzerland is delivered at 15,000 volts $16^2/_3$ cycles; in northern France at 25,000 volts 50 cycles; in Italy and Belgium at 3,000 volts DC; and the Netherlands and southern and central France at 1,500 volts DC. The Etoile du Nord TEE locomotives carried four pantographs, one for each electric system. When cruising through Belgium under 3,000-volt catenary, the pantograph would be lowered when approaching the French frontier. Coasting across the border at 70 mph (112 kph), the 25,000-volt pantograph was raised, and after confirmation of contact with the correct pantograph, the throttle was

Last-spike ceremonies were de rigueur, and this group has gathered on a temporary bridge to drive the last spike in the Sunset Route of the Southern Pacific Railroad on January 12, 1883. The location is 2.5 miles (4 km) west of the Pecos River in Texas. The private car of the construction superintendent Col. Tom Pierce, of the "Texas Lines," and Oneonta, *belonging to Collis P. Huntington, of the Southern Pacific, are a part of the ceremony.*

again advanced and the train accelerated back up to 100 mph (160 kph) under French power—without a stop. When crossing the Spanish border, the Geneva-to-Barcelona Catalan Talgo stops for a short time to have its wheel sets changed to match the Spanish gauge of 5 feet 6 inches.

The Ontario Northland of Canada purchased one of the diesel-powered TEE train sets from the Dutch railways in 1977, assigning the equipment to their Northlander service between Toronto and Timmins.

across the snow by sled, and at one time the party had to outrun a pack of wolves. All three locos were put into service in October 1837, after being duly baptized by the Russian Orthodox Church. The first trunk line, covering the 400 miles (640 km) from St. Petersburg, the capital, to Moscow, opened in November 1851 through flat country, on a route selected by the czar. He simply placed a ruler on the map and drew a straight line between the two points.

The Crimean War (1854–1856) exposed the weaknesses of the poorly organized, privately held systems, and nationalization was begun. By 1900, one third of the system had been acquired and two thirds by 1914. Locomotive and rolling stock works were organized so that self-sufficiency would be possible and standard designs were adopted. Much American equipment was delivered during World War I, including the famous Russian Decapod, a shipment of which wound up on American roads after they were embargoed following the Bolshevik Revolution.

The building of the 5,900-mile (9,440 km) Trans-Siberian Railway was a truly immense undertaking. It was begun under the czar in 1891, at Vladivostok. By 1903, the 5-foot Russian standard-gauge line was complete except for a ferry crossing

U

USSR Railways

As the future of this federation has not been fully resolved, the largest railway system in the world is presented as an integrated system, although the formation of the new republics will have obvious impact.

With 85,700 route miles (140,000 km), the unified system is twice as large as any other, extending 6,000 miles (9,600 km) east to west and 3,000 miles (4,800 km) north to south. This great system all began with a 15-mile (24 km) railway designed for pure pleasure. The line was authorized by the czar, after he saw John Blenkinsop's engines on a visit to the Middleton Colliery railway in England. An Austrian engineer, in Russia to examine mines, proposed the St. Petersburg to Pavlovsk Railway, which ran from the capital to the royal resort of Tsarskoye Selo.

Three English locomotives were bought, one each from Timothy Hackworth, Robert Stephenson, and Tayleur & Company. Hackworth's adventures in locomotive delivery in the dead of the Russian winter are worth recounting. All normal routes were frozen over, and the locomotive was landed at an open port in the Baltic. The large and handsome 2-2-2 was carried

Above: Riding the railway across Siberia was similar to riding across the early American West. This Trans-Siberian Railway 4-6-2 and passenger train of 1906 illustrate the similarities. Below: Delivery of two hundred American-built 5-foot-gauge 2-10-0 Decapods was interrupted by the Bolshevik Revolution of 1917. These locomotives, known as the "Russian Decapods," were ultimately equipped with wider steel tires to reduce the gauge to standard and were sold in the United States. The Erie Railroad bought seventy-five, eleven of which were later sold to the New York, Susquehanna & Western. NYS&W No. 2492 is seen here in Little Ferry, New Jersey, in 1948.

of Lake Baikal, although one section ran on the Chinese Eastern Railway through Manchuria. It was not until 1905 that the loop around Lake Baikal was completed and another ten years before the Amur River line was finished north of the Chinese border, allowing a completely Russian route.

By the time of the revolution, the network was half-complete, although the majority of trackage had been built in European, rather than Asian, Russia. With 60 percent of the country's landmass, Asia had only 20 percent of the railway. The new government made expansion of the railway a prime goal, and great progress was made. Air brakes and automatic couplers were standard by 1939, and much of the below-standard track had been relaid. The Trans-Siberian was double-tracked from end to end and new lines were put down, particularly in Asia.

The war devastated the European portions of the Soviet railroads. Fortunately, there was enough time to evacuate both rolling stock and shop equipment, so once the damage had been repaired, expansion was rapid. In the postwar years, 30,000

Above: The Soviet railway was dominated by ten-coupled locomotive designs. The Class LV 2-10-2 was representative of the enormous workhorses of the freight-hauling fleet.

Below: A large fleet of 2-10-0 Decapods typified Russian steam-locomotive power. This Class L appears to have been converted to burn oil.

miles (48,000 km) of new line were built, steam was retired, and 25,000 miles (40,000 km) of electrification supported half of all traffic.

The original Soviet locomotives were imported, frequently from Britain, but in the 1840s, domestic production began in St. Petersburg under direction of the son of the famous American locomotive builder Ross Winans of the Baltimore & Ohio. Steam locomotive design was treated with great importance and standardization was paramount, frequently based on American designs. The best of these were then modified and built upon until the Soviet steam fleet was unmatched in development of standard designs.

Not all developments were successes. In an attempt to provide great tractive effort on the light rail typical of 1934, a 33-foot

(10 m) wheelbase 4-14-4 was built. It was the longest nonarticulated locomotive ever built, but the long wheelbase damaged the track on curves. Another experiment was the Teploparovozy, a combined steam-diesel locomotive that used steam for starting (where the power is most efficient) and diesel plus steam for running. The steam was generated with the waste heat from the diesel. Theoretically, the thermal efficiency could exceed the diesel alone, and the complications of electric motors or hydraulic transmissions were bypassed, but three attempts over a number of years did not produce a working locomotive.

On the other hand, 13,000 0-10-0s of the E class, the largest class of locomotives ever built, were toiling on the railroad. In the 1920s, an order for these placed with the Swedish builder Nohab was paid for

The enormous 4-14-4 of the Soviet railway was the longest nonarticulated locomotive ever built. Unfortunately, this behemoth, which had a 33-foot (10 m) wheelbase, had the habit of straightening the track on curves and was scrapped.

with gold bars that were unloaded from the hold of a ship as the locomotives were put aboard. Freight traffic was otherwise basically hauled by two wheel arrangements: 13,000 locomotives of the 2-10-0 and 2-10-2 types along with 2,000 German 0-10-0s captured during the war. Passenger service was dominated by 4,000 S class Prairies (2-6-2s) built between 1910 and 1953. There were also 2-8-4s and 4-8-4s on the heaviest trains. At the peak

Above: Soviet railway Class FD 2-10-2 illustrates the often mixed appearance of Russian steam power, where a very American locomotive design has been adorned with European buffers. The ten-coupled type—some 28,000 of the 0-10-0, 2-10-0, and 2-10-2 wheel arrangements —constituted the largest group of locomotives on the world's largest fleet, which numbered 35,000 at its peak. Right: Passengers could spend a comfortable evening in the dining car as the Russia sped across the vast Siberian wilderness.

in 1957, the steam fleet was the world's largest, at 35,000 locomotives. Thirty thousand were included in just ten classes. Then Kaganovitch, the commissar of transportation, disappeared, and steam development was halted.

Reliable diesel locomotives were not to be found until American units were delivered during World War II and domestic production based on these designs began immediately. Starting with 1,000-hp units, a 2,000-hp unit was put into production when steam was dropped, and ultimately a 3,000-hp diesel was produced. Reliable statistics were state secrets, but fleet size was estimated at 10,000 units.

Electric locomotives are numerous; the original technology was developed from three-axle trucked General Electric designs that were imported in 1929. Prototype designs were also imported from France, Germany, and Sweden; production locomotives came from Czechoslovakia. Domestically produced locomotives dominate the fleet, however, and operate on both 3,000 volts DC and 25,000 volts AC.

The scale of the Russian rail system is huge by every measurement. The equipment itself is oversize, with clearance allowances of 17 feet 2 inches (5.2 m) in height and 11 feet 2 inches (3.4 m) in width. For many years, trackwork standards lagged behind the equipment, and these large loading capabilities were rarely used. Despite the vast distances the rail line covers, and the many substantial rivers that are crossed, there are no great bridges; the longest is less than a mile (1.6 km). The longest tunnel is the Suram Tunnel, boring 2.5 miles (4 km) through the Caucasus on the Baku-Poti line.

As could be expected, freight service dominates operations within excess of 2 million ton-miles annually, more than all other world systems combined. It has been estimated that 250,000 freight cars are dispatched daily in trains averaging 3,000 tons (2,700 t). Passenger train speed limits are set to match the freights, so they are not fast. The Trans-Siberian Express, more properly called the Russia, averages 30 mph (48 kph) on the 5,900 miles (9,440 km) between Vladivostok and Moscow, and the journey takes almost seven days. There are no "classes" in passenger trains, only "hard" and "soft" cars, and attendants keep the cars heated and cleaned. The heavily used service moves 3.5 billion riders per year, the second most in the world.

The impressive depot at Vladivostok is the final stop on the Trans-Siberian Express route, a seven-day, 5,900-mile (9,440 km) journey that starts in Moscow.

invention of a "car replacer" and "reversible railway frog," both of which enabled minor derailments to be quickly corrected. While in Pittsburgh to arrange for manufacture of his devices, Westinghouse realized that here—in "the Workshop of the World," a place of sweat, soot, and industry—was where a hardworking man of ideas could prosper. It was where Westinghouse would produce his first significant invention, the railroad air brake, and where he would make his fortune.

Before the air brake, trains were slowed and stopped by steam brakes, which acted only on the locomotives; hand brakes were operated by men scrambling across the roofs of the cars and turning the brake wheels one at a time. These methods were slow and unreliable: runaway trains on mountain grades caused great loss of life; brakemen often slipped and fell from the roofs of the cars; trains could not be stopped quickly if an obstruction was on the tracks.

The use of compressed air–powered tools in the drilling of the 7-mile (11 km) Mont Cenis Tunnel, in the European Alps, inspired Westinghouse to design a compressed air–powered railroad braking system. In 1869, the Panhandle Railroad (later part of the Pennsylvania Railroad) agreed to try his "automatic air brake" as an experiment on a special three-car train, with the provision that he bear the entire cost of installation and accept full financial responsibility for damage to the railroad's equipment. Despite desperate financial circumstances, Westinghouse agreed.

As the special train accelerated out of the Pittsburgh Depot, it passed through Grant's Hill tunnel at 30 mph (48 kph) and immediately encountered a teamster who had disregarded warning signals and crossed in front of the oncoming train. Daniel Tate, the engineer, gave the brake handle a twist and, accompanied by the rush of expelled air, the train jerked to a stop 4 feet (1.2 m) short of the terrified man and rearing horse. The railroad officials and guests were thrown about their car, but jumped up excitedly, rubbing their bruised elbows and heads. Thus, the test of the first air brake was the first true emergency application; and the invention that was to "save more lives than Napoleon lost in all his battles" had saved its first.

George Westinghouse was awarded his first patent at age nineteen, founded the Westinghouse Air Brake Co. at the age of twenty-two, and went on to earn 360 additional patents for a wide variety of devices in the railroad, electrical, natural gas, and public transportation fields.

That night, a proud Westinghouse wrote to his father: "My air brake had a practical trial today on a passenger train on the Panhandle Railroad and proved a great success."

On July 29, 1869, the twenty-two-year-old Westinghouse organized the Westinghouse Air Brake Company (later known as WABCO), with an initial 105 employees, to manufacture the new device, which went through several modifications and improvements. The "triple valve" of 1872 made automatic braking possible, since a break in the air hose connections between cars (caused by a broken coupling or derailment) would cause the instant application of brakes as the air dumped from the system. The runaway car, the railroader nightmare, became a thing of the past. The "quick-action brake," patented in 1887, allowed for the simultaneous braking of all cars in a fifty-car freight train.

Demand for the air brake, from both American and European railroads, was high, and the new endeavor quickly outgrew its first two facilities. Westinghouse

Before the automatic air brake became standard, railroad brakemen scrambled across freight car roofs to apply mechanical brakes manually upon whistle-signaled commands from the engineer. This dangerous occupation required men to be on the ladders and roofs of swaying, jerking cars, frequently in terrible conditions for extended periods of time.

was well known for his progressive views, and he chose a site east of Pittsburgh, named Wilmerding, for his new headquarters and plant, which would be surrounded by company-built workers' housing. The streets were paved and electricity was installed in all the homes, a novelty even for the wealthy at the time. Saturday afternoon was a holiday for the workers, a company tradition. The labor organizer Samuel Gompers said of Westinghouse: "If all employers of men treated their employees with the same consideration as he does, the American Federation of Labor would have to go out of existence."

Once the problem of stopping trains had been solved, Westinghouse turned to the problem of electrically powered signaling

and switching. He acquired the Union Electric Signal Company of Boston, which owned the patent rights to Dr. William Robinson's closed-track circuit, along with patents for several safety and signaling appliances. Purchase of the Interlocking Switch and Signal Company (of Harris-

burg, Pennsylvania) provided patents for the interlocking machines of Saxeby & Farmer and Youcey & Buchanan. These were consolidated into a new Westinghouse venture, the Union Switch & Signal Company in 1881, and quickly became a leader in railroad signaling and safety devices.

Westinghouse had interests outside of railroads, and pursued his work with electric power and, defying conventional scientific wisdom of the day, developed the alternating current system, which is today the basis of the power and light industry. On a whim, he drilled for natural gas on the grounds of his estate (although some say he was drilling for water) and unleashed a geyser that, when lit to test its quality, shot a flame 100 feet (30 m) into the sky. Ordered to control this torch by city officials, he devised a method of capping the well and piping the gas over a great area, and then organized the Philadelphia Company to supply natural gas for domestic and industrial use throughout Pittsburgh.

Other significant Westinghouse inventions include the railroad friction draft gear, an electrical street railway, high-powered gas engines, an automated telephone system, and air springs to improve automotive suspensions.

During his lifetime, Westinghouse was awarded the French Legion of Honor, the Order of the Crown of Italy, the Order of Leopold of Belgium, the John Fritz Medal, and the Edison Gold Medal, and was the first American to receive Germany's Grashof Gold Medal. Despite these and countless other awards and recognitions, he remained a modest man, disdaining publicity and rarely allowing himself to be photographed. He would not permit the press to print his biography until he was past fifty. Although always a genial and generous host, while entertaining, Westinghouse would often get a familiar "far-away look in his eyes" and begin to sketch on his ever-present paper—another invention having come to mind.

On March 12, 1914, George Westinghouse died unexpectedly, from heart disease, in New York. On February 24 he had been awarded his 346th patent, and fifteen more were to follow his death. His

The Chinese steam-locomotive industry developed from imported American designs, and that influence continued for many years. The Chinese Peoples Republic Railways still produced new steam power well into the 1980s at their Datong Works, 168 miles (270 km) west of Beijing, although there are signs that even there diesel and electric power will soon prevail. No. 2551 (left) is a Q J class (quian jin, or "advance forward") 2-10-2 based on the Russian LV class of 1952, but with many American features; it represents the world's most populous class of locomotive, numbering over four thousand. No. 8225 (inset) is a Russian-influenced 2-8-2 photographed in Kansu Province, in northern China.

industrial empire continued to innovate, and the Westinghouse name was applied to household appliances, diesel and electric locomotives, electrical transformers, and nuclear power. The company exists today as an international conglomerate that continues to prize research and development, creatively solving problems by developing additional products and industries to meet the needs of the modern world.

See also: *Electrification; GG1 Electric Locomotive; High-speed Rail Travel.*

Whyte System

The Whyte System of steam locomotive identification by wheel arrangement evolved as the standard of North American railroading. Developed in 1900 by Frederick Methven Whyte, a New York Central mechanical engineer, and subsequently adopted by the chief mechanical officers of the time, the system endured through the steam era and is still used today.

The Whyte System uses numerals divided by hyphens to represent the number of wheels (on both sides) in each grouping, starting at the front end with the leading truck, progressing through the drivers (or groups of drivers), and finishing with the trailing truck: 0-4-0, 2-6-0, 4-6-2, 2-6-6-2, and so on.

Before Whyte, other, more complex systems were in use. Alco (American Locomotive Works) left out the hyphens but

also appended a "C" for compound, an "S" for superheated, a "T" for tank, and then a number representing the weight of the loco rounded to the nearest thousand pounds. Under Alco, a 4-6-2, superheated and weighing 247,000 pounds (112,000 kg), would be designated 462S247. Other systems developed that may be even more obscure. There are five alternate ways to designate a 4-4-2 (in addition to Atlantic, a "nickname"): 22.1; bBa; 2-B-1 (German or Continental); 2-2-1 (French, which counts axles instead of wheels).

In addition to the numerical designations, names became attached to many of the arrangements. At first, they were very logical: 4-4-0 American Standard or American; 4-4-2 Atlantic; 4-6-2 Pacific. As more designs developed, the names evolved to represent significance to the railroad that first introduced them—Hudson, for the New York Central; Jubilee, for the Canadian Pacific—and in the case of the 4-8-4, many railroads chose their own names instead of the standard, Northern (Northern Pacific, 1926). The Louisville and Nashville called their 4-8-4s Dixies, in deference to their route through America's South. The Chesapeake & Ohio used Greenbrier in honor of their famous resort (and its namesake river); the New York Central continued with their own river tradition by calling them Niagaras. Big Boy, generally accepted as the largest American locomotive, was named when a shop worker chalked that apt description on the smoke box.

Wilcox's Uprising

In May 1911, the International Workers of the World, commonly known as "the Wobblies," involved the San Diego & Arizona Railroad, which was then under construction, in a bloody attempt to take over Tijuana, Mexico, in order to form their own society. The workers' army requisitioned supplies from the railroad (giving worthless receipts), imprisoned railroad workers, and commandeered entire trains.

After steaming southward on a stolen train, the "soldiers" were attacked and overwhelmed by Mexican troops. The survivors, fearing capture by the Federales, retreated northward in their bullet-ridden stolen train, and negotiated a surrender to the American authorities. At noon on June 22, 1911, the train was positioned so that the caboose exactly straddled the international border, and the insurrectionists, standing on the Mexican end facing Captain Wilcox of the U.S. Army at the other, laid their guns on a table in the center and surrendered to American custody.

Z

Zephyr

Named for the classical god of the wind, Zephyrus, the first American diesel streamliner was built in 1934 for Chicago, Burlington & Quincy service from Chicago to Minneapolis-St. Paul. The stainless steel shovel-nosed fixed train set was built by General Motors' fledgling Electro-Motive Division along with the Budd Company. In May of that year, Zephyr made a highly publicized nonstop demonstration run from Denver to the Century of Progress Exposition in Chicago. Several more Zephyrs followed, including the overnight sleeper-equipped Denver Zephyr.

The name became legendary, representing the best of the new postwar streamliners, and continued in use with the coming of Amtrak, which still operates the California Zephyr from Chicago to San Francisco.

With its dedicated train set and integral power plant, the stainless steel Denver Zephyr (of the Chicago, Burlington & Quincy) was typical of the early streamliners. The train's sleek styling and light weight contrasted sharply with the (often) grimy steam locomotives and heavyweight passenger cars of the day.

Appendix I: Diesel Locomotive Production in North America

To attempt to enumerate all of the railroad locomotives produced by individual builders would be a formidable task indeed, and in fact many fine books and periodicals have already been devoted to this material. Nonetheless, a distillation of the vast amount of available data into chart form provides important insight into the design and development processes. Since steam locomotives of the major builders tended to be custom designs produced for individual railroads, the following charts have been limited to represent only the products of certain American diesel locomotive build-

ers. (The railroad industry, however, is rapidly developing new technologies and changing market strategies. In addition, many older locomotives are being recycled —emerging from the shops of rebuilders such as Morrison-Knudsen—into virtually brand-new machines. Furthermore, the surviving builders EMD and GE are constantly designing for more fuel efficiency and power, and Amtrak is experimenting with European locomotive designs.)

These charts provide a glimpse of the growth of the industry, from the earliest switchers and streamlined passenger train

sets to the 6000-hp locomotives of the late 1980s. The *very* latest designs and experiments aren't here, but the material that *is* here will enable a better understanding of the history of the diesel locomotive.

The dates shown represent the production period of the locomotive; a date followed by a hyphen indicates that the locomotive was still being produced in 1989 (sales figures not included).

This streamlined EMD E7 passenger cab is resting between runs in Pittsburgh in 1948.

AMERICAN LOCOMOTIVE WORKS (INCLUDING MONTREAL LOCOMOTIVE WORKS) DIESELS

Model	Hp	Cyl	Engine	Period Produced	U.S.	Can	Mex
Boxcabs (Alco)							
60 ton	300	6	IR 10x12	1924–1928	26	—	—
60 ton	300	6	M&S 9.5x10.5	5/31	1	—	—
100 ton	600	12	(2) IR 10x12	1925–1928	7	—	—
Experiment	900		M&S 14x18	1928	1	—	—
Experiment	300		IR 10x12	1928–1936	2	—	—
Experiment	750		IR 14x16	1928–1941	4	—	—
Switchers (Alco)							
—	300	6	M&S 9.5x10.5	1931–1935	7	—	—
0900	600	6	531	1931	1	—	—
HH600	600	6	531	1931–1939	78	—	—
HH900	900	6	531 Turbo	1937–1939	21	—	—
HH660	660	6	539	1939–1940	43	—	—
HH1000	1000	6	539 Turbo	1939–1940	34	—	—
S-1	660	6	539	4/40–6/50	535	—	5
S-2	1000	6	539	4/40–6/50	1376	103	23
S-3	660	6	539	3/50–11/57	128	164	—
S-4	1000	6	539	8/50–1/61	636	146	15
S-5	800	6	251	6/54	7	—	—
S-6	900	6	251A,B	5/55–12/60	93	—	33
T-6	1000	6	251B	3/58–1/69	55	—	2
" " (MLW)							
S-7	1000	6	539	6/57–8/57	—	29	—
S-10	660	6	539	1/58–6/58	—	13	—
S-11	660	6	539	6/59–7/59	—	10	—
S-12	1000	6	539 Turbo	5/58–8/58	—	11	—
S-13	1000	6	251C	1/59–7/67	—	56	—
M420TR	2000	12	251C	4/72	—	2	—
M420TR-2	2000	12	251C	7/75	—	—	15
Light road switchers (Alco)							
RS-1	1000	6	539	3/41–3/60	353	—	64
RSD-1	1000	6	539	11/42–5/46	144	—	6
" " (MLW)							
RSC-13	1000	6	539	6/55–11/57	—	35	—
RS-23	1000	6	251C	8/59–7/66	—	40	—
RSC-24	1400	12	244	4/59–5/59	—	4	—
Road switchers (Alco)							
RS-2	1500	12	244	10/46–2/50	335	17	—
RS-2	1600	12	244	2/50–5/50	31	—	—
RS-3	1600	12	244	5/50–8/56	1265	98	7
RSC-2	1500	12	244	10/46–11/49	65	—	—
RSC-2	1600	12	244	3/50–4/50	5	—	—
RSC-3	1600	12	244	11/50–6/52	11	8	—
RSD-4	1600	12	244	3/51–8/52	36	—	—
RSD-5	1600	12	244	3/52–3/56	167	—	37
RS-11	1800	12	251B	2/56–4/64	327	—	99
RS-27	2400	16	251B	12/59–10/62	27	—	—
RS-36	1800	12	251B	2/62–8/63	40	—	—
RS-32	2000	12	251C	6/61–6/62	35	—	—
C-415	1500	8	251F	4/66–12/68	26	—	—
C-420	2000	12	251C	6/63–8/68	129	—	2
C-424	2400	16	251B	4/63–5/67	53	92	45
C-425	2500	16	251C	10/64–12/66	91	—	—
Road switchers (Alco) Cont.							
C-430	3000	16	251E	7/66–2/68	16	—	—
C-628	2750	16	251C	12/63–12/68	135	—	46
C-630	3000	16	251E	7/65–7/69	77	56	—
C-636	3600	16	251E	12/67–11/68	34	—	—
C-855	5500	32X	251C (2)	6/64	2	—	—
C-855-B	5500	32	251C (2)	6/64	1	—	—
" " (MLW)							
RS-18	1800	12	251B	12/56–6/68	—	351	—
RS-10	1600	12	244	12/54–2/57	—	128	—
M420	2000	12	251C	5/73–2/77	—	92	—
M420B	2000	12	251C	6/75–7/75	—	8	—
M420R	2000	12	251C	2/74–5/75	5	—	—
HR412	2000	12	251C	9/81–11/81	—	11	—
M630	3000	16	251E	11/69–11/73	—	55	20
M636	3600	16	251E	11/69–4/75	—	95	16
M640	4000	18	251E	2/71	—	1	—
HR616	3000	16	251E	2/82–8/82	—	20	—
Diesel hydraulic							
DH-643	4300	24	251C (2)	9/64	3	—	—
Cab units (including passenger variations)							
Black Maria (A)	1500	12	241	1945	2	—	—
Black Maria (B)	1500	12	241	1945	1	—	—
FA-1	1500	12	244	1/46–10/50	372	36	4
FA-1	1600	12	244	3/50–6/50	20	—	1
FB-1	1500	12	244	1/46–10/50	209	24	—
FB-1	1600	12	244	3/50–8/50	16	—	—
FA-2,FPA-2	1600	12	244	10/50–6/56	291	58	46
FB-2,FPB-2	1600	12	244	10/50–6/56	164	29	34
FPA-4	1800	12	251B	10/58–5/59	—	36	—
FPB-4	1800	12	251B	10/58–3/59	—	14	—
Passenger units							
GM&N 352,353[1]	600	6	539	1935	2	—	—
GM&N 354[1]	600	6	539	1937	1	—	—
DL-109	2000	12	539 (2)	1/40–4/45	74	—	—
DL-110	2000	12	539 (2)	2/42–8/42	4	—	—
PA-1	2000	16	244	9/46–6/50	170	—	—
PB-1	2000	16	244	9/46–8/49	40	—	—
PA-2	2250	16	244	4/50–8/52	28	—	—
PB-2	2250	16	244	8/50–9/50	2	—	—
PA-3	2250	16	244	4/52–12/53	49	—	—
PB-3	2250	16	244	4/52–6/53	5	—	—
Miscellaneous locomotives							
MRS-1[2]	1600	12	244	3/53–10/53	83	—	—
DL-535E[3]	1200	12	251	5/69, 12/71	10	—	—

[1] Power cars for the streamlined Rebel train set

[2] Also manufactured by EMD, these adjustable-gauge locomotives were custom-made for the U.S. Army

[3] These were narrow-gauge locomotives built for the White Pass & Yukon Railroad. The DL-535 was Alco's only North American export locomotive

GENERAL ELECTRIC COMPANY DIESELS

Model	Hp	Cyl	Engine	Period Produced	No. Sold U.S.	Can	Mex
Demonstrators							
Original	200	V-8	GE	1918	Disposition unknown		
60 Ton	300	6	IR	1924	Disposition unknown		
Experimental number 750							
Cab	1200	8	CB	1954	1	—	—
Booster	1200	8	CB	1954	1	—	—
Cab	1800	12	CB	1954	1	—	—
Booster	1800	12	CB	1954	1	—	—
Switchers							
Boxcab 60 T	300	6	IR	1928–1930	2	—	—
Boxcab 100 T	600	12	IR	1928–1930	11	—	—
Oil-Battery	300	6	IR	1930	7	—	—
Oil-Batt-Electric	300	6	IR	1930	38	—	—
Boxcab	800	6	IR	1931	1	—	—
60 Ton Hood	300	6	IR	1931	7	—	—
Centercab	600	12 (2x6)	IR	1933–1935	7	—	—
"Model Y" Hood	600	8	IR/CB	1936	10	—	—
Transfer	1800	12 (2x6)	IR	1936	1	—	—
Transfer	2000	10	Busch-Sulzer	1936	1	—	—
Center cab	1000	12 (2x6)	CB GN-6	1937–1940	9	—	—
Center cab	1500	16 (2x8)	CB GN-8	1939–1940	4	—	—
Center cab	680	12 (2x6)	CB EN-6	1941	2	—	—
Center cab	1100	12 (2x6)	CB GS-6	1942–1945	3	—	—
44 Ton	400	16 (2x V-8)	Cat D17000	1940–1956	334	9	5
70 Ton	500-660	6	CB FWL-6T	1946–1958	193	37	8
95 Ton	500-660	6	CB FWL-6T	1949–1956	46	1	—
SL80	600	2x6		11/76–	5	—	—
SL110	600	2x6		8/74–	30	—	9
SL144	1100	2x6		12/75	16	—	13
Light road switchers							
U18B	1800	8	FDL-8	3/73–10/76	118	—	45
U18D	1800	12	FDL12	1956	—	—	10
Medium road switchers							
U23B	2250	12	FDL-12	8/68–6/77	425	—	40
U23C	2300	12	FDL-12	3/68–?	60	—	—
B23-7	2250	12	FDL-12	9/77–12/84	411	—	125
BQ23-7	2250	12	FDL-12	10/78–1/79	10	—	—
High horsepower road switchers: 4-wheel trucks							
U25B	2500	16	FDL-16	4/59–2/66	478	—	—
U28B	2800	16	FDL-16	1/66–12/66	148	—	—
U30B	3000	16	FDL-16	12/66–3/75	291	—	—
U33B	3300	16	FDL-16	9/67–8/70	137	—	—
U36B	3600	16	FDL-16	1/69–12/74	125	—	—
B30-7	3000	16	FDL-16	12/77–5/81	199	—	—
B30-7A	3000	12	FDL-12	6/80–2/82	58	—	—
B30-7A1	3000	12	FDL-12	4/82–5/82	22	—	—
B30-7A(B)	3000	12	FDL-12	6/82–10/83	120	—	—
High horsepower road switchers: 4-wheel trucks (cont.)							
B36-7	3600	16	FDL-16	11/80–9/85	222	—	—
B32-8	3150	12	FDL-12	1/84	3	—	—
B36-8	3800	16	FDL-16	10/82	1	—	—
B39-8	3900	16	FDL-16	1/84–2/88	143	—	—
Dash 8-40B	4000	16	FDL-16	5/88–	89	—	—
High horsepower road switchers: 6-wheel trucks							
U25C	2500	16	FDL-16	9/63–12/65	113	—	—
U28C	2800	16	FDL-16	12/65–12/66	71	—	—
U30C	3000	16	FDL-16	1/67–9/76	592	—	8
U33C	3300	16	FDL-16	1/68–1/75	375	—	—
U36C	3600	16	FDL-16	10/71–4/75	124	—	94
C30-7	3000	16	FDL-16	9/76–12/85	783	—	354
C36-7	3600	16	FDL-16	6/78–12/85	129	—	40
C30-7A	3000	12	FDL-12	5/84–6/84	50	—	—
C32-8	3150	12	FDL-12	9/84–	10	—	—
C39-8	3900	16	FDL-16	3/83–12/87	162	—	—
Dash 8-40C	4000	16	FDL-16	12/87–	100	30	—
Miscellaneous locomotives							
U50	5000	2x16	(2) FDL-16	9/63–8/65	26	—	—
U50C	5000	2x12	(2) FDL-12	9/69–	40	—	—
Steam Turbine	2500	gross	Experimental	1939	2	—	—
Gas Turbine 101	4500	gross	Experimental	1948	1	—	—
Gas Turbine[1]	4500	gross		1952	10	—	—
Gas Turbine[1]	4500	gross		1954	15	—	—
Gas Turbine	8500	gross		1958–1961	30	—	—
WP&Y 3ft Gauge	800-900		Alco 251	1954–1956	11	—	—
Passenger versions of primarily freight locomotives							
U34CH	3430	16	FDL-16	11/70–1/73	32	—	—
U36CG	3600	16	FDL-16	4/74–5/74	—	—	20
Cowl units (passenger units)							
U30CG	3000	16	FDL-16	11/67	6	—	—
P30CH	3000	16	FDL-16	8/75–1/76	25	—	—
Electric locomotives							
Boxcab	1100	DC	2400v	6/14–11/16	—	6	—
Boxcab	1100	DC	2400v	1924–1926	—	9	—
Center cab	1100	AC	2400v	7/50	—	3	—
E35B	2500	AC/DC	25kv, 60hz	5/76–2/79	7	—	—
E44	5000	AC/DC	11kv, 25hz	12/60–7/63	66	—	—
E50C	5000	AC/DC	25kv, 60hz	5/68	2	—	—
E60C	6000	AC	50kv, 60hz	12/72–10/76	6	—	—
E60CH	6000	AC	25kv, 60hz	10/74–8/75	26	—	—
E60C-2	6000	AC	25/50kv, 60hz	8/82–1/83	2	—	39

[1] Chassis components used on U50s

GENERAL MOTORS' ELECTRO-MOTIVE DIVISION

Switchers

Model	Hp	Cyl	Engine	Period Produced	U.S.	Can	Mex
SC[1]	600	8	201-A	2/35–3/35	2	—	—
SC[2]	600	8	201-A	5/36–1/39	42	—	—
SW	600	8	201-A	12/36–1/39	77	—	—
NC[3]	900	12	201-A	3/35	1	—	—
NC	900	12	201-A	5/37–1/38	5	—	—
NC1[4]	900	12	201-A	3/37	5	—	—
NC2[4]	900	12	201-A	7/37	2	—	—
NW[4]	900	12	201-A	9/37–12/38	8	—	—
NW1[5]	900	12	201-A	11/37–1/39	27	—	—
NW1A[6]	900	12	201-A	12/38–1/39	3	—	—
T	1800	24[7]	201-A	5/36	1	—	—
TR1	1350	16	567	4/41–5/41	4	—	—
SW1[8]	600	6	567(A)	1/39–11/53	660	—	1
NW2[8]	1000	12	567(A)	2/39–12/49	1119	24	—
SW8	800	8	567B	9/50–1/54	306	65	—
SW600	600	6	567C	2/54–1/62	15	—	—
SW900	900	8	567C	1/54–11/65	260	97	—
SW7	1200	12	567A	10/49–1/51	493	—	—
SW9	1200	12	567B	2/51–12/53	786	29	—
SW1200	1200	12	567C	1/54–5/66	737	287	—
SW1000	1000	8	645E	6/66–10/72	118	—	—
SW1001	1000	8	645E	9/68–6/86	151	4	19
SW1500	1500	12	645E	7/66–1/74	807	—	—
SW1504	1500	12	645E	5/73–8/73	—	—	60
MP15DC	1500	12	645E	2/74–11/80	237	4	5
MP15AC	1500	12	645E	8/75–8/84	226	4	25
MP15T	1500	8	645E	10/84–11/87	42	—	—

Light road switchers

Model	Hp	Cyl	Engine	Period Produced	U.S.	Can	Mex
NW4	900	12	201-A	8/38	2	—	—
NW3	1000	12	567	11/39–3/42	7	—	—
NW5	1000	12	567B	12/46–2/47	13	—	—
GMD1	1200	12	567C	1958–1960	—	101	—
RS1325	1325	12	567C	10/60	2	—	—
GP15-1	1500	12	645E	6/76–3/82	310	—	—
GP15AC	1500	12	645E	11/82–12/82	30	—	—
GP15T	1500	8	645E	10/82–4/83	28	—	—

Road switchers: 4-wheel trucks

Model	Hp	Cyl	Engine	Period Produced	U.S.	Can	Mex
BL1	1500	16	567B	2/48	1	—	—
BL2	1500	16	567B	4/48–5/49	58	—	—
GP7	1500	16	567B	10/49–5/54	2610	112	2
GP7B	1500	16	567B	3/53–4/53	5	—	—
GP9	1750	16	567C	1/54–12/59	3436	646	10
GP9B	1750	16	567C	2/54–12/59	165	—	—
GP18	1800	16	567D1	12/59–11/63	350	—	40
GP28	1800	16	567D1	3/64–11/65	16	—	10
GP20	2000	16	567D2	11/59–4/62	260	—	—
GP20[9]	2000	16	567C	9/55–10/69	75	—	—
GP30	2250	16	567D3	7/61–11/63	906	2	—
GP30B	2250	16	567D3	4/63–7/63	40	—	—
GP35	2500	16	567D3A	10/63–1/66	1250	26	57
GP38	2000	16	645	1/66–12/71	466	21	6
GP38-2	2000	16	645	1/72–12/87	1801	254	133
GP38P-2	2000	16	645E	6/75	—	—	20
GP39	2300	12	645E	35/69–7/70	21	—	—
GP39DC	2300	12	645E	6/70	2	—	—
GP39-2	2300	12	645W	8/74–12/87	249	—	—
GP39X	2600	12	645	11/80	6	—	—
GP49	2800	12	645	8/83–5/85	9	—	—
GP59	3000	12	710	6/85	3	—	—

Road switchers: 4-wheel trucks (cont.)

Model	Hp	Cyl	Engine	Period Produced	U.S.	Can	Mex
GP40	3000	16	645E3	11/65–12/71	1201	24	18
GP40-2	3000	16	645E3	4/72–11/86	812	275	44
GP40TC	3000	16	645E	11/66–12/66	—	8	—
GP40P-2	3000	16	645E	11/74	3	—	—
GP40X	3500	16	645F	12/77–6/78	23	—	—
GP50	3500	16	645F	5/80–11/85	278	—	—
GP60	3800	16	710G	10/85–			

Road switchers: 6-wheel trucks

Model	Hp	Cyl	Engine	Period Produced	U.S.	Can	Mex
SD7	1500	16	567B	2/52–11/53	188	—	—
SD9	1750	16	567C	1/54–6/59	471	—	—
SD18	1800	16	567D1	4/60–3/63	54	—	—
SD24	2400	16	567D3	7/58–3/63	179	—	—
SD24B	2400	16	567D3	7/59–9/69	45	—	—
SD28	1800	16	567D1	7/65–9/65	6	—	—
SD35	2500	16	567D3A	6/64–1/66	360	—	—
SD38	2000	16	645E3	5/67–10/71	52	1	—
SD38-2	2000	16	645E3	11/72–6/79	74	7	—
SD39	2300	12	645E	8/68–5/70	54	—	—
SDL39	2300	12	645E	3/69–11/72	10	—	—
SD40	3000	16	645E3	1/66–7/72	883	330	62
SD40-2	3000	16	645E	1/72–2/86	3131	719	107
SD40T-2	3000	16	645E	6/74–11/80	315	—	—
SD45	3600	20	645E3	2/65–12/71	1260	—	—
SD45-2	3600	20	645E3	5/72–9/74	136	—	—
SD45T-2	3600	20	645E	2/72–6/75	247	—	—
SD45X	4200	20	645E3	1970–1971	7	—	—
SD40X	3500	16	645F	9/79	4	—	—
SD50	3500	16	645F	5/81–7/84	230	—	—
SD50	3600	16	645F	11/84–5/85	131	—	—
SD50F	3600	16	645F	4/85–7/87	—	60	—
SD50S	3500	16	645F	9/79	4	—	—
SD60	3800	16	710G	5/84–	365	—	—
SD60F	3800	16	710G	10/85	—	4	—
DD35B	5000	32[10]	567D3A	9/63–9/64	30	—	—
DD35A	5000	32[10]	567D3A	4/65–5/65	15	—	—
DDA40X	6600	32[10]	645E3A	4/69–4/71	47	—	—

Cab units and boosters

Model	Hp	Cyl	Engine	Period Produced	U.S.	Can	Mex
FTA	1350	16	567(A)	11/39–11/45	555	—	—
FTB	1350	16	567(A)	11/39–11/45	541	—	—
F2A	1350	16	567B	7/46–11/46	60	—	14
F2B	1350	16	567B	7/46–11/46	16	—	14
F3A	1500	16	567B	7/45–2/49	1107	4	—
F3B	1500	16	567B	7/45–2/49	694	2	—
F7A	1500	16	567B	2/49–12/53	2261	80	25
F7B	1500	16	567B	2/49–12/53	1420	47	16
F9A	1750	16	567C	1/54–12/56	77	—	10
F9B	1750	16	567C	1/54–4/57	98	46	10

Power cars[11]

Model	Hp	Cyl	Engine	Period Produced	U.S.	Can	Mex
UP M-10000	600	12	191-A	2/34	1	—	—
CB&Q 9900	600	8	201-A	4/34	1	—	—
BM-MEC 6000	600	8	201-A	2/35	1	—	—
CB&Q 9901	600	8	201-A	4/35	1	—	—
CB&Q 9902	600	8	201-A	4/35	1	—	—
CB&Q 9903	600	8	201-A	4/35	1	—	—
IC 121	1200	16	201-A	3/36	1	—	—
SAL 2027	600	8	201-A	4/36	1	—	—
SAL 2028	600	8	201-A	4/36	1	—	—
CB&Q 9908	1000	12	567	4/39	1	—	—

GENERAL MOTORS' ELECTRO-MOTIVE DIVISION

Model	Hp	Cyl	Engine	Period Produced	No. Sold U.S.	Can	Mex
Custom-built passenger locomotives[11]							
UP M-10001	1200	16	201-A	10/34	1	—	—
UP M-10002[12]	1200	16	201-A	5/36	1	—	—
UP M-10003[13]	1200	16	201-A	5/36–8/36	5	—	—
RI 601-606	1200	16	201-A	8/37–10/37	6	—	—
EMD 511,512	1800	12[14]	201-A	5/35	2	—	—
B&O, Alton 50	1800	12[14]	201-A	8/35	1	—	—
ATSF 1,1A	1800	12[14]	201-A	9/35	1	—	—
CB&Q 9904,9905	1800	12[14]	201-A	11/36	2	—	—
CB&Q 9906A/B[15]	1800	12[14]	201-A	10/36	2	—	—
Aerotrain 1000,1001[16]	1200	12	567C	1956	2	—	—
RI 1[17]	1200	12	567C	1956	1	—	—
Production passenger locomotives							
EA	1800	12[14]	201-A	5/37–6/38	6	—	—
EB	1800	12[14]	201-A	5/37–6/38	6	—	—
E1A	1800	12[14]	201-A	6/37–4/38	8	—	—
E1B	1800	12[14]	201-A	6/37–3/38	3	—	—
E2A	1800	12[14]	201-A	1/37–12/37	2	—	—
E2B	1800	12[14]	201-A	1/37–12/37	4	—	—
E3A	2000	12[14]	567	3/39–6/40	16	—	—
E3B	2000	12[14]	567	3/39–9/39	2	—	—
E4A	2000	12[14]	567	10/38–12/39	14	—	—
E4B	2000	12[14]	567	10/38–12/39	5	—	—
E5A	2000	12[14]	567	2/40–6/41	11	—	—
E5B	2000	12[14]	567	2/40–3/40	5	—	—
E6A	2000	12[14]	567	11/39–9/42	92	—	—
E6B	2000	12[14]	567	4/40–2/42	26	—	—
E7A	2000	12[14]	567A	2/45–5/49	428	—	—
E7B	2000	12[14]	567A	2/45–4/49	82	—	—
E8A	2250	12[14]	567B	8/49–12/53	418	3	—
E8B	2250	12[14]	567B	12/49–5/53	39	—	—
E9A	2400	12[14]	567C	5/54–12/63	100	—	—
E9B	2400	12[14]	567C	5/54–12/63	44	—	—
FP45	3600	20	645E	12/67–12/68	14	—	—
F40PH	3000-3200	16	645E	3/76–1/88	278	6	—
F40PH-2	3000	16	645E	3/85–	61	30	—
F40PH-2C	3000	16	645E	7/87–5/88	26	—	—

Model	Hp	Cyl	Engine	Period Produced	No. Sold U.S.	Can	Mex
Passenger versions of primarily freight locomotives							
SDP35	2500	16	567D3A	7/64–9/65	35	—	—
SDP40	3000	16	645E3	6/66–5/70	6	—	14
SDP40F	3000	16	645E3	6/73–8/74	150	—	—
SDP45	3600	20	645E3	5/67–8/70	52	—	—
FP7	1500	16	567B	6/49–12/53	301	57	18
FP9	1750	16	567C	1954–1959	—	54	25
FL9	1750	16	567C	10/56–11/57	30	—	—
FL9	1800	16	567D1	6/60–11/60	30	—	—
Electric locomotives							
SWi1200MG[18]	1200	AC/DC	2300v, 60hz	1963–1971	—	9	—
AEM7	7000	AC	25kv, 60hz[18]	11/79–	65	—	—
GM6	6000	AC/DC	11kv, 25hz	4/75–	11	—	—
GM10	10,000	AC/DC	11kv, 25hz	7/76	1	—	—
GF6C[19]	6000	AC	50kv, 60hz	11/83–7/84	—	7	—

[1] Original experimental version, assembled at General Electric plant, Erie, Pennsylvania

[2] General Electric or Westinghouse motors and generator

[3] Original experimental version, assembled at Bethlehem Steel, Wilmington, Delaware

[4] Westinghouse motors and generator

[5] General Electric motors and generator

[6] EMD motors and General Electric generator

[7] Two 12-cylinder engines—center cab design for transfer service

[8] Production suspended 1942 to 1945 by War Production Board

[9] "Omaha" model turbochargers factory applied to GP9s as influenced by Union Pacific experiments. Nine of these GP20s had the 567D2 engine

[10] Two 16-cylinder engines

[11] Power cars and custom-built locomotives were designated by the initials of the railroad that purchased the machines and a number

[12] This locomotive had a 900-hp booster articulated to the cab by a span bolster

[13] The M-10003 to M-10007 were all alike; each had a 1200-hp booster articulated to the cab by a span bolster

[14] These locomotives had two 12-cylinder engines each, doubling the power output

[15] The 9906A/B and its twin the 9907A/B each had a 1200-hp booster powered by a 16-cylinder 201-A engine that was semipermanently coupled to the cab

[16] Demonstrated on UP, NYC, ATSF, and PRR, these complete train sets were sold to the RI

[17] This was the last Aerotrain locomotive built; it was used by the RI to power the Talgo Jet Rocket

[18] Originally 11kv, 25hz. Current changed in Northeast Corridor, 1983

[19] Built by GMD (Canada)

MISCELLANEOUS NORTH AMERICAN DIESEL LOCOMOTIVE BUILDERS[1]

Builder	Location	Primary business	Loco Era	Models
Atlas Car & Manufacturing	Cleveland, OH	Industrial rail equipment	1930s–1940s	Army 65-ton; Navy 50-ton
Bethlehem Steel Co.	Bethlehem, PA	Steel making and fabrication	1930s	Gas electric switcher
J.G. Brill	Philadelphia, PA	Streetcars, doodlebugs	1920s	Box cab
Canadian Locomotive Co.	Kingston, ON	Steam, licensed diesel designs	1940s	44-ton torque converter
Cummins Engine Co.	Columbus, IN	Engine supplier to others	1937	90-ton Steeple cab
Euclid Road Machinery Co.	Euclid, OH	Road-building equipment	1935	35-ton; 55-ton
Harland & Wolf (Belfast) & National Steel Car	Hamilton, ON	Power plants and railcars	1937	550-hp unit
Heisler Locomotive Works	Erie, PA	Steam, geared logging locos	1932	60-ton w/Buda engine
Ingalls Shipbuilding Co.	Pascagoula, MS	Shipbuilding	1945	1500-hp turret cab w/Superior engine[2]
Midwest Locomotive Works	Hamilton, OH		1933	65-ton w/Cummins engine
St. Louis Car Company	St. Louis, MO	Streetcars	1929	Diesel-electric-battery
Vulcan Locomotive Works	Wilkes-Barre, PA	Steam-powered industrials	1920s–1954	25-ton; 31-ton; 45-ton; 65-ton (military); 70-ton center cab

[1] Unable to compete with giants GM and Alco in most areas, smaller companies saw the industrial locomotive niche as an opportunity for them; this chart summarizes some of those builders and their designs

[2] Ingalls also designed, but never built, other diesel locomotives of 6 to 8 cylinders with power outputs of 660 to 2000 hp

Appendix II: The Whyte System

This 4-6-2, built for the Illinois Central by Alco's Schenectady facility in 1906, was also called a Pacific (see chart below).

LOCOMOTIVE WHEEL ARRANGEMENTS AND NAMES ACCORDING TO THE WHYTE SYSTEM

Wheel Arrangement	Name	Wheel Arrangement	Name	Wheel Arrangement	Name	Wheel Arrangement	Name
0-4-0		2-10-2	Santa Fe	4-6-2	Pacific	**Other local and regional variants**	
0-6-0		2-10-4	Texas	4-6-4	Hudson, Baltic (Milwaukee Road)	2-8-2	MacArthur (during WWII)
0-6-2				4-8-0	twelve-wheeler	2-8-4	Kanawha (Chesapeake & Ohio)
0-8-0		2-6-6-0		4-8-2	Mountain	2-8-4	Lima (Boston & Maine)
0-8-2	(ex-2-8-2)	2-6-6-2		4-8-4	Northern	2-10-2	Decapod (Southern Pacific)
0-10-0		2-6-6-4		4-10-0	Mastodon	2-10-4	Colorado (Burlington)
0-10-2	Union	2-6-6-6	Allegheny	4-10-2	Overland	4-8-2	Mohawk (New York Central)
0-6-6-0		2-6-8-0		4-12-2	Union Pacific	4-8-4	Confederation (Canadian National)
0-8-8-0		2-8-8-0				4-8-4	Confederation (National of Mexico)
		2-8-8-2		4-4-4-4	(Duplex, Pennsylvania)	4-8-4	Dixie (New York, Chicago & St. Louis)
2-4-0		2-8-8-4	Yellowstone	4-4-6-2		4-8-4	Golden State (Southern Pacific)
2-4-2	Columbia	2-10-10-2	Virginian	4-4-6-4	(Duplex, Pennsylvania)	4-8-4	Greenbrier (Chesapeake & Ohio)
2-6-0	Mogul	2-8-8-8-2	Triplex	4-6-4-4		4-8-4	Niagara (New York Central)
2-6-2	Prairie	2-8-8-8-4		4-6-6-2		4-8-4	Pocono (Lackawanna)
2-6-4	Adriatic	4-2-4	Bicycle	4-6-6-4	Challenger	4-8-4	Potomac (Western Maryland)
2-8-0	Consolidation	4-4-0	American, eight-wheeler	4-8-8-2	(Cab Forward, Southern Pacific)	4-8-4	Wyoming (Lehigh Valley)
2-8-2	Mikado	4-4-2	Atlantic	4-8-8-4	Big Boy		
2-8-4	Berkshire	4-4-4	Reading, Jubilee (Central Pacific)				
2-10-0	Decapod	4-6-0	ten-wheeler				

Appendix III: Major North American Railroad Mergers

MERGERS AND CONSOLIDATIONS OF THE MAJOR NORTH AMERICAN RAILROADS[1]

Pennsylvania
New York Central
New York, New Haven & Hartford — 1968 Central
Erie
Delaware, Lackawanna & Western — 1967 Erie-Lackawanna
Central of New Jersey
Lehigh Valley
— 1976 Conrail

Reading
Western Maryland
Baltimore & Ohio
Chesapeake & Ohio — 1973 Chessie System
Pere Marquette
Seaboard Air Line
Atlantic Coast Line — 1967 Seaboard Coast Line
Louisville & Nashville
Nashville, Chattanooga & St. Louis
Chicago, Indianapolis & Louisville (Monon)
Chicago & Eastern Illinois — 1967 Family Lines
Richmond, Fredericksburg & Potomac
Clinchfield

1980 CSX — 1992 CSX
P&LE
(trackage only)

New York, Chicago & St. Louis (Nickel Plate)
Virginian
Wabash
Akron, Canton & Youngstown
Norfolk & Western — 1964 Norfolk & Western
Wheeling & Lake Erie
Pittsburgh & West Virginia
Southern — 1963 Southern
Central Georgia
Cincinnati, New Orleans & Texas Pacific
— 1982 Norfolk Southern

Chicago, Burlington & Quincy
Fort Worth & Denver
Colorado & Southern
Great Northern — 1970 Burlington Northern — 1980 Burlington Northern
Northern Pacific
Spokane, Portland & Seattle
St. Louis-San Francisco (The Frisco)

Missouri-Kansas-Texas
Spokane International
Union Pacific — 1982 Union Pacific — 1988 Union Pacific
Western Pacific
Texas & Pacific
Missouri Pacific

Illinois Central
Gulf, Mobile & Ohio
Alton — 1972 Illinois Central Gulf — 1985 Illinois Central (less GM&O)

Denver & Rio Grande Western
Southern Pacific — 1988 Rio Grande Industries (Anschutz Corporation)[2]
St. Louis Southwestern (Cotton Belt)

Grand Trunk Western
Detroit, Toledo & Ironton — 1980 — 1981 Grand Trunk Western (Canadian National)
Detroit & Toledo Shore Line

Duluth, Missabe & Iron Range
Bessemer & Lake Erie
Elgin, Joliet & Eastern — 1986 USX[3]
Union RR

Minneapolis, St.Paul & Saulte Ste. Marie — 1961 Soo Line — 1985 Soo Line — 1990 Canadian Pacific[4]
Duluth, South Shore & Atlantic
Wisconsin Central
Chicago, Milwaukee, St. Paul & Pacific

Maine Central
Boston & Maine — 1981 — 1982 — 1984 Guilford System[5]
Delaware & Hudson

[1]Railroads not involved in recent major mergers: Atcheson, Topeka & Santa Fe; Florida East Coast; Long Island; Amtrak; C&NW; KCS. Major railroads that have disappeared through abandonment or sale: New York, Ontario & Western; Chicago, Rock Island & Pacific; Pittsburgh & Lake Erie
[2]These railroads are owned and managed by Rio Grande Industries, which in turn is controlled by Anschutz Corporation
[3]These railroads serve the mills of U.S. Steel, which is now controlled by USX
[4]These railroads still operate as the Soo Line, which is controlled by the Canadian Pacific
[5]The D&H was let go by the Guilford System and bought by the Canadian Pacific

Glossary of Railroad Terminology

Adhesive weight: On a locomotive, the portion of the total weight that is resting on the driving wheels.

Air brake: A braking system that operates using the action of compressed air.

Alternating current (AC): An electric current that reverses its direction of flow at regular intervals, called cycles.

Articulated locomotive: A steam locomotive that uses a single boiler mounted on a chassis that is (usually) composed of two sets of driving mechanisms and cylinders connected by a pivot, so each mechanism can function and swivel independently from the other but under single control. A compound articulated (Mallet) uses exhaust steam from one set of high-pressure cylinders to drive the larger low-pressure cylinders on the other mechanism. A simple articulated uses direct boiler steam at high pressure to drive all cylinders.

Auto rack: A flatcar with fixed steel racks for shipping automobiles. Racks have two or three levels and are equipped with tie-down devices. The racks are typically fitted with metal screens on the sides, and sometimes with roofs, to protect the vehicles from vandals.

Backhead: The rear surface of a steam locomotive boiler, on which are mounted the controls, valves, and gauges necessary for the operation of the locomotive.

Ballast: The granular material, usually crushed rock, that supports the trackage on the roadbed. The ballast allows for quick drainage of rainwater away from the cross ties (sleepers) and provides a method of easily resetting the level or alignment of the track.

Bogie: The British and Australian term for a truck, the set of wheels and suspension components that supports a railroad car.

Boiler: That portion of a steam locomotive, usually a horizontal cylinder, in which the steam is produced. Boilers may also be installed in diesel or electric locomotives to produce steam for passenger-car heating systems.

Boxcar: A rectangular, fully enclosed freight car with side and/or end doors, designed for hauling general merchandise.

Brakeman: Crew member who was originally responsible for clambering over car roofs to apply hand brakes. Also responsible for throwing switches and "flagging," the practice of carrying a red lantern or flag to a point far enough from the rear, or head end, of a stopped train to warn an approaching train.

Broad gauge: Trackage spaced farther apart than the standard gauge of 4 feet 8 1/2 inches.

Buffers: A primarily British term for shock-absorbing devices located on the ends of railway carriages that help minimize bumping between cars. Also, an end-of-track protection device—a bumper.

Cab forward: A steam locomotive type extensively used by the Southern Pacific. In response to problems with smoke accumulation in the lengthy tunnels and snowsheds of the Sierra Nevadas, the SP arranged an articulated locomotive with the tender coupled at the smoke-box end of the boiler. The controls in the cab were reversed, and a new flat front, with appropriate lights, whistle, and bell, was applied to the former rear of the cab. This left the stack (and its smoke) behind the crew, who had fresh air to breath. This reversal was made possible only because the SP used fuel oil, rather than coal, in their fireboxes.

Caboose: A car in which the conductor has an office and, in the early days, living quarters. The caboose marked the traditional end of a train, but has fallen into disuse in recent years, as modern electronic communication has reduced the need in many countries.

Cab-unit: Also called a cowl-unit, a diesel locomotive on which the body is flush with the outside of the frame, and there are no exterior walkways, access to the engine compartment being from the interior of the locomotive cab.

Carriage: An early term for a passenger coach, which continued in use for a much longer time in Britain than elsewhere.

Catenary: The supporting wire and structure for an overhead cable used to provide electricity to electric locomotives.

Chimney: British term for the exhaust stack of a steam locomotive.

Class 1 railroad: In the United States, a railroad of sufficient traffic density to earn revenues in excess of a figure set by the Interstate Commerce Commission. In 1991, that figure was $93.5 million and there were thirteen Class 1 systems, plus Amtrak. See also **Regional railroads.**

Compound locomotive: A steam locomotive in which exhaust steam is directed to additional, larger cylinders that are designed to operate at lower pressure. This is a method of increasing steam locomotive efficiency.

Conductor: In the United States, the official in charge of a train. Once called captain, this person was responsible for receiving train orders, keeping paperwork on freights, and collecting fares on passenger trains.

Consist: The composition—cars, loads, locomotives, and so on—of a train.

Container on flatcar (COFC): A system that allows closed containers, usually compatible with maritime requirements, to be carried on a flatcar.

Continuously welded rail (CWR): Steel rail was traditionally rolled in 39-foot (11.8 m) lengths so that it could be loaded into the common 40-foot (12.1 m)-long cars of the day. The wheels rolling over the resultant bolted joints produced the rhythmic "clickety-clack." Most of today's main-line rail is factory-welded into lengths of a quarter mile (0.4 km) and transported on trains of specially rigged flatcars that hold the rail, but allow it to flex around curves.

Covered hopper: Similar to an open hopper, a covered hopper has sloped ends that direct granular material toward discharge chutes in the car bottom and a weatherproof roof with hatches for loading.

Cow and calf: A diesel locomotive set made up of a regular cab-equipped control unit (cow) that is semipermanently coupled to a cabless booster unit (calf) and usually used for yard switching.

Crew change: The crew from point A leaves the train at point B and turns it over to a rested crew who takes the train to point C; the process continues until the train arrives at its destination. Crew-change points are normally at terminals where the relieved crew lives, or spends the night at railroad expense.

Crown sheet: The roof over the firebox of a steam boiler. Most steam is generated from the water directly over this spot, and failure to keep the water level over the crown sheet was the most common cause of boiler explosions.

Cylinder: The bore in which a piston moves. The piston could be powered by steam or internal combustion (as in a diesel) to produce power, or be driven by air to apply brakes.

Direct current (DC): An electric current that flows continuously in one direction.

Doghouse: A telephone booth–sized enclosure, mounted on the top rear of a steam locomotive tender, that provided shelter for the head brakeman.

Doodlebug: A motor car, usually passenger-carrying, powered by an internal-combustion engine that provided service on lightly traveled lines where a full train was not justified. These began as converted passenger coaches but evolved into sophisticated machines like the Budd RDC and the McKeen Car.

Doubleheading: The practice of using two locomotives (traditionally steam powered) with separate crews on the head end of a train.

Double-stack car: A recent development in intermodal technology that uses specially designed well-hole flatcars that are semipermanently coupled in articulated sets and carry standard marine containers stacked two high.

Draft gear: The energy-absorbing component, usually rubber, of the coupling, friction, or hydraulic systems that reduces jerking or bumping shocks during coupling or slack action. These shocks can be severe enough to damage lading, and thus must be dampened.

Drumhead: A sign, usually illuminated, mounted on the rear of a passenger train that provides a graphic image advertising the name of the train or railroad.

Dynamic braking: A method of train braking wherein the truck-mounted traction motors of diesel electric locomotives are reversed so the wheels actually turn the motors on a downhill run. The motors then act as generators, and the resultant electrical current is directed to a bank of resistor grids, where it is converted into heat and dissipated into the air. This process absorbs a tremendous amount of energy, slowing the train while saving wear and tear on the braking system.

EMD: The Electro-Motive Division of General Motors, once the largest American diesel-electric locomotive builder.

Engineer: The operator of a locomotive. In some countries this person is called the engine driver.

Exhaust pipe: A vertical pipe attached to the cylinders of a steam locomotive that directs the exhaust steam toward the stack, creating a vacuum that draws the combustion products from the firebox through the boiler tubes so all is propelled out through the stack, producing the unique steam-locomotive "smoke."

Feedwater heater: A device on a steam locomotive that uses exhaust steam to preheat the incoming boiler water, thus improving efficiency.

Firebox: The portion of the steam locomotive, normally at the rear of the boiler, in the cab, where the fuel is burned.

Fireman: Originally, the member of the locomotive crew that fed the fuel into the fire. This was a training position for engineer. On diesels and electrics, the fireman is responsible for assisting the engineer and minor maintenance.

Flange: The projecting lip on a railroad wheel that rides (typically) inside the rails and guides the wheel set along the track.

Flatcar: A freight car that has only a flat deck, with no sides. Used for bulky or unwieldy loads that are difficult to maneuver through a boxcar door.

Third rail: A non-running "rail" mounted between or beside the running rails, used for the supply of current to an electric locomotive through a pickup "shoe."

Tie (or cross tie): Wood, concrete, or metal slats placed perpendicular to the rail to support the rail, hold it in gauge, and distribute the load to the roadbed.

Torpedo: An explosive device with two moldable tabs that can be attached to the top of the rail. A wheel contacting the torpedo will set off a loud explosive report, warning the engineer of a track obstruction immediately ahead.

Tractive effort: The measurement of the energy exerted by a locomotive at the point where the wheel tread meets the rail.

Trailer on flatcar (TOFC): A system of intermodal transport that uses highway trailers carried on flatcars for part of the journey.

Turbine: A rotary engine in which the power is derived from the force of expanding gases applied against blades or fans that turn a central shaft.

Two-stroke cycle: The operating cycle of an internal combustion (as in a diesel locomotive) in which there is one power stroke during each revolution of the crankshaft.

Unit train: A freight train made up entirely of a single type of car and carrying a single commodity, usually coal or grain. The trains normally operate from shipper to unloading point in a continuous round-trip cycle.

Valve gear: On a steam engine, the mechanism that controls the operation of the valves that coordinate the intake or exhaust steam with the position of the piston in the cylinder.

Valves: The devices that allow the intake of fuel or the expulsion of exhaust in an engine—steam in a steam engine or fuel in a diesel.

Van (or brake van): The terminology for caboose often used in Britain, Canada, and Australia.

Wagon: Also called a "goods wagon," the British term for freight car.

Yard: A network of parallel tracks, connected by switches on at least one end, arranged so trains can be disassembled and the cars rearranged into new trains. Sometimes called a classification yard or a marshaling yard, it allows the trains to be "shuffled" so each car gets to its proper destination. A storage yard holds cars until they are needed.

Glossary of Railroad Slang

Advertised: Time "advertised" in the schedule or timetable.

Air monkey: Air brake mechanic.

"Anchor them": Set the brakes. "Tie 'em down."

Ashcat: Locomotive fireman.

Backhead: The rear surface of a locomotive boiler, usually inside the cab, to which the gauges, valves, and controls are mounted. Also a nickname for a fireman.

Bakehead: Fireman.

Ballast scorcher: Locomotive engineer noted for high-speed running.

Beanery: Depot restaurant, or nearby eatery.

Beanery queen: Waitress.

Bend the iron: To throw, or alter the position of, a switch.

Big E: Brotherhood of Locomotive Engineers.

Big hole: Emergency brake application by the engineer.

Big hook: Wrecking crane.

Big O: Order of Railway Conductors.

Big Ox: Conductor.

Big Rock Candy Mountain: The hobo's paradise.

Bindle stiff: A tramp or vagrant carrying his own bundle.

Black diamonds: Coal.

Black snake: A train of coal cars.

Blazer: A hot box—a journal with its packing on fire.

B.O.: For "bad order," chalked on a car requiring repairs.

'Bo: Abbreviation of hobo.

Bob tail: Switch engine.

Boomer: A railroader who roamed North America from job to job, division to division, and railroad to railroad.

Brains: Conductor.

Brass collars: Railroad officials.

Brass hats: Railroad management officials.

Brass pounder: Telegraph operator.

Brownies: Demerits given out for rules infractions.

Caboose: Ambulance, anchor, buggy, brain box (the conductor was "the brains"), bazoo wagon, cabin, chariot (although more properly an official's business car), crummy, cripple's home, den, diner, glory wagon (dead railroaders "went to glory"), go-cart, hack, kitchen, mad-house, monkey cage or monkey hut, palace, parlor, perambulator, rest room, treasure chest, van, zoo, and many more unprintable and derogatory names.

Car toad or car knocker: Car mechanic.

Cherry picker: Switchman, named after the red lights on the switch stands.

Cinder dick: Railroad policeman.

Clock: Locomotive steam gauge.

Clown or club winder: Brakeman.

Cock loft: The cupola on a caboose.

Color-blind: Employee unable to distinguish between his own and company money—dishonest.

Company bible: Rule book.

Company jewels: Trainman's hat badge, switch key, etc.

Company notch: The position on the control device that indicates the most fuel-efficient adjustment of the valves.

Cornfield meet: Head-on collision.

Cowcatcher: An inclined frame mounted on the front of a locomotive for the purpose of scooping obstacles off the track. It is also called the pilot.

Cripple: A bad order car.

Cushions: Passenger cars.

Dance the carpet: To appear before the superintendent for investigation or discipline.

Deadhead: Employee riding on a pass; any non-paying passenger; empty equipment being moved to shops or a new location.

Delayer or detainer: Dispatcher.

Diamond: The crossing of railroad tracks.

Dinky: A small steam locomotive, usually a tenderless tank engine or a steam dummy.

Diploma: Letter of service provided when one qualifies for a job.

Dishwasher: A roundhouse engine wiper.

Dog house: The cupola of a caboose. Also sun porch.

Doodlebug: Gasoline railcar for passenger service or carrying section gangs.

Dope: Material, usually wool or cotton waste mixed with oil, used to lubricate wheel bearings; a preparation used to reduce foaming in a locomotive boiler.

Dope monkey: A car inspector.

Drummer: A yard conductor.

Eagle eye: An engineer.

Eye: A trackside signal.

Ferroequinologist: A rail fan, or student of the "iron horse."

First reader: Conductor's train book.

Fishtail: The notched blade on a semaphore.

Flimsy: A train order.

Gandy dancer: A track laborer. Legend is that this name derives from the Gandy Manufacturing Co., which supplied nineteenth-century track tools, and the rhythmic "dance" of driving the spikes.

Garden: A freight yard. Also the radial tracks outside of a roundhouse.

Grazing ticket: Meal book.

Grease monkey: A car oiler.

Groundhog: Brakeman or yardmaster.

Hand bomber: Hand-fired locomotive.

Hat: An incompetent railroader whose head is of no use except as a place to hang a hat.

Highball: To run a train at high speed; an all-clear or go-ahead signal, derived from the top position of the old "ball" signal.

High iron: The main line.

Hog: A locomotive.

Hogger (or hoghead): An engineer.

Selected Bibliography

Archer, Eric H., ed. "Streamlined Steam: A Pictorial Review of Streamstyled Steam Locomotives." *Quadrant Press Review 1,* 1973.

Beebe, Lucius, and Charles M. Clegg. *Mixed Train Daily.* New York: E. P. Dutton, 1947.

Brignano, Mary, and Hax McCullough. *The Search For Safety: A History of Railroad Signals and the People Who Made Them.* Pittsburgh: The Union Switch & Signal Division, American Standard Inc., 1981.

Carroll, Brian. *Australia's Railway Days.* South Melbourne: The Macmillan Company of Australia Pty. Ltd., 1976.

Cunningham, Frank. *Big Dan: The Story of a Railroad Man.* Salt Lake City: The Deseret News Press, 1947.

Ellis, Hamilton. *The Pictorial Encyclopedia of Railways.* Middlesex, England: Hamlin Publishing Group, Ltd., 1968.

Frew, Tim. *Locomotives: From The Steam Locomotive to the Bullet Train.* New York: Mallard Press, 1990.

Galloway, John Debo, ed. *The First Transcontinental Railroad.* New York: Dorset Press, 1989.

Hayden, Bob. *Model Railroader Cyclopedia: Diesel Locomotives.* Vol. 2. Milwaukee: Kalmbach Books, 1980.

Hollingsworth, Brian. *Model Railroads.* New York: Galahad Books, 1981.

Hollingsworth, J. B. *The History of American Railroads.* New York: Exeter Books, 1983.

Knapke, William F. *The Railroad Caboose.* San Marino, Calif.: Golden West Books, 1968.

Lyle, Katie Letcher. *Scalded to Death by the Steam.* Chapel Hill, N.C.: Algonquin Books, 1983.

Marre, Louis A., and Jerry A. Pinkepank. *The Contemporary Diesel Spotter's Guide.* Milwaukee: Kalmbach Books, 1989.

Marshall, John. *The Guinness Railway Book.* 2nd ed. Enfield, England: Guinness Publishing Ltd., 1989.

Mulhearn, Daniel J., and John R. Taibi. *General Motors F-Units: The Locomotives That Revolutionized Railroading.* New York: Quadrant Press Inc., 1982.

Nock, O. S. *Railways Then and Now: A World History.* New York: Crown Publishers, Inc., 1975.

Phillips, Lance. *Yonder Comes the Train.* New York: A. S. Barnes and Co., 1965.

Pinkepank, Jerry A. *The Second Diesel Spotter's Guide.* Milwaukee: Kalmbach Books, 1973.

Thompson, Anthony W., ed. *Learning from the Prototype.* Pittsburgh: The Pittsburgh Limited, 1990.

————. *Symposium On Railroad History.* Chattanooga, Tenn.: A. C. Kalmbach Memorial Library (NMRA), 1990.

Zimmerman, Karl R. "The Remarkable GG-1." New York: *Quadrant Press Review 6,* 1977.

Index